Rating Occupations on a Civility Scale

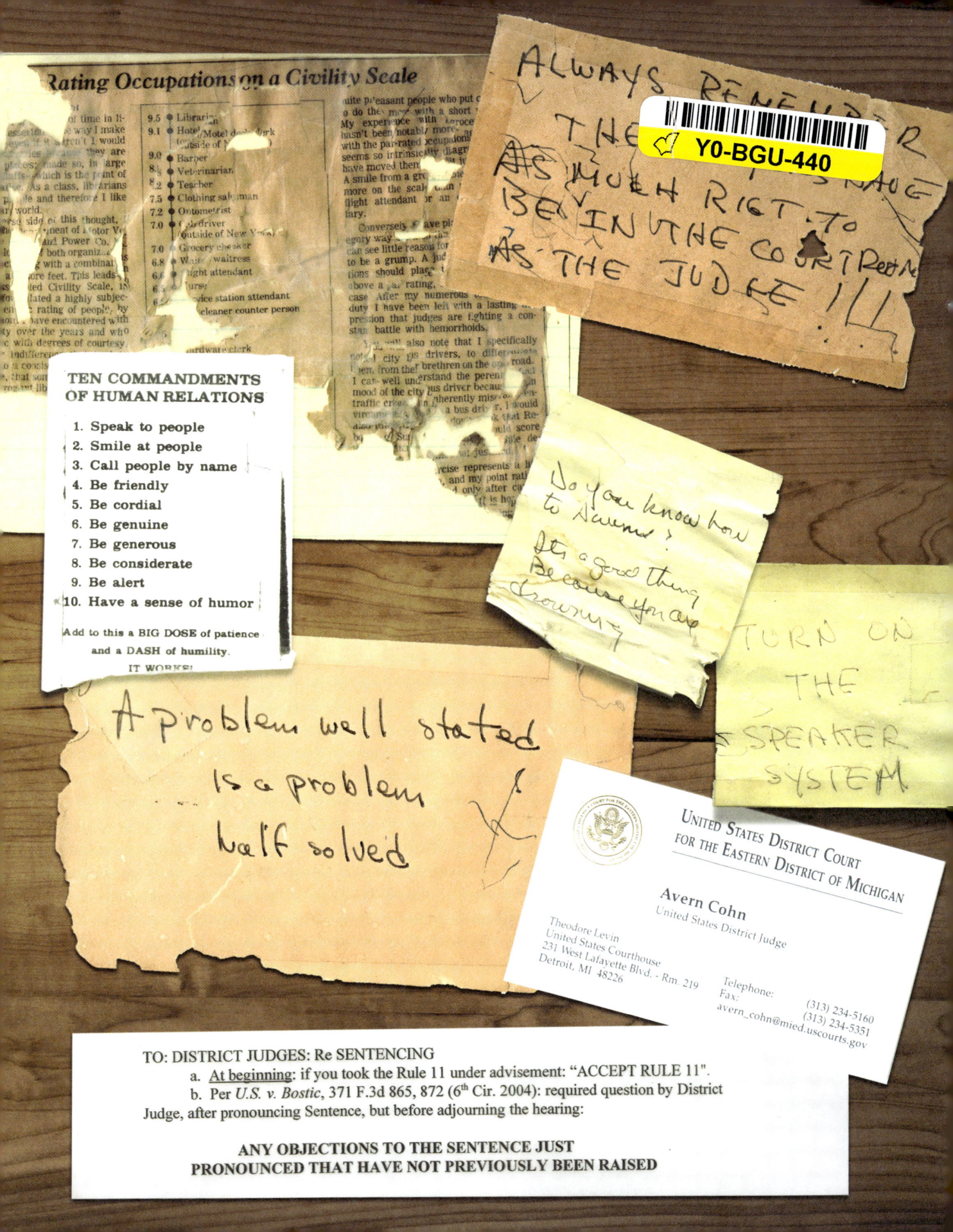

9.5	Librarian
9.1	Hotel/Motel desk clerk (outside of N...)
9.0	Barber
8½	Veterinarian
8.2	Teacher
7.5	Clothing salesman
7.2	Optometrist
7.0	Cab driver (outside of New York)
7.0	Grocery checker
6.8	Waiter/waitress
6.6	Flight attendant
6.5	Nurse
	...vice station attendant
	...cleaner counter person
	...rdware clerk

ALWAYS REMEMBER THE ... HAS ~~AS~~ ✓MUCH RIGT TO BE IN THE COURTROOM ^AS THE JUDGE IS

TEN COMMANDMENTS OF HUMAN RELATIONS

1. Speak to people
2. Smile at people
3. Call people by name
4. Be friendly
5. Be cordial
6. Be genuine
7. Be generous
8. Be considerate
9. Be alert
10. Have a sense of humor

Add to this a BIG DOSE of patience and a DASH of humility.
IT WORKS!

Do you know how to swim? It's a good thing because you are drowning

TURN ON THE SPEAKER SYSTEM

A problem well stated is a problem half solved

UNITED STATES DISTRICT COURT
FOR THE EASTERN DISTRICT OF MICHIGAN

Avern Cohn
United States District Judge

Theodore Levin
United States Courthouse
231 West Lafayette Blvd. - Rm. 219
Detroit, MI 48226

Telephone: (313) 234-5160
Fax: (313) 234-5351
avern_cohn@mied.uscourts.gov

TO: DISTRICT JUDGES: Re SENTENCING
    a. <u>At beginning</u>: if you took the Rule 11 under advisement: "ACCEPT RULE 11".
    b. Per *U.S. v. Bostic*, 371 F.3d 865, 872 (6th Cir. 2004): required question by District Judge, after pronouncing Sentence, but before adjourning the hearing:

ANY OBJECTIONS TO THE SENTENCE JUST PRONOUNCED THAT HAVE NOT PREVIOUSLY BEEN RAISED

Thinking About 'the Other Fella'

U.S. District Judge Avern Cohn at 95

Thinking About 'the Other Fella'

Avern Cohn's Life and the Law

Jack Lessenberry and Elizabeth Zerwekh

ACB

Copyright by Auld Classic Books, 2021.
Published in the United States of America by
Auld Classic Books
All rights reserved

Published in the United States of America by
Auld Classic Books
Manufactured in the United States of America

This book may not be reproduced, in whole or in part, including illustrations, in any form (beyond that copying permitted by Sections 107 and 108 of the U.S. Copyright Law and except by reviewers for the press or media) without written permission from the publisher; additional permissions may be required for those portions that are reprints from previously printed publications.

ISBN 978-0-578-95241-3

Cover design by Anne Zimanski

Auld Classic Books
13165 Ludlow Ave.
Huntington Woods, MI 48070

This book is dedicated to my wife, Lois, to my three children—Sheldon, Leslie and Tom—and to all those who have done so much to assist me during my forty years on the federal bench, my case managers, law clerks, court reporters and secretaries.

I could not have done it without all of you.

- Avern Cohn

Contents

From the Editors — ix
Foreword — xi
Introduction: Justice, Community, and Compassion — xiii

About the Judge

An Interview That Began Like Very Few Others — 1
Michigan Lawyers in History — 3
Timeline — 7

Some Notable Cases in a Long Career

Dozier v. Automobile Club, 1976 — 13
Butcher v. Evening News Association, 1981 — 17
Odgers v. Ortho Pharmaceutical Corporation — 19
Doe v. University of Michigan, 1989 — 23
Bradley v. Milliken, 1989 (The Detroit School Busing Case) — 27
The Kearns Patent Cases, 1987-1995 — 31
U.S. v. Jake Baker, aka Abraham Jacob Alkhabaz, 1995 — 37
Immigrants and Justice: Three Cases — 43
United States of America v. Nada Nadim Prouty, 2008 — 49
U.S. v. City of Detroit, Michigan and the Detroit Police Department — 53
U.S. v. Matthew David Kuppe, 2017 — 55

Two Notable Dissents	59
U.S. District Judge Avern Cohn: Former Law Clerks and Key Staff Members	67

A Selection of Avern Cohn's Articles

Constitutional Interpretation and Judicial Treatment of Blacks in Michigan Before 1870	75
Doe v. University of Michigan: A Somewhat Personal View	85
Judging the First Amendment	97
A Federal Trial Judge Looks at Academic Freedom	107
A Century of Local Jews in Politics: 1850's to 1950's	127
General Accounting Office Report to Congressional Committees Sentencing Guidelines-A Reaction	139
Vignette	143
Prosecutors and Voters Are Becoming Smart on Crime	147
My Passion for History	155
Three Frenchmen Three Centuries Across Michigan	161
The Detroit Banking Crises of 1933	183
A Jewish Judge—Or a Judge Who Is Jewish?	187

More letters, etc: Judge Cohn's Journalism, 2015-2020

Letters	197
Judge Avern Cohn Awards and Honoraria	207

Afterword	221
About the Editors	223

From the Editors

Thinking About 'the Other Fella' - Avern Cohn's Life and the Law, is a second volume collecting and celebrating his life's work. In 2015, Elizabeth edited and published *Letters, etc.,* a privately published collection of the judge's journalism in both legal and popular publications over thirty years of his career, 1976-2005.

This book is a much fuller treatment of his entire career, including essays about the judge, some of the best of his previously published articles as well as a number of new, never-before-published works—and more.

Perhaps most significantly, we also take an in-depth look at some of his most important cases, including two highly relevant decisions involving free speech and the internet; a spy case that drew the attention of *60 Minutes*, and a patent case that inspired international attention and a major Hollywood movie, *Flash of Genius*.

This book has been both intellectually fascinating and a labor of love, for both of us and, hopefully, for U.S. District Judge Avern Cohn as well.

- Jack Lessenberry and Elizabeth Zerwekh
September 2021

FOREWORD

⇢―――――――――⇠

Wisdom too often never comes, and so one ought not to reject it merely because it comes late.

- U.S. Supreme Court Associate Justice
Felix Frankfurter

Avern Cohn is a man who knows something about wisdom. Above is one of his favorite quotations, from a dissent the Supreme Court justice wrote in 1949[1]—the year this book's subject graduated from law school and was first admitted to the bar.

This book, *Thinking About 'the Other Fella,'* is a second collection of works by and about U.S. District Judge Avern Cohn, who presided in federal court in Detroit for forty years.[2] Though he took senior status in 1999, he did not reduce his caseload until he fully retired at the end of 2019, after a fascinating career on the bench.

His judicial years included a number of important and highly prominent cases worth remembering. He was indeed a "good judge," which is how he says he would like to be remembered. But he has also had a multifaceted life that went far beyond that; a long pre-judicial career as an attorney, as a force in Michigan Democratic politics, in government, as a philanthropist, and in the Jewish community.

He is a consummate history buff, who has belonged to the Historical Society of Michigan longer than anyone now alive, and has a special interest in the travels of Alexis De Tocqueville in Michigan. Cohn also is passionate about literature; in an amusing footnote, his name once ended up in an Elmore Leonard novel (*Mr. Paradise*) after he was the winning

---

1. *Henslee v. Union Planters National Bank, 1949*
2. The first volume, *Letters, etc.,* edited and privately published by Elizabeth Zerwekh, was privately published in 2015, and contains many of Cohn's earlier articles and journalism, primarily letters to the editors of newspapers.

bidder in a Michigan Opera Theater charity auction.[3]

He was also a journalist in his own right, contributing a stream of essays, articles and letters to both legal and general interest publications, from the *Federal Sentencing Reporter* to the *New York Times.*

This volume includes an essay that traces the sweep of a life that began when Calvin Coolidge was President and which still continues to have an impact today.

That is followed by a look at Avern Cohn the lawyer, in an article reprinted with permission from the *Michigan Bar Journal*, a look at some of Judge Cohn's most interesting and important cases, and a selection of his writings, some published here for the first time. Finally, there's a selection of his recent journalistic endeavors.

In addition to thanking the *Michigan Bar Journal* for permission to reprint "Michigan Lawyers in History," we want to thank Tom Kirvan, editor-in-chief of the *Detroit Legal News* for permission to reprint his story, "An Interview Like Very Few Others." We also want to acknowledge the sources where the following articles written by Judge Cohn first appeared: "Constitutional Interpretation and Judicial Treatment of Blacks in Michigan:" *Detroit College of Law Review*, 1986; "Doe vs. University of Michigan: A Somewhat Personal View," *Wayne Law Review*, 1991; "Judging the First Amendment:" *Detroit College of Law Review,* 1991.

Also, "A Federal Trial Judge Looks at Academic Freedom," a 1996 lecture included in *Freedom in American Intellectual Life*, edited by Peggie J. Hollingsworth, (University of Michigan Press, 2000;) "A Century of Local Jews in Politics: 1850s to 1950s:" *Michigan Jewish History,* Fall 1999; "The General Accounting Office Report … on Sentencing Guidelines—A Reaction and Reflections," *Federal Sentencing Reporter,* April 2017. Finally, "Vignette," *Michigan Bar Journal.* November 2011, and "Prosecutors and Voters Are Becoming Smart on Crime," *Litigation*, Fall 2019.

Also included is a chart of the key dates in Judge Cohn's life, a roster of his staff members and law clerks over the years, and an updated list of his honors and awards.

There has never been anyone quite like Avern Cohn in Michigan legal history. Whether or not you are a lawyer, and regardless of where your own life has taken you, we hope you enjoy what follows.

- Jack Lessenberry and Elizabeth Zerwekh

---

3. Avern Cohn in the novel is, as Ann Beattie said in her *New York Times* review (Feb. 1, 2004), a "thoroughly corrupt lawyer." When told this after the review was published, Judge Cohn reportedly said "Oy. Oy, Oy, Oy. Oy." When he was asked if it bothered him that his name had been used for a contemptible character, he said "No. They spelled my name right, and the only person who would have been offended is my mother, and she is deceased."

Introduction: Justice, Community, and Compassion

By Jack Lessenberry

Justice Louis Brandeis, one of the most influential justices ever to sit on the U.S. Supreme Court, supposedly said that the core of his judicial philosophy is that "you have to think about the other fellow."

In other words, you have to be devoted to justice, but also have compassion.

That is certainly how he lived his life. That is also what Avern Cohn did as well, throughout thirty years as a lawyer and forty years as a federal judge in Detroit.

It has been a life devoted to the law, justice and his community—make that *communities*; the legal community; the Jewish community; various other communities in Metropolitan Detroit, and his professional home for slightly more than four decades, the United States District Court for Eastern District of Michigan.

He may have scared more than a few young lawyers and law students over the years, but he was also a very good mentor, as generations of his former clerks will testify. Cohn also was both happy and proud in September, 2020, when he had the privilege of swearing in his career law clerk of twenty years, Kimberly Altman, when she became a federal magistrate judge for the Eastern District.

Cohn would never claim to be in the same league with Brandeis, the first Jewish Supreme Court justice in U.S. history.[1] If you know Avern Cohn, you can imagine that he might well

---

1. Brandeis (1856-1941) was nominated to the U.S. Supreme Court by Woodrow Wilson in 1916, and served until 1939. He is best remembered as a lawyer for battling for social justice and as a judge for defending free speech and declaring that there is a right to privacy.

bark at me for daring to make this comparison.

But Brandeis and Cohn have more than a few things in common.

Each practiced law for many years, and both were appointed to the federal bench relatively late in life; Cohn was 55; Brandeis 59, and both had long careers as activist attorneys beforehand. Brandeis fought against monopolies and pushed for investigations into conditions in the poorhouses. Cohn defended people arrested for alleged looting during the Detroit riot of 1967 and argued cases pro bono for the American Civil Liberties Union, and served on the Michigan Social Welfare and Civil Rights Commissions, and finally the Detroit Board of Police Commissioners.

Both Brandeis and Cohn were influenced by the moral and ethical traditions of their Jewish faith—the declaration in the Torah that "Justice, justice you shall pursue."[2] For years, Cohn liked to say that there are judges who are Jewish, in the way that others might be Methodists or Presbyterians. But there are also *Jewish judges*, meaning those for whom their Jewishness informs how they see the world.

There is no doubt that Avern Cohn was a truly Jewish judge.

Many, perhaps most young people have no idea what they want to do with their lives, when they leave high school, even perhaps when they finish college.

That wasn't true for Avern Cohn.

His father, Irwin Cohn, was a Detroit lawyer who had gone to the University of Michigan for undergrad and law school. Avern Cohn always said that growing up, he never had any doubt he would follow in his father's footsteps.

World War II intervened, however, and led him to a brief flirtation with medical school. Cohn, who was a not-yet-19-year-old student at the U of M when he was drafted, was clearly very bright, and was selected for the Army Specialized Training Program, and sent to pre-engineering, then pre-medical training and finally medical school.

When the war ended, he went back to medical school—but after about six weeks, he said "I realized I wasn't cut out for medicine," once he faced having to memorize the amino acids, and went to law school instead. He got his JD in 1949, passed the bar and went to work with his father, taking various criminal and civil assignments, some pro bono, as he learned the full spectrum of the practice of law.

In 1962, his father merged his firm with what became the much larger Honigman, Miller, Schwarz and Cohn. By that time, Avern had married a vivacious and dynamic woman, the former Joyce Ann Hochman, with whom he had three children, Sheldon, Leslie and Thomas. For many lawyers, a family and a successful practice would have been enough. But it was not enough for Avern Cohn.

For one thing, he took the Jewish concept of *tikkum olam* seriously—the idea that you

---

2. Deuteronomy 16:20. In Hebrew: ***Tzedek, tzedek tirdof*** צדק צדק תירדף

have to work to make this a better world. For another, he had an ambition, one he realized from the time he first had a case in U.S. District Court in Detroit: He wanted to be a federal judge. "There's a Yiddish word *yiches,* which loosely translated means honor," he told oral historian Judith Christie in 2005,"honor plus prestige."[3] Federal judges are appointed, not elected, as are state judges. They are appointed, for life, in fact, by Presidents of the United States after a recommendation from the senior U.S. Senator from their state. Actually, *yiches* encompasses learning, virtue, philanthropy, service to the community. Cohn knew that he would have to demonstrate a considerable record of all those things, and pay his dues in the political world, to merit a chance.

This he did. He began his career in politics as a volunteer for Adlai Stevenson's presidential campaign in 1952; by 1960, he was treasurer and the effective leader ("in fact I ran it") of a Michigan group called Citizens for Kennedy and Johnson.

John F. Kennedy's narrow victory in Michigan that year was a key part of his narrow victory nationwide, and Cohn's efforts were noticed. When Michigan Attorney General Paul Adams resigned to take a seat on the Michigan Supreme Court in 1961, Avern Cohn came close to being appointed to succeed him—but then-Gov. John Swainson chose Frank Kelley, then practicing law in Alpena, instead.

"I won't deny I was disappointed at the time, but in the end, Frank got the job he should have and I got the one I should have gotten, eventually," Cohn said.

Meanwhile, Avern Cohn continued to pay his dues, political and otherwise. His only attempt at elective office had come earlier in 1961, when he sought election as a delegate to the "Con-Con"—the only Michigan Constitutional Convention held in our lifetimes. Unfortunately, it was a heavily Republican district, and while he won the primary, he didn't come close in the general election. After that, he worked behind the scenes, helping raise money and serving as treasurer for a number of Democratic campaigns, including two for the U.S. Senate.

He also contributed financially to more political campaigns than anyone could easily count. In 1972, he joined in filing an election-night lawsuit to keep the polls open past the normal closing time, though it did not make much difference in that Republican year. But while Cohn was active in partisan politics, his service to the community went far beyond. Gov. George Romney appointed Cohn, even though he was a Democrat, to a seat on the Michigan Social Welfare Commission, a body that disappeared when the new state constitution took effect in 1963.

Another Republican, Gov. William Milliken, appointed Cohn to the Michigan Civil

---

3. *"Conversations with Avern Cohn,"* Oral History Interviews conducted by Judith K. Christie, United States District Court, Eastern District of Michigan and The Historical Society for the United States District Court, Eastern District of Michigan, July 18, 2005. p. 36.

Rights Commission, where he worked hard to shape state policy on civil rights issues, which at least once led to his being picketed for several days.

Cohn also did *pro bono* work for the ACLU in a number of cases, including suing Wayne State University over an effort to deny unpopular organizations space on campus, and an unsuccessful effort to get the Automobile Club of Michigan from moving out of Detroit, or at least to integrate their board of directors. He did, however, succeed in forcing the board to move to a system where rank-and-file members elected board members; until then, only the existing board decided who sat on it.

But perhaps Avern Cohn's most vital community work came when he was a member, and then chair, of the Detroit Board of Police Commissioners from 1975-79, at a time when that body displayed more autonomy and had more prestige than it does today. He was appointed at a time when there was considerable tension between the commission, which was, at least theoretically, responsible for managing and overseeing the police department, and the mayor.

That was back in Coleman Young's first term as mayor of Detroit. Both Avern Cohn and the feisty mayor sometimes clashed, but they respected each other—and Cohn earned Coleman Young's trust and support by strongly backing his integrating what had been an overwhelmingly white police force via a policy of hiring one black and one white officer every time there was a vacancy.

But there was more to Avern Cohn's life than politics, the law, family and government. He has been deeply involved and heavily invested in the Jewish community. "There's a strong ethic in the Jewish religion and the Talmud teaches that those more fortunate have an obligation to look out for those less fortunate.

"That's the principle of a good Jewish life," he once said.[4]

Cohn has been looking out for the less fortunate and the Jewish community his entire life. His earliest memory of a charitable contribution is putting coins in a basket when the cornerstone was laid for Congregation Shaarey Zedek's synagogue at Lawton and Chicago on May 25, 1930—more than ninety years ago.

By the early 1950s, he was active in organizations from the Allied Jewish Campaign to the Jewish Community Council to the Hebrew Free Loan Association, and a frequent early visitor to the state of Israel.

His service led to his eventually becoming President of the Jewish Welfare Federation of Metropolitan Detroit in 1981, probably the most important office in the Jewish community. He also combined his respect for his religion and history by becoming the founding chairperson of the Leonard Simons Jewish Community Archives.

Among his other efforts was the establishment of the Samuel and Maly Cohn Millennium Fund, named in honor of his grandparents, to aid Orthodox educational institutions; he also

---

4. "Conversations with Avern Cohn," *op. cit.* p. 116

designated that funds his father had left with the Federation should be used to establish the Irwin I. Cohn Cemetery Index.

Though a member of a conservative congregation (Shaarey Zedek in Southfield) Cohn has said "you can't have a strong Jewish community without a strong Orthodox component. "You have to keep the core strong. The core is the Orthodox community." [5]

Avern Cohn's many services to the legal community and the state bar prior to his being named a federal judge are ably covered in the opening essay in this volume: *"Michigan Lawyers in History: Judge Avern Cohn."*

His service to all these communities, plus a steady stream of entertaining and informative articles on a wide range of aspects of the law, undoubtedly were a factor in his nomination to the federal bench in 1978, at a time when two seats were vacant and three new federal judgeships were about to be created for Michigan's Eastern District.

Though President Jimmy Carter would formally recommend five names to the U.S. Senate, the tradition is that the state's senior senator actually selects the names, especially when the President and the senator are in the same party.

They were that year, and both U.S. Sen. Donald Riegle and President Carter were Democrats, which was certainly something in Avern Cohn's favor.

Eleven attorneys went through the selection process successfully. Nobody questioned Cohn's credentials or intelligence, but there was a one slight problem. To quote Avern Cohn himself, "Riegle was concerned that I lacked judicial temperament, and he was right. I still do… I had never been a potted palm. I was militant, excitable, forceful, occasionally probably interrupted people, occasionally irritated people."

"And as my very wise wife Lois sometimes says, I am sometimes rhetorically promiscuous." Despite that, Avern Cohn was nominated, and in October, 1979, confirmed by the U.S. Senate and began his judicial career.

Nobody is born a judge, and as he said candidly, "it took some time to adjust, to develop a routine … eventually you settle in."

He did more than that.

Before he had been on the bench for a year, he was named to a three-judge panel assigned to settle *Bradley v. Milliken*, the famous long-standing Detroit school desegregation case that was filed in 1970.

Known locally as the "cross-district busing case," it was highly controversial until the U.S. Supreme Court ruled in 1974 that the courts could not order students to be bussed outside their own districts for purposes of integration, but the case dragged on.

Eventually, the other two judges left Cohn with the case, and he settled it by closing it by saying that it was up to the Detroit Board of Education to apply the agreed-upon remedies.

---

5. Interview by Charlotte Dubin for the Leonard M. Simons Jewish Community Archives, Aug. 4, 2004

In 2014, he ended another long-running case, *U.S. v. City of Detroit*, which since 2003 had mandated federal oversight of the Detroit Police Department—at a cost to the taxpayers of $87,000 a month.

But though Cohn presided over virtually every type of case, criminal as well as civil, during his career, he may be best known for two types of cases. First, those involving free speech in an academic setting—most notably in *Doe v. University of Michigan* (1989) and *United States v. Alkhabaz* (1995), known as the "Jake Baker" case.

In both cases, he ruled that freedom of speech as guaranteed by the First Amendment is a constitutional right, even where that speech is offensive.

However, his only case—actually, cases—that became a Hollywood movie was a patent case. Eccentric engineer Robert Kearns invented the first intermittent windshield wiper system and sued the major auto companies for infringing his patent.

That led to the movie "*Flash of Genius*" (2008) starring Greg Kinnear, in which the movie judge was, unfortunately, not called Avern Cohn. Kearns was awarded more than $12 million in his case against Ford and another $20 million from Chrysler, but failed in the other cases, principally because he tried to be his own lawyer and failed to file needed paperwork on time.

"Most judges don't like patent cases. They can go on for years, and they require the judge to not only research a lot of law, but often to acquire a lot of very specialized knowledge about particular technology," Cohn once told this writer.

"However, I like them for exactly that reason. They forced me to learn new things and keep my mind active," he said.

Cohn had a number of notable other cases, including *Odgers v. Ortho Pharmaceutical Corp.*, (1985) in which he held that the manufacturer of a drug has the duty to inform consumers of their possible side effects.

Not that he ever lobbied for any particular case. "I've always believed that a judge who wants a case shouldn't have it," he said, meaning that impartiality is essential to administering justice. "When I began the Kearns cases, I knew nothing about intermittent windshield wipers and hence had no preconceived opinion, which is how it should be. He had other notable cases too, including one in which he decided the fate of an FBI agent turned CIA operative (*U.S. v. Nada Nadim Prouty, 2007*).

Cohn also occasionally sat by invitation on the U.S. Court of Appeals for the Sixth Circuit, an experience he feels helps enhance every district judge's understanding of how the system works.

Earlier in his career on the bench, he often heard cases in other districts and other states, when the need arose and Michigan's Eastern District could lend a judge.

Once, in a case in Kentucky, there were anonymous threats made against the judge—which led to the case being reassigned to an out-of-district judge, who turned out to be Avern

Cohn. When the defendant told Cohn in somewhat scatological terms that he was scared, Cohn replied "that makes two of us!" an honest sentiment that helped lessen the tension and lead to a resolution of the case.

Nor did Cohn shrink from controversy when necessary; late in his career, he was vilified when he ruled that Matthew Kuppe, who had secretly taken pictures of little boys and placed them on an internet porn site, was not a danger to the community, and did not need to be confined prior to trial.

"Being occasionally attacked goes with the territory," he said. *(A more in-depth look at some of Avern Cohn's significant cases appears later in this volume.)*

While this essay was in progress, James Churchill, a former chief judge in the Eastern District who served with Avern Cohn for years, died in Harbor Springs; like Cohn, he was a World War II veteran born in 1924. According to his obituary, when asked how he wanted to be remembered, Churchill said "as a good judge.

'Good judge' covers everything," he said.

Reading that, Avern Cohn told me, "that would do it for me, too. That's all that need be said about my life and career."

To that, I need to file a dissent. Avern Cohn *was* a good judge. His written opinions are well-crafted and show both a mastery of the law—and occasional flashes of wit. His oral remarks in court and his temper sometimes got him in mild trouble; as his wife Lois said, he is sometimes 'rhetorically promiscuous.'"

He would, however, usually extricate himself, sometimes by recognizing he had a temper and apologizing in open court, and sometimes with a humorous twist.

Many of his remarks were so priceless that a group of his clerks collected and published a hardcover volume called *Cohnisms*.[6]

He did not suffer fools gladly, to put it mildly. But at times, he could be quite humble. On March 25, 2021, Michigan Chief Justice Bridget McCormack presided at ceremonies presenting him with the Michigan History Foundation's Avern L. Cohn Distinguished Michigan Civic Historian Award. "I truly care what he thinks of my work," she said, "because I admire him and want him to be proud of me and because he has a historian's view of the Michigan Supreme Court."

Afterwards, clearly moved, Cohn told me, "when I started out as a lawyer, the last thing I ever dreamed was that I would get an honor like that from the chief justice."

Avern Cohn was, indeed, a good judge. But he was something more, too.

In my opinion, he was, and is, a mensch.

---

6. Edited by Bryan Anderson, privately published, 2005.

About the Judge

Detroit LEGAL NEWS

Posted February 3, 2021

An interview that began like very few others

Tom Kirvan
Legal News, Editor-in-Chief

I must admit that I miss U.S. District Judge Avern Cohn, who retired from the federal bench in December 2019 after a 40-year judicial career that by any measure could be described as "distinguished" and "significant."

We became acquainted with one another in the fall of 2009 during an "interview" that had been arranged by then Chief Judge Gerald Rosen, who wanted his colleague to be duly featured for marking a series of milestones that fall – 30 years as a judge and 60 years as a member of his graduating class at the University of Michigan Law School. And for good measure that year, the federal jurist was saluted by the State Bar of Michigan with the Founder's Award, which recognizes lawyers who exemplify professional excellence and outstanding community contributions.

Collectively, the two anniversaries and the coveted State Bar award warranted a full-page feature on Cohn, except for the fact that the Detroit native wanted no part of it. He made as much known within seconds of me sitting down in his office, doing his best to shut down the interview before it even started.

"As you can see, I'm busy," Judge Cohn barked at me from behind his trademark scowl. "I really don't have time for this interview. Enough has been written about me already, and you're going to be wasting your time and my time if this goes any further."

My problem, aside from sitting across from a very unwilling interviewee, was that I had scheduled our photographer to sit in on the proceedings in hopes that he could snap a few candid photos of the judge, who was acting particularly "judgy" at this point of our get-acquainted session.

So, I persisted, trying to convince someone firmly planted in the catbird seat that it would behoove him to come down from his perch even for a minute, perhaps long enough for the taking of an especially candid photo of him chewing out a well-intentioned writer from The Detroit Legal News.

Magically, that may have done the trick, as a small crack in his less-than-friendly façade began to emerge. The crack turned to earthquake-like proportions a minute later when I asked him to tell me a bit about his late father, Irwin Cohn, an "entrepreneurial type of lawyer" who gained legal fame as one of the principal partners in the Detroit firm of Honigman Miller Schwartz & Cohn.

With that simple question, I had opened the floodgates, prompting Judge Cohn to treat me to story after story about the family patriarch, whose legacy is firmly preserved at the U-M Law School with an endowed professorship.

An hour or so later in an interview that somewhat miraculously had gained full traction, Judge Cohn even felt comfortable enough to take me into his courtroom, where his bench was lined with hand-written sticky notes that served as a daily reminder of his important duties as a jurist.

Among the messages: "Keep cool!"

Another was "A problem well stated is a problem half solved."

A third, perhaps the most telling, read: "Be reasonable. Do it my way!"

That, in the strictest of Cohn terms, may have said it all.

Until he shared another: "No matter how high the throne, there sits but an ass."

There, in his own self-deprecating way, Judge Cohn had struck the right chord with me, beginning a bond of friendship that I continue to treasure.

Michigan Lawyers in History

Judge Avern Cohn

By John R. Runyan and Carrie Sharlow

The state of Michigan was built by the lumber and auto industries, agriculture, and the lawyers who lived, studied, and practiced here. The articles in this occasional series highlight some of those lawyers and judges and their continuing influence on this great state.

Chances are good that if your P number begins with a seven or even a high six, Avern Levin Cohn has always been known to you as a federal court judge. However, although he is probably most often associated with his work since 1979 on the U.S. District Court for the Eastern District of Michigan, Judge Cohn was, and always has been, first and foremost a lawyer.

Judge Cohn has been known to say that his path to the federal bench began with his selection of Irwin Isadore Cohn and Sadie Levin as his parents.[1] Both were children of immigrants. The Cohns and Levins were Eastern Europeans who emigrated to the United States before the turn of the twentieth century. The Cohns settled in Detroit; the Levins in Chicago.[2]

Irwin Cohn attended the University of Michigan, obtaining a law degree in 1917. He joined the firm of Selling & Brand and practiced there until opening his own law firm in the mid-1920s.[3] In later years, he attributed much of his success to luck and guts, and that's essentially how he met Sadie Levin.[4] He happened to be at a Lake Michigan resort at the same time she was, and jumped into the lake to rescue her when she started to drown; it was particularly gutsy because Irwin couldn't swim.[5] A second rescuer dove in after Irwin, and everyone survived. Irwin and Sadie were married on January 14, 1923.[6]

Avern Cohn was born July 23, 1924. His was "a typical middle-class Jewish upbringing"[7] in Detroit's "golden ghetto."[8] His parents were involved in Jewish community affairs, sometimes at the forefront, sometimes behind the scenes. Irwin Cohn would write "a check for a school or a hospital or a church, [and] few people ever hear[d] of it."[9] The family believed that with privilege came a responsibility to help those less fortunate.

The "golden ghetto" was a tight-knit community; Judge Cohn recalled that he "had almost no non-Jewish friends or associations" growing up.[10] Much of his early life can be traced in the *Detroit Jewish News* and *Detroit Jewish Chronicle*. The Cohns were frequently mentioned, with "Mr. and Mrs. Irwin I. Cohn and son Avern" wishing friends and family a happy new year, or Irwin donating trees to be planted in Palestine in honor of Avern and his sister, Rita. When the family celebrated Avern's bar mitzvah in 1937, the paper included an announcement and an extensive invitation.[11]

The Cohns were a close-knit family. Avern walked to his grandparents' home regularly and often attended Saturday services with his grandfather at the Congregation Shaarey Zedek. But Irwin and Sadie Cohn were by no means "helicopter parents"; as Judge Cohn describes it, "there was more freedom and independence than today."[12] He rode his bike all over northwest Detroit and played ball on vacant lots with friends. He spent summers at sleepaway camps beginning at the tender age of six, or at the family cottage on Pine Lake in Oakland County.[13] He recalled one summer on Pine Lake in the

Avern L. Cohn portrait, HS12848, University of Michigan Alumni files, Bentley Historical Library, University of Michigan

Michigan Lawyers in History

Judge Avern Levin Cohn

"I was fortunate in that I had both the time and resources so I could devote myself to public service, including activities relating to the bar."

mid-1930s when he and his future law partner's older brother tied Alan Schwartz to a tree in an effort to rid themselves of an annoying younger sibling.[14]

Of course, to the surprise of no one who knows him now (or knew him then), Avern was an excellent student. He read everything he could get his hands on and was particularly interested in history.[15] He also had an early interest in politics, listening on the radio to the nomination of Franklin D. Roosevelt at the 1936 Democratic National Convention (which he later regularly attended as a delegate). He attended Winterhalter Elementary School, Tappan and Durfee intermediate schools, and finally, Detroit Central High School, where he graduated with honors in January 1942.[16] Immediately after graduation, Avern started college. He knew from an early age that he would follow in his father's footsteps and attend the University of Michigan—"I didn't know there was any other university in the United States"[17]—and then join him in the Cohn law firm.

The world intervened with such designs that Judge Cohn very nearly became Dr. Cohn instead. The attack at Pearl Harbor had brought the United States into World War II, and each week, another U-M fraternity brother would receive his draft notice, put his civilian clothes up for sale, and report for duty.

Cohn waited for his draft notice (he might have enlisted if his eyesight had not been so poor). When the notice finally arrived in 1943, he reported for infantry training at Fort Custer near Battle Creek. He aced the Army's General Classification Test that was administered to all new inductees and was selected for the Army Specialized Training Program. He was sent to Stephenville, Texas, for pre-engineering training at John Carlton Agricultural College.[18] The training program was soon suspended in anticipation of the need for reserves to replace casualties expected in Europe, but Cohn was one of a fortunate few who were instead sent to Stanford University for pre-medical training.[19]

After fetching bed pans for eight months as a ward boy while waiting for a spot to open,[20] Cohn started Loyola School for Medicine in 1945 but dropped out in the spring of 1946 after deciding that he was better suited for the law.[21] He entered the University of Michigan Law School that fall, graduated in 1949, and immediately joined his father's practice.[22]

Irwin Cohn's law firm was in the Hammond Building. It was a general civil practice firm with an emphasis on bankruptcy, real estate, business transactions, and labor relations; clients included Federated Department Stores, Wrigley's Supermarkets, Sinai Hospital, and the Michigan Hospital Association. Avern did debt collection, evictions, and labor arbitrations; examined abstracts; and took criminal assignments. In 1962, Irwin Cohn's practice combined with the law offices of Honigman, Miller & Schwartz to form Honigman, Miller, Schwartz & Cohn.[23]

In 1954, Avern met his future wife, Joyce Ann Hochman, who was, by her own account, "such a good Democrat when she met her husband at the young and idealistic age of 21, that 'if [Avern] had been a Republican, [she] would not have gone out with him a second time.'"[24] The couple married in December 1954[25] and would eventually have three children. After Joyce passed away in 1989, Avern married Lois Pincus, an art dealer, in 1992.[26]

The Cohns were politically active. Avern worked with Volunteers for Stevenson as a precinct delegate and then ran Citizens for Kennedy and Johnson.[27] In the 1960s, he managed the reelection campaigns of Justice Paul Adams and Justice Otis Smith—both appointees to the Supreme Court by Gov. John Swainson—and later served as treasurer for the Senate campaigns of G. Mennen Williams and Frank Kelley.[28] He was also involved in the campaigns of his cousins Sander and Carl Levin.[29]

Avern also volunteered to serve on several State Bar of Michigan committees, including the Character & Fitness Committee,[30] Civil Liberties Committee,[31] Committee on Legal Aid, and the Committee on Judicial Selection & Tenure.[32] In 1978, he was appointed chair of a committee that authored a controversial "Report of the Special State Bar Committee on Court Congestion," which recommended that the Michigan Supreme Court become more transparent in its operations and fulfill the promise of "one court of justice" under the 1963 constitution, requiring greater uniformity and the exercise of greater supervisory authority over the lower courts in Michigan.[33] The recommendations were quite revolutionary at the time and caused a firestorm.

(Continued on the following page)

Michigan Lawyers in History

In between law practice, political activities, State Bar activities, and personal relationships, Cohn served on several commissions, including the Michigan Social Welfare Commission,[34] the Michigan Civil Rights Commission, and the Detroit Board of Police Commissioners.[35] He was also active in Jewish organizations like the Jewish Community Council.[36] And through it all, he sent scores of thought-provoking letters over the years to editors of legal journals and various newspapers.

But Cohn was always a lawyer first, and during his 30 years in private practice, he often used his skills to further the public interest. When the Automobile Club of Michigan moved its headquarters and 1,200 jobs from downtown Detroit to Dearborn in 1974, there was an uproar. While others were attacking this discrimination directly, Cohn tried a more subtle approach. In *Dozier v Automobile Club of Michigan*,[37] he challenged the legality of the club's bylaws, which allowed for nomination and election of the club's directors (in a self-perpetuating fashion) by the directors themselves rather than by the membership.[38] Despite being opposed by former Michigan Supreme Court Justice Theodore Souris, Cohn successfully persuaded the Court of Appeals to reverse a decision by then Wayne Circuit Judge James. L. Ryan. Although the club amended its bylaws in response to the lawsuit, Cohn was unsuccessful in his attempts to persuade the club to add an African American to its board.[39]

Later, he "stirred the pot" again when he questioned the applicability of the state's Open Meetings Act to Michigan Supreme Court meetings on administrative matters.[40] His letter to the Court asking when it was next scheduled to meet prompted the Court's sua sponte opinion, *In re "Sunshine Law"*, declaring unconstitutional that portion of the act applicable "to a court while exercising rule-making authority and while deliberating or deciding upon the issuance of administrative orders."[41]

It's no wonder that his name came to the forefront when there were vacancies on the federal bench in the late 1970s. For 30 years, Cohn had groomed himself for such an appointment. He was a senior partner in an established, well-regarded law firm; active in the general, political, and religious communities; and supported by both organized labor and the African-American community.[42] To top it off, there was a Democratic president and congressional majorities. To no one's surprise, his investiture to the federal court was a highly attended event.

When describing his career before he ascended to the federal bench, Judge Cohn said: "I was fortunate in that I had both the time and resources so I could devote myself to public service, including activities relating to the bar."[43] Michigan is also fortunate that a man who could easily have devoted himself to other pursuits chose instead to put his considerable intellectual gifts to work to benefit those around him. When Justice Charles Levin retired from the Michigan Supreme Court in 1996, Judge Cohn noted that Levin might not have had a perfect heart, but he surely did not have an imperfect one. About Judge Cohn, it can be said that while he might not have had a perfect heart, any imperfection is not reflected in the generosity of his spirit nor in his compassion for others. ■

John R. Runyan is of counsel to Nickelhoff & Widick, PLLC. He is immediate past president of the College of Labor and Employment Lawyers and a past president of the Detroit Bar Association and the Federal Bar Association's Eastern District of Michigan chapter. Runyan is also chair of the SBM Michigan Bar Journal Committee and vice chair of the Labor and Employment Law Section Council.

Carrie Sharlow is an administrative assistant at the State Bar of Michigan.

ENDNOTES
1. Judge Avern Cohn Oral History with Judy Christie (July 18, 2005), housed in the U.S. Courthouse in Detroit, p 2.
2. Judge Avern Cohn Oral History with Charlotte Dubin (August 4, 2004), housed in the Leonard M. Simons Jewish Community Archives, pp 1–2.
3. Judge Avern Cohn Oral History with Judy Christie, p 3.
4. Cook, *In a Quiet Way, He's a Detroit Power*, Detroit Free Press (June 8, 1958), p 2-C.
5. Sachs, *Strength of Commitment*, Detroit Jewish News (April 14, 2000), p 178.
6. *Id.*
7. Judge Avern Cohn Oral History with Judy Christie, p 5.
8. *Id.* at 4.
9. *In a Quiet Way, He's a Detroit Power.*
10. Judge Avern Cohn Oral History with Judy Christie, p 5.
11. *Social and Personal*, The Detroit Jewish Chronicle & The Legal Chronicle (June 18, 1937), p 6.
12. Judge Avern Cohn Oral History with Charlotte Dubin, p 8.
13. *Id.* at 4.
14. *Id.* at 5.
15. Judge Avern Cohn Oral History with Judy Christie, p 7.
16. *Id.* at 4.
17. Judge Avern Cohn Oral History with Charlotte Dubin, p 7.
18. *In the Realm of Local Society*, The Detroit Jewish Chronicle & The Legal Chronicle (October 29, 1943), p 10.
19. *Pvt Cohn Sent to Stanford U*, The Jewish News (June 16, 1944), p 24.
20. Judge Avern Cohn Oral History with Judy Christie, p 10.
21. *In the Realm of Local Society.*
22. Judge Avern Cohn Oral History with Judy Christie, pp 11–14.
23. *News About Lawyers*, 41 Mich State B J 45 (1962).
24. Welch, *Avocation on the Bench*, The Detroit Jewish News (February 14, 1986), p 15.
25. *Honeymoon in Jamaica After Dec. 30 Wedding*, The Detroit Jewish News (January 21, 1955), p 12.
26. Ghannam & Dozier, *Joyce Cohn loved Grandkids, Civic Work*, The Detroit Free Press (December 13, 1989), p 7B and *Party Line*, The Detroit Free Press (October 7, 1992), p 2G.
27. Judge Avern Cohn Oral History with Judy Christie, p 16.
28. *Id.* at 17.
29. *Id.*
30. *Committees on Character & Fitness*, 34 Mich St B J 52 (1955).
31. *Committees for 1957–1958*, 36 Mich St B J 37 (1957).
32. *Committees for 1959–1960*, 38 Mich St B J 42 (1959).
33. See *Assert Greater Authority, Supreme Court Urged: Court Congestion Committee Reports*, 57 Mich St B J 826–827 (1978).
34. Judge Avern Cohn Oral History with Charlotte Dubin, p 13.
35. Mitchell, *Cohn Replaces Fraser: Lawyer Named to Police Panel*, Detroit Free Press (September 24, 1975), p A3.
36. *Outdoor Rally*, The Detroit Jewish News (April 25, 1969), p 6.
37. *Dozier v Automobile Club of Michigan*, 69 Mich App 114 (1976); 224 NW2d 376.
38. *Id.*
39. Judge Avern Cohn Oral History with Judy Christie, pp 20–21.
40. *In re "Sunshine Law,"* 1976 PA 267, 400 Mich 660, 662 (1977); 255 NW 2d 635.
41. *Id.* at 662.
42. Judge Avern Cohn Oral History with Charlotte Dubin, p 12.
43. Interview with authors (March 7, 2019).

Lois and Avern Cohn, c. 2000

Timeline

(Notable Dates In the Life of Avern Cohn)

Parents

Isadore Irwin Cohn (1896-1984)   Attorney

Sadie Levin Cohn (1899-2000)   Homemaker

Grandparents

Samuel and Malka Cohn,

Louis and Rachel Levin, of Chicago

All were immigrants from lands now part of Lithuania, Poland or Russia

Avern Cohn

July 23, 1924:   Born at old St. Mary's Hospital at Clinton and St. Antoine, Detroit

1937:   Bar Mitzvah: Congregation Sharrey Zedek

1939-41:   Summers at Camp Tamakwa, Algonquin Park, Ontario

January 1942:   Graduates Central High School

January 1942:   Enrolls at the University of Michigan, joins Sigma Alpha Mu

March 1943:	Leaves U of M; inducted into the Armed Forces at Fort Custer, near Battle Creek. Selected for Army Specialized Training Program in engineering; attends John Tarleton Agricultural College in Texas; transfers to pre-med at Stanford University. Works at Vaughn General Hospital in Chicago; attends Loyola University School of Medicine in Chicago
1946:	Discharged from the U.S. Army; briefly returns to medical school before leaving to attend law school at the University of Michigan
1949:	Graduated from law school; admitted to the bar. Begins practicing in the Law Office of Irwin I. Cohn
1951:	First trip to Israel
1952:	Active member of Volunteers for Stevenson
December, 1954:	Marries Joyce Ann Hochman. Three children follow: Sheldon, Leslie and Tom
1960:	Treasurer, Citizens for Kennedy and Johnson
1961:	Democratic nominee for delegate to Michigan Constitutional Convention. Narrowly misses appointment as Michigan Attorney General
1961:	Merger; now member of Honigman Miller Schwartz and Cohn
1962:	Campaign Chairman for Michigan Supreme Court Candidates Otis Smith and Paul Adams
1962:	Becomes Commodore, Great Lakes Yacht Club
1963-64:	Serves on the Michigan Social Welfare Commission for nine months until commission is abolished by the new state constitution
1966:	Treasurer, G. Mennen Williams U.S. Senate Campaign
1971-75:	Serves on the Michigan Civil Rights Commission; last year as chair; resigns because he perceives a conflict of interest

1972:	Treasurer, Frank Kelley U.S. Senate Campaign
1975:	Appointed to the Detroit Police Commission. Became chair 1979; serves until appointed a U.S. District Judge
1979:	Nominated by President Carter to be a judge for the United States District Court for the Eastern District of Michigan
1979:	Confirmed by the U.S. Senate
1982-83:	President of the Jewish Federation of Metropolitan Detroit.
1989:	Death of Joyce Cohn
1992:	Marries Lois Padover Pincus
2019:	Retires after more than 40 years on the bench

His "first case." Judge Cohn's children present him with a case of Stroh's beer, an iconic Detroit brand, at ceremonies celebrating his becoming a federal judge, October 1979. (*From left*: Sheldon, Leslie and Thomas Cohn.)

Some Notable Cases in a Long Career

Dozier v. Automobile Club, 1976[1]

(May 27, 1976)

I initially sued the Automobile Club of Michigan because it was trying to move out of Detroit. It had a set of bylaws that provided for directors electing directors without the members really having any say. I forced a change.

- Judge Avern Cohn

    This case is different from the other cases considered in this book, because it illustrates Avern Cohn's legal skills and as well as his commitment to justice during the thirty years he was a practicing attorney before being appointed a U.S. District Judge.

    The Automobile Club of Michigan,[2] founded in 1916, was, as the Michigan Court of Appeals noted in its eventual ruling, "a non-profit corporation existing to promote automobile travel and safety and provide various services to its members," of whom, the court determined, there were more than 1.1 million by the early 1970s.

    However, these members had essentially no say in the club's governance. Beginning in 1933, the board of directors was chosen and elected solely by the board itself, without any member input. That continued until 1973 and resulted, not surprisingly, in a board that consisted entirely of 15 white businessmen.

    This became an issue in the late 1960s, when the board decided that the Automobile Club should move out of Detroit, where it had been founded, to Dearborn, taking some

---

1. *69 Mich. App. 114 (Mich Ct. App 1976 244 N.W. 2d 376)*
2. The club is now known as the Auto Club Group and is affiliated with AAA—the American Automobile Association.

1,200 jobs with it. This was at a time when Detroit was desperately trying to stem a massive flight from the city of both people and jobs.

Cohn believed that the Auto Club's decision to leave Detroit was totally unjustified, since the million-plus members had no say in what was decided. He said in an interview, "the desire to move out of Detroit was illegally determined."[3] He first attempted to file suit to stop the move, but said "I finally gave up trying to keep them from moving out of Detroit," because he lacked support.

However, he still thought the Automobile Club's bylaws were patently illegal, because they effectively prevented the members from participating in making the club's policies, or any other meaningful decisions. So in 1971, Cohn found a plaintiff who had standing, and in *Dozier v. Automobile Club*, sued both the club and a reciprocal insurance exchange, which was controlled by the same board of directors.[4]

Perhaps because of this suit, the Automobile Club's directors did amend their bylaws in early 1972 to provide for election of the board by the membership.

However, while acknowledging that this was an improvement, Cohn, who was then in private practice with Honigman, Miller, Schwartz and Cohn, noted that this still was a long way from effective democracy. The board of directors still nominated all candidates for the board. There was, theoretically, a way in which rank-and-file members could collect petition signatures for a candidate. But he argued that the barriers to doing so were still unreasonably hard. While the board could nominate anyone it chose, candidates not picked by the directors had to secure the signatures of 5,775 members.

Since Automobile Club members were widely scattered and did not traditionally gather in groups, getting such signatures would hardly be easy, he argued.

Nevertheless, Cohn lost in what later became Wayne County Circuit Court.[5] Judge James L. Ryan, who later would also become a federal judge, ruled that the bylaws relating to the election of directors were reasonable, and granted no relief.

But the Michigan Court of Appeals reversed that decision, at least as far as the process for electing directors was concerned. A three-judge panel unanimously held that "the club's present bylaws are invalid because they are unreasonable."

"Much is at stake in the direction of the club," the Appeals Court found. "It is clear that the club wields considerable power in establishing transportation policies in this state and in the financial community through its deposits and investments. Those on the board who control this power should not be allowed to perpetuate themselves in office indefinitely. There

---

3. "Conversations with Avern Cohn," Oral history interview conducted by Judith K. Christie for the Historical Society for the United States District Court, Eastern District of Michigan, July 18, 2005
4. It was called the Detroit Automobile Inter-Insurance Exchange, or DAIIE. Its subsidiaries were also included in the suit. Neither the trial court nor the appellate court agreed with Cohn that it was an alter ego of the club.
5. Formerly the 3rd Circuit Court, before the abolition of Detroit Recorders' Court.

should be more director accountability and more access to the board given to non-management candidates."

With that, the appellate panel sent the case back to the trial judge. At length, a settlement was worked out that called for the members to elect the board of directors.

Today, as a result, the directors are a far more diverse body, and include women and people of African-American, Arab-American, and other diverse groups. In this instance, attorney Avern Cohn used the law to effect positive and meaningful change.

BUTCHER V. EVENING NEWS ASSOCIATION, 1981[1]

(Rulings on Motions on May 27, 1981; June 11, 1981)

There is no doubt Ms. Butcher's lawsuit was the catalyst that sped up these improvements (women hired, promoted and honored) at a pace that would not have occurred without it.

- Mary Lou Butcher's citation, Michigan Journalism Hall of Fame

A landmark case in gender equality in journalism occurred early in Judge Cohn's career on the bench. Mary Lou Butcher, at the time the only female news reporter at the *Detroit News*, then Michigan's largest-circulation newspaper, claimed that she had been banished to a suburban bureau after she complained about unfair treatment.

Eventually, she and two other women employees filed a federal lawsuit, both on behalf of themselves individually and as a class action suit, charging the newspaper, then privately owned, with illegal discrimination in hiring, promotion and reporting assignments.

The case, which was filed in 1979, was assigned to Judge Cohn by random draw. Butcher had, as the law required, initially filed a discrimination charge with the Equal Employment Opportunity Commission.

But by the time she received the necessary letter from the EEOC granting her the right to sue, she had resigned to take another job. In June 1980, the women then filed a motion for their case to be certified as a class action suit.

However, with Butcher no longer a *Detroit News* employee, the question became whether

---

1. *Butcher v. The Evening News Ass'n,* No. 79-70987 (E.D. Mich. May 27 and June 11, 1981).

the case still qualified for class action status, On March 5, 1981, Judge Cohn expressed concern as to whether the named plaintiffs—Butcher, Diane Dunn and Vivian Moore—could represent female "editorial staff" employees, since none were then employed as *News* editorial staff members. (Moore and Dunn worked in the *Detroit News* reference department, and claimed they had been denied a chance to join the editorial staff because of their gender.)

However, another female editorial employee, Marcia Biggs, filed a motion to establish her right to intervene as a plaintiff charging the Evening News Association with sex discrimination, both on behalf of herself and as a class representative in a class action lawsuit under both federal law and the Michigan Civil Rights Act.

The defendant and employer, the Evening News Association, opposed this motion on both grounds, and claimed Biggs was procedurally ineligible because she had never filed any charge of discrimination with the EEOC, and consequently had never been given a letter from the commission giving her the right to sue.

After reviewing the case law cited by both parties, Judge Cohn ruled decisively that "in the court's opinion, the law is clear that a class action may be maintained on behalf of aggrieved individuals who have not filed charges with EEOC and they may later intervene as parties plaintiff," and added that the record "appears to clearly demonstrate the timely filing of a discrimination charge by the named plaintiffs; a clear statement that more than an individual act of discrimination was being asserted," and included other necessary elements for establishing that a class action suit was legitimate.

"It is unfortunate that so much time should be devoted to matters preliminary to the substantive allegations of the complaint," Judge Cohn added, a thought that undoubtedly has been shared by many litigants in many cases over the years.

Eventually, after further arguments in early June, Judge Cohn ruled that it was a proper class action case. Days later, on June 11, 1981, the Equal Employment Opportunity Commission sought to intervene on behalf of the plaintiffs.

The Evening News Association opposed this, arguing that it was not timely and would serve no purpose. But Judge Cohn disagreed, ruling that the case was still in its early stages and that the EEOC was entitled to intervene.

Procedural battles in the case went on until February, 1984, when the parties entered into an agreement under which the Evening News Association paid more than $330,000 to 90 female employees to settle the case.

Even before it was decided, the case, from the time it was certified as a proper class action lawsuit, sparked major changes and more opportunities for women at newsrooms in Detroit and across the country; the case also led to other successful sex discrimination suits being filed by female newsroom employees nationwide.

Odgers v. Ortho Pharmaceutical Corporation[1]

(Ruling May 27, 1985)

…a manufacturer of oral contraceptives has a duty to warn users of its product for birth control purposes directly of any risks inherent in their use.

- Judge Avern Cohn

Does a pharmaceutical company have a duty to warn consumers of possible side effects that its products—in this case, a birth control pill—might cause?

That was the question posed in this landmark product liability case. The essential facts were not in dispute. Susan Odgers believed that her use of Ortho-Novum, a birth-control pill manufactured by Ortho Pharmaceutical Corp. caused a blood clot that partly paralyzed her. She claimed that Ortho had failed to adequately warn her and had failed to adequately warn her doctor that the contraceptive could cause blood clotting.

Accordingly, she sued them for the damages she suffered.[2]

There was also agreement that under common law, drug manufacturers had a duty to warn physicians of any potential risks in the drugs they might prescribe.

But did they have a duty to warn the patient?

Before proceeding further, U.S. District Judge Avern Cohn posed this question to the Michigan Supreme Court:

---

1. 609 F. Supp. 867;(E.D. Mich. 1985)
2. In June, 1980, Odgers prevailed in a trial before a jury, but that verdict was set aside because the judge gave the jury erroneous instructions under Michigan law. Judge Avern Cohn then granted Ortho, the defendant, a new trial.

"Does the manufacturer of an oral contraceptive, which is a prescription drug, in addition to its duty under the common law of Michigan to warn physicians of any risks inherent … which it knows or should know to exist … have a duty under the common law of Michigan to provide adequate warnings directly to persons using the oral contraceptives?" A duty, that is, in cases where the decision to take the drugs is based on the patient's "informed choice," and not just the decision of the doctor?

The Michigan Supreme Court took a year and a half to reply. When it did, it told Judge Cohn that there was no "rule of law" in Michigan that would answer the question; the state's highest court also declined to volunteer what rule of law *would* answer it.

Though three of the seven judges would have attempted to answer that question, a majority of four said that was up to lawmakers—in effect, passing the buck.

"The allocation of the duty to warn patients is a public policy question involving the marketing system and economics of a major industry and the everyday practice of an essential profession. We believe that the legislature is in a better position to allocate these duties," the Michigan Supreme Court said.

Not surprisingly, Ortho Pharmaceutical then filed a motion asking Judge Cohn to grant summary judgment and decide the case in their favor. Their case was strengthened because Susan Odgers' physician, Dr. Joan Wake, testified that even if she had been warned more strongly by Ortho that women with certain blood types were at greater risk, she would still have prescribed Ortho-Novum for Susan Odgers.

However, Judge Cohn wasn't impressed with the reasoning of the majority of the state's highest court. Despite their opinion, he wrote "I conclude, however, that the Michigan Supreme Court's deference to the legislature is, in the area of tort duties, clearly excessive," and added that as far as he was concerned, it could be discounted.

After quoting several well-respected authorities, one of whom wrote that "American courts have a great responsibility for participation in the creative adaptation of law to current needs… Where a need for reform is clear but no reforming statute has yet been enacted, courts must choose …"[3]

Judge Cohn went on to note that "as a general rule, the manufacturer of a product has a duty to warn the user of known dangers inherent in the use of that product. Courts have treated prescription drugs as an exception to this rule on the assumption that it is reasonable for the manufacturer to rely on the prescribing physician," who becomes a so-called "learned intermediary" to inform the patient of potential side effects.

However, oral contraceptives are a different matter, the judge reasoned, primarily because those using them tend to be only minimally involved with their doctors.

Women do make an appointment to see a physician to undergo a physical examination

---

3. Robert E. Keaton, "Creative Continuity in the Law of Torts." *Harvard Law Review,* January 1962, pp 484-6,

in order to receive the initial prescription, as required by law. But afterwards they return only when they must to automatically renew their prescriptions, thereby lessening the "learned intermediary" function of the presiding physician.

Judge Cohn also relied on two recent cases in which each court had ruled that manufacturers of birth control pills had a duty to warn the user, and that despite extensive federal regulation of these drugs, there was still a common-law duty on the part of the manufacturer to provide warnings to the consumer.

"I am of the opinion that the FDA's (Food and Drug Administration) regulation of oral contraceptives was not intended in any way to preclude imposition of tort liability for failure to warn," Judge Cohn found. "In sum, I have no doubt that the better rule of law is that the manufacturer of an oral contraceptive has a duty to warn the user of the possible side effects."

Cohn added, "not only is the rule establishing a duty to (directly) warn the user of oral contraceptives the more reasoned rule of law, I am satisfied that it is the rule of law that the Michigan Supreme Court would most likely adopt. He did grant Ortho Pharmaceutical's request for a summary judgment as to Odgers' physician, based on her deposition testimony and sworn affidavits.

But he said Ortho still had a duty to have warned Susan Odgers herself.

That ruling has stood the test of time—as far as Odgers was concerned. Legal articles have cited the case as showing that in the case of the potential side effects of oral contraceptives, drug companies have a duty to warn, not only to the prescribing physicians, but also those for whom the drugs may be prescribed.[4]

Earlier that same year, the late Horace Gilmore, also a U.S. District judge for the Eastern District of Michigan, had also similarly ruled that Michigan law requires makers of oral contraceptives to warn patients directly of the potential risks and side effects.

But six years later, U.S. District Judge John Feikens disagreed. In *Reaves v. Ortho Pharmaceutical Corp.*,[5] he ruled that "given the testimony presented and my reading… I find that oral contraceptives do not differ significantly from other prescription drugs.

"Therefore, I hold that the learned intermediary doctrine applies equally to oral contraceptives under Michigan law. This finding is consistent with a majority of decisions in other jurisdictions, which also guide this result."

Following Judge Cohn's ruling, Susan Odgers eventually settled her case with Ortho and went on to graduate studies in psychology. She has taught at a number of universities in Michigan and France, became a popular newspaper columnist, and ran unsuccessfully as a Green Party candidate for a university board position. "This case did change the way they

---

4. "Prescription Drugs and the Duty to Warn: An Argument for Patient Package Inserts." Alan R. Styles, *Cleveland State Law Review*, 1991.
5. *Reaves v. Ortho Pharmaceutical Corp.*, 765 F. Supp. 1287 (E.D. Mich. 1991).

(pharmaceutical companies) do business, and spared some women from going through what I did, and I'm proud of that," she said in October, 2020.

There is general agreement that pharmaceutical companies did begin supplying more written information to women who use oral contraceptives.

However, in the years following Judge Cohn's ruling in *Odgers v. Ortho Pharmaceutical*, neither the Michigan Legislature nor the Michigan Supreme Court has taken action to resolve the question of whether the manufacturers of birth control pills are legally obligated to directly warn those who use them of any potential risks.

Doe v. University of Michigan, 1989[1]

(September 25, 1989)

It is an unfortunate fact of our constitutional system that the ideals of freedom and equality are often in conflict. The difficult and sometimes painful task of our political and legal institutions is to mediate the appropriate balance between these two competing values.

It is fundamental that statutes regulating First Amendment activities must be narrowly drawn to address only the specific evil at hand.

-Judge Avern Cohn

Today, battles over whether or not "hate speech" should be banned are commonplace everywhere in society from political campaigns to college campuses.

But that wasn't true in the late 1980s, when the University of Michigan made an attempt to deal with what seemed to be a rising tide of ugly racial harassment incidents on campus. These included racist jokes broadcast on a campus radio station; Ku Klux Klan robes hung from a dormitory window, and a flier distributed anonymously declaring "open season" on "saucer lips, porch monkeys and jigaboos."

The University found itself under considerable pressure to do something about all this, and the Board of Regents responded by adopting a complex and complicated three-tiered

---

1. *721 F. Supp.852 (E.D. Mich., 1989)*

policy that attempted to regulate speech and conduct, and prescribed a range of sanctions or penalties for violating provisions that were not always clear.[2]

Though a number of students were sanctioned during the slightly more than a year that the policy was in effect, "John Doe" was not one of them.[3] Rather, he was a graduate student specializing in biopsychology, which studies possible biological differences in personality traits and mental abilities on certain fields.

He was worried that he might get into trouble for legitimately discussing certain controversial theories about biologically-based differences between the races and the sexes, and feared he might be denounced and reported, and that his right to freely and openly discuss these theories would be impermissibly chilled.

The American Civil Liberties Union (ACLU) agreed—and lawyers for the ACLU assisted him in filing a suit in federal court asking that the policy be declared unconstitutional because it was both too vague and overboard.

The University of Michigan disagreed—and questioned Doe's standing to challenge the policy. They claimed that it had never been used to sanction classroom discussion of legitimate ideas and Doe had not shown that had any reason to believe it might be applied to his work or to him.

After studying the arguments on both sides and reviewing the relevant case law, Judge Avern Cohn concluded that "were the Court to look only at the plain language of the Policy, it might have to agree with the University that Doe could not have realistically alleged a credible threat of enforcement" against him for discussing theories.

But the judge added, "The slate was not so clean, however."

Cohn had reviewed the record of how the policy had been enforced at the U of M, and found that "as applied by the University over the past year, the Policy was consistently applied to reach protected speech," i.e., speech protected as freedom of expression by the First Amendment to the United States Constitution.

This included a number of examples, including a case involving another graduate student in social work who stated in class that he thought homosexuality was a disease and that he intended to find a way to change his gay clients to straight.

Cohn archly noted that the University "saw no First Amendment problem in forcing the student to a hearing to answer for allegedly harassing statements made in the course of academic discussion and research."

Having concluded that Doe indeed had standing to challenge the policy, the judge then

---

2. The university also published a Guide to the Policy, both of which appeared in pamphlet form with contrasting maize and blue color schemes. The Guide, which had a yellow cover, was later quietly withdrawn, although the university did not publicize that it had done so. On learning the Guide had been withdrawn, Judge Cohn quipped that they were "taking the maize out of the maize and blue," which are the university's colors.
3. The university did not object to his choosing to remain anonymous.

found that policy both too broad and hopelessly vague.

In terms of breadth, Cohn noted that "the Supreme Court has consistently held that statutes punishing speech and conduct solely on the grounds that they are unseemly or offensive are unconstitutionally overbroad."

He quoted a relatively recent decision[4] in which the nation's highest court said "the mere dissemination of ideas, no matter how offensive to good taste on a state university campus may not be shut off in the name alone of conventions of decency."

The University of Michigan's policy, the judge ruled, was indeed too broad to pass Constitutional muster, since it was clear "that the state may not prohibit broad classes of speech, some of which may indeed be legitimately regulable, if in so doing, a substantial amount of constitutionally protected conduct is also prohibited.

Judge Cohn also agreed that the policy as written was too vague to be constitutional. "The University never articulated any principled way to distinguish sanctionable from protected speech, and it was simply impossible to discern any limitation on its scope of any conceptual distinction between protected and unprotected conduct."

***

Accordingly, the judge then issued a permanent injunction striking down the provisions of the policy applying to what could be said—but left intact those portions forbidding any physical contact that could be construed as harassment.

"While the court is sympathetic to the University's obligation to ensure equal educational opportunities for all its students, such efforts must not be at the expense of free speech. Unfortunately, this is precisely what the University did," he ruled.

***

More than thirty years after it was decided, *Doe v. University of Michigan* is still cited today. It has had a lasting impact in that it established the ground rules for any "speech codes" that might be adopted on any campus. It was clear from Judge Avern Cohn's ruling that, in addition to not violating speech clearly protected by the First Amendment, any such policy provisions must be clearly and specifically outlined, defined, and be perfectly clear and comprehensible to faculty, staff and students.

---

4. *Papish v. University of Missouri, 410 U.S. 667 (1973)*

Bradley v. Milliken, 1989[1] (The Detroit School Busing Case)

(Final Judgment: Feb. 24, 1989)

The remedial plan has been formally completed … none of this is to say the Detroit system is problem-free. Indeed, it is not.

- Judge Avern Cohn

Milliken v. Bradley[2] is a landmark school desegregation case in which the United States Supreme Court effectively ruled in July, 1974 that cross-district busing of Detroit public school students for purposes of integration was unconstitutional.

But as *Bradley v. Milliken*, the case went on in federal court in the Eastern District of Michigan for many years, ultimately being ended by Judge Avern Cohn.

Much has been written about this case, especially on the federal level,[3] but much less about how it all played out in the city of Detroit and its suburbs after the U.S. Supreme Court's 1974 ruling. Ten years after the initial lawsuit was filed, the case had gone through many twists and turns that included more than a thousand docket entries, two trips to the U.S. Supreme Court, the death of Stephen Roth, the first federal judge assigned to the case, and the recusal of the second, Robert DeMascio.

Finally, in late 1980, a three-judge panel was assigned to the case: Chief Judge John

---

1. Case No. 70-3527 was the civil case number in the Eastern District of Michigan.
2. *Milliken v. Bradley*, 418 U.S. 717 (1974).
3. See, for example, *The Detroit School Busing Case: Milliken v. Bradley and the Controversy over Desegregation*, by Joyce A. Baugh, University Press of Kansas, 2011.

Feikens, Judge Patricia Boyle, and Judge Avern Cohn.[4]

Bradley v. Milliken was unquestionably important; it was the first case dealing with a deliberately segregated public school system in the United States since school segregation itself had been found unconstitutional by the U.S. Supreme Court in *Brown v. Board* in 1954.[5]

The *Brown* decision famously ordered schools to desegregate with "all deliberate speed." But as time went on and *de facto* school segregation continued, those opposed to it pursued further legal remedies. In 1970, the NAACP filed suit in U.S. District Court for the Eastern District of Michigan arguing that deliberately discriminatory policies had created segregation in the Detroit public schools, and challenging that as unconstitutional.

The case was initially assigned to U.S. District Judge Stephen Roth, who in 1971 found that the Detroit Public Schools were indeed illegally and deliberately segregated, and ruled that any plan dealing with only the Detroit schools was bound to be inadequate, and ordered a solution that required cross-district busing with suburban districts.

That led to the first U.S. Supreme Court ruling, which held that the courts could not order cross-district busing unless it could be shown that the suburban districts had engaged in deliberate segregation. Nevertheless, the Detroit schools also were still required to develop a school desegregation plan within the district's own boundaries.[6]

Three years later, the nation's highest court unanimously reaffirmed a Detroit-only solution, and also held that the State of Michigan could bear some of the costs of the remedial educational programs Judge DeMascio ordered adopted by the Detroit Public Schools.

***

After U.S. Supreme Court returned the case to Detroit, the plaintiffs claimed that DeMascio was biased against them, and at the suggestion of the Sixth Circuit Court of Appeals, he recused himself in August 1980, which led to the appointment of the previously mentioned three-judge panel to oversee the case.

Disputes continued over various issues, from the cost of various programs to legal fees, to an independent Monitoring Commission and a student code of conduct. In 1984, the panel dissolved the commission, arguing that it was an unnecessary duplication of the elected Detroit Board of Education, and said that administering the educational components should be the responsibility of the Detroit board.

Interviewed years after the case, Judge Cohn said: "When we did all this, we said … "we are of the opinion that our oversight responsibility under the remedial orders and the manner

---

4. Judge Boyle left the court in 1983 to take a seat on the Michigan Supreme Court. She was replaced on the *Bradley v. Milliken* panel by Judge James Churchill.
5. Formally, *Brown v. Board of Education of Topeka* (Kansas) 347 U.S 483 (1954).
6. University of Michigan Law School, Civil Rights Litigation Clearinghouse, *Milliken v. Bradley*

in which courts usually operate to enforce such orders might distort the political processes which govern elected boards of education."[7]

However, the panel's decision was overturned by the Sixth Circuit, which sent the case back to the District Court panel and ordered it to 1) reinstate the Monitoring Commission and to retain authority for a school community relations program and a code of conduct. Following that, Judges Churchill and Feikens left the panel in 1985 and turned sole responsibility for the case over to Judge Cohn.

Meanwhile, population shifts (continuing "white flight" and demographic changes) meant that by the late 1980s, the student population of the Detroit Public Schools, 70 percent white when the case began, had become nearly all African-American, meaning that busing to achieve racial balance there had become an exercise in futility.[8]

Recognizing this, the Detroit Board of Education then filed a motion in late 1988, asking Judge Cohn to declare that the schools had achieved "unitary status" and that the court should terminate its jurisdiction and enter a final order dismissing *Bradley v. Milliken*, with the exception of a 1988 order regarding vocational education.

On January 11, 1989 Cohn did just that, issuing a memorandum stating that "the remedial plan … has been formally completed and the vestiges of past *de jure* segregation have been eliminated from the Detroit school system. In so doing, he wrote, "The changing demographics of Detroit have eliminated the evils which formed the basis for the finding of liability; the Detroit school system has achieved "unitary status" as that term is commonly used in school segregation cases."

In granting the motion, he noted that "ordinarily, political processes should be sufficient to make the Detroit Board of Education accountable for its actions, and any failures can best be responded to by such processes, or by the State Board of Education, which bears ultimate responsibility," for Michigan's constitutional guarantee that "every school district shall provide for the education of its pupils without discrimination." [9]

Cohn was not starry-eyed about the future, however: "None of this is to say the Detroit school system is problem-free. Indeed, it is not," he wrote, noting the system itself had reported "massive deficiencies in the Detroit school system which the Detroit board must deal with in the future."

Judge Cohn then entered a final judgment formally dismissing the case on Feb. 24, 1989. The problems he cited were never really solved, and indeed became much worse. The district passed in and out of emergency management by the state several times in the following years. Enrollment in the Detroit Public Schools, which was 182,332 in 1990, the year after he

---

7. Baugh, *The Detroit School Busing Case,* op. cit, p. 189-190
8. In the 2019-2020 school year, the student population was 82 percent black, 14 percent Hispanic and 3 percent white, a figure that, apart from an increasing Hispanic population, has little changed in recent decades.
9. Constitution of the State of Michigan of 1963, Section VIII, Education.

ended the case, fell to fewer than 48,000 in 2015.[10]

Looking back with the hindsight of more than thirty years, Avern Cohn's closing comments reflect a certain poignancy. He had been educated in the Detroit public schools, as was his father before him, in an era when the schools were among the finest in the country. Managing what had then become a severely distressed school system was not a happy or satisfying task for him, even when he ended oversight of the two programs the court had been supervising, community relations and the student code of conduct.

His dismissal of the case meant the district was now on its own, and responsibility for problems both present and future returned to the Detroit Board of Education.

But he was left with a real concern that the schools had a tough road ahead, especially when it came to adequately educating its pupils. That concern, alas, was more than justified by what happened during the next few decades.

No one knows what might have happened had the suburban districts been included in a school desegregation plan. But in an interview twenty years after *Bradley v. Milliken* ended, Cohn said "I'm not a sociologist and not an educator, but I am also not sure the case really hastened white flight in from Detroit by much. Detroit, because of the age of its housing stock and the layout, simply became a less attractive place to live. Those who could afford to move into the new suburban communities and (enjoy) the amenities they offered did so. School environment was a part of that, but a small part.

"The city had aged, and those could escape its wrinkles did so, while leaving those who couldn't afford it behind, but not because of *Bradley v. Milliken.*"[11]

---

10. Echoes of the continuing issues that led to the original *Bradley v. Milliken* lawsuit can be heard in *Gary B. v Whitmer,* also known informally as the Detroit literacy case, in which seven poorly educated Detroit public school students filed suit in federal court, claiming they had a right to an adequate education that included making sure they were literate. The case was at first dismissed, but on appeal, in April 2020 a three-judge panel for the Sixth Circuit ruled in the students' favor. There was speculation that this would be overruled by the Sixth Circuit sitting *en banc,* but before that could happen, the state settled with the plaintiffs and provided more money for what is now called the Detroit Public Schools Community District. There will almost certainly be more such cases, both in Michigan and nationally.
11. Baugh, *op cit.* p. 195

The Kearns Patent Cases, 1987-1995[1]

This is a complex patent validity and infringement case.

- Judge Avern Cohn

Avern Cohn had many interesting cases during the more than forty years he was a federal judge. But the patent saga involving Robert Kearns, the quixotic former engineering professor who invented the technology behind the intermittent electronic windshield wiper, was the only one that has been made into a Hollywood movie.[2]

"How often does a judge find himself with a case that becomes a *New Yorker* article, a book, and a movie?" Judge Cohn said years later. "But this case had romantic appeal—it was David vs Goliath, the little guy against the big guy in the public mind."

Kearns, the "little guy," received numerous patents in the 1960s for a wiper system that would pause between swipes in light rain or mist, an idea he said was based on the way in which the human eye blinked. He tried to interest various automakers in his invention, but his true desire was to build plants and manufacture the wipers himself—a theme that drove his position throughout the cases.

---

1. Judge Cohn presided over five Kearns patent cases in Detroit, the details of which can be easily found on the internet. However, nearly all the pertinent facts and information pertaining to the claims and defenses can be found in the decision in *Kearns v. Chrysler Corp.* 32 F.3d 1541; (Fed. Cir. 1994) and *Kearns v. Ford Motor Co.*, 726 F. Supp 159 (E.D. Mich. 1989).
2. *Flash of Genius (*2008), a Universal Pictures film starring Greg Kinnear as Kearns. The film was well received by the critics, but a box office flop, earning less than a quarter of the $20 million spent to make the film. Though Cohn was the judge in reality, the judge in the movie was named Michael Franks. A penetrating and entertaining factual narrative can be found in the book *Flash of Genius, and Other True Stories of Invention,* by John Seabrook; St. Martin's Press, 2008.

The automakers declined to come to such an agreement with Kearns, and soon began manufacturing intermittent wipers on their own, without acknowledging Kearns as the inventor or paying him any royalties. This led him to file a patent suit against Ford Motor Co. in 1978, the first company he approached about his invention, and then to sue other automakers, including Chrysler and General Motors. In addition to the cases against Detroit's Big Three automakers, Kearns filed two other cases.[3]

Initially, the cases were assigned to U.S. District Judge Philip Pratt. It was only after he succumbed to cancer in early 1989 that the cases were assigned to Judge Cohn. Besides the complexity of the issues, the potential dollar amounts at stake were also huge; Kearns asked for $325 million from Ford alone.

The cases at times took on the trappings of a spy melodrama, as when early in the saga, Kearns' son Dennis, a private detective, seduced a paralegal at a law firm for confidential documents in the Daimler-Benz and Porsche case. After this was discovered, Judge Pratt ordered a $10,000 sanction on Kearns, in addition to attorney fees and interest. That brought the eventual total he was ordered to pay to $198,310.83.[4]

Pratt did not, however, entertain a motion to dismiss the lawsuits as a result. However, he stayed progress in all the cases until Kearns paid. The inventor had neither the money nor the inclination to do so, and so all cases were at a standstill at the time of Pratt's death. When Cohn got the cases, he determined that those against Ford, Chrysler and General Motors were "uncontaminated" by what Dennis Kearns had done, and that those cases should go forward.

The Ford case was the first to go to trial. Chrysler agreed that it would then be bound by any decision on the validity of Kearns' patents in the Ford case. In January, 1990 a jury found that Ford had indeed infringed those patents.[5] A further trial was needed to determine the amount of damages Ford had to pay.

The first attempt at assessing damages ended in a mistrial in May, 1990, with the jury unable to agree on damages. A second jury in November awarded Kearns $5.2 million. Interest of roughly an equivalent amount was added to the award.[6] Ironically, Ford had offered to settle the case for $30 million before the verdict, but Kearns indignantly refused. He wanted the automaker to agree to buy all its future intermittent wiper assemblies from Kearns, which Ford declined to do.

Afterwards, Kearns threatened to challenge the verdicts, but instead settled for $10.2 million. His original demand for much more was based on claims that he intended to

3. *Robert Kearns v. Wood Motors, Inc., Daimler-Benz and Porsche*, (106 F.3rd 427, Fed.Cir. 1997) and *Kearns v. Ferrari*, 752 F. Supp 749 (E.D.Mich. 1990)
4. Much later, Kearns managed to acquire other documents by going through an opposing law firm's waste paper; Cohn ruled that trash was open to the public. Neither the papers found in the trash nor those purloined earlier were of any legal importance.
5. "Ford Loses Patent Suit on Wipers," By Edmund L. Andrews, *New York Times,* Jan. 31, 1990.
6. "Ford to Pay $10 million to Settle Suit By Windshield Wiper Inventor," *Buffalo News,* Nov. 15,1990.

manufacture intermittent windshield wiper systems himself, and also that he was entitled to all of the mark-up over manufacturing costs Ford charged for every vehicle it produced with an intermittent wiper system.

Judge Cohn had previously ruled, however,[7] that neither claim was valid. Instead, Kearns was entitled to a reasonable royalty for Ford's having infringed on his patents.

As to the claim of all the profits Ford made from marking up the cost of a vehicle, Cohn said "it is clear that Kearns is not entitled to lost profits as a measure of damages because he cannot meet the test articulated in *Panduit v. Stahlin Bros. Fibre Works.*"[8] This was a 1978 case in which the Court of Appeals for the Sixth Circuit ruled that anyone in Kearns' position must "show the existence of a demand for the patented product … the manufacturing and marketing capability to exploit the demand, and the amount of profits he would have made."

Similarly, Cohn ruled at the same time that Kearns could not claim the loss of profits he might have made from manufacturing intermittent systems because he never demonstrated that could have raised the capital or take the other steps that would have been needed to do so.

Cohn noted that Kearns' statements "lack sufficient detail to even suggest that producing electronic IWW control circuits would have been a realistic option."

Years later, after Kearns died an unhappy and bitter man, Cohn told the *Associated Press* that while Kearns had "established the fact that he had made a contribution to the auto industry that was unique, his zeal got ahead of his judgment."[9]

***

Kearns v. Chrysler Corporation[10]

Kearns filed a patent infringement suit against Chrysler in 1982 similar to the one he had brought against Ford and several other automakers.

As noted above, Chrysler stipulated that it would be "bound by the judgment (excluding a consent judgment) in the Ford case as to validity and enforceability of the patents." With the end of the Ford trial, the Chrysler case returned to active status. At the beginning, because of the verdict in Ford, Judge Cohn issued a pre-trial order stating that the issues to be decided at trial would include "infringement, damages and willfulness."[11]

This, of course, excluded validity. Chrysler, notwithstanding the prior agreement, then

---

7. *Kearns v. Ford Motor Co.* 726 F. Supp. 159 (E.D. Mich, 1989)
8. 575 F.2d 1152 (6th Fed. Cir. 1978)
9. "Robert Kearns, 77, Inventor of Intermittent Wipers, Dies." *Associated Press,* Feb, 26, 2005.
10. 771 F. Supp.190 (E.D.Mich. 1991) The case was decided by a jury in October, 1992. Cohn denied Chrysler's motion for a directed verdict or for a new trial. The Federal Circuit affirmed Cohn and the jury in all respects, and declined in September, 1994 to rehear the entire case *en banc.*
11. Feb. 20, 1991

filed a motion to have the validity of Kearns' patents as an issue. The automaker claimed that the Ford outcome should be counted as a "consent judgment" because it ultimately ended in a settlement, and thus the stipulation no longer applied. Judge Cohn denied the motion, noting that the question of "validity" had indeed been hotly contested in the Ford trial—the result being a jury verdict and a final judgment in favor of Kearns.

As with Ford, Cohn split the Chrysler case into two separate jury trials, one to consider liability and the second, assuming Chrysler was found liable, to award damages. The liability trial ended in December 1991, with the jury finding that Chrysler had infringed three of the Kearns patents. Six months later, the same jury ruled that Chrysler's infringement was not willful, and assessed a royalty of 90 cents per vehicle that Chrysler had made with intermittent wipers—some 12.6 million cars and trucks.

In the damages trial which followed, Kearns elected to act as his own lawyer. In the light of the substantial award, he apparently did a good job. When interest and costs were added, a judgment of $18,740,465 was entered against Chrysler.

The automaker then appealed the case, and lost in the Court of Appeals, which upheld the judgment "in all respects." The U.S. Supreme Court declined to hear the case.

Meanwhile, the money Chrysler had to pay had swollen to $30 million. However, there were various claims on the award, including the sanction award and one from Kearns' ex-wife, who, as part of the divorce settlement, was supposed to get ten percent of any total award, and several sets of attorneys, whom the inventor had discharged at various times since his cases began.

When the case was returned to his docket, Cohn appointed a magistrate judge to adjudicate the claims. Kearns declined to take part in the proceedings. The judgment had been paid directly to the court by Chrysler to avoid further interest. When the claims were settled, about $12 million remained in the court's account. Kearns was notified, but did not pick up the deposited amount for many months.

"After he picked up the money on deposit, three days later, he called and said he had lost the check." Cohn said. When so advised, Cohn ordered payment on the check stopped and had a new check issued to Kearns.

***

As noted earlier, Ford and Chrysler were not the only companies Kearns sued, as previously described. After Ford and Chrysler, the General Motors case was next in line. However, the General Motors case was eventually dismissed by Cohn, largely because Kearns at that time refused to retain lawyers and had decided to represent himself—something he proved to be incapable of doing.

Additionally, the other cases were dismissed for the same reason. When Cohn advised him that he needed counsel and asked if he intended to get a lawyer, Kearns told him "I'd sooner have my arms fall off." [12] Kearns appealed the dismissal of his suits to the Federal Circuit, which, in stinging language, affirmed Judge Cohn's actions. The appeals court noted that Kearns not only failed to file his appeal on time, he filed it in the wrong court. Kearns's quixotic lawsuits soon evaporated after that. His patents had expired,[13] and he had become bitter and disillusioned.

"All my friends are saying, 'you won.'" he told the *New York Times*. [14] "In truth, I lost," he said, complaining that the lengthy litigation deprived him of the time he would have needed to start his own manufacturing business.

Kearns also claimed a court should extend his exclusive patent rights for an extra 12 years, the time he spent in litigation, and that the industry should be forbidden from making intermittent wipers, and be required to buy them from him.

This claim was denied.

Eventually, Kearns moved to Maryland, where he continued to talk of reclaiming his patents until the effects of a brain tumor and Alzheimer's Disease ended his life in February 2005. In his final years, he drove two aging vehicles, a 1978 Ford pickup and a 1965 Chrysler. Neither had intermittent windshield wipers.[15]

---

12. As the Federal Circuit noted in affirming Cohn, "the district court dismissed Kearns' suit with prejudice on the grounds that he was unable to adequately represent himself and that he refused to retain counsel." *Kearns v. Toyota*, 53 F. 3rd 345 (E.D. Mich. 1995).
13. Patents then generally expired after 17 years; that has since been extended to 20 years
14. "Patents: An Inventor Wins, but Isn't Happy," By Edmund L. Andrews, *New York Times*, Dec. 14, 1991.
15. "Accomplished, Frustrated Inventor Dies. By Matt Schudel, *Washington Post,* Feb. 26, 2005.

U.S. v. Jake Baker, aka Abraham Jacob Alkhabaz, 1995[1]

(June 21, 1995)

While new technology such as the Internet may complicate analysis and may sometimes require new or modified laws, it does not in this instance qualitatively chance the analysis under the statute or under the First Amendment.

- Judge Avern Cohn

What has become known as the "Jake Baker case" is important for two reasons. *Baker* was one of the first major cases involving free speech, the law and the then-new medium of the internet, which was in its infancy when the case was filed in the District Court for the Eastern District of Michigan in 1995.

To this day, *Baker* is frequently cited as setting a precedent for free speech in cyberspace. This is believed to have been the first time anyone had been charged with a crime in connection with what was then the fledgling internet.[2]

But the case is also notable for an example of a judge who chose to follow an interpretation of fairness and the law in a highly publicized and emotionally charged case in which his rulings went against much of public opinion.

---

1. 890 *F. Supp.1375 (E.D. Mich. 1995)*
2. While the internet itself had been around since 1969, it only became widely available to the public in the early 1990s, after the invention of the World Wide Web. Prosecutors in the Baker case took pains to explain to some grand jurors what the internet was. A May 29, 1995 *New York Times* story cited by Cohn quoted an expert as saying the internet had fewer than 40 million users worldwide. ("Technology: On the Net") by Peter Lewis.

The origins of the case began when a University of Michigan alumnus living in Moscow contacted the school in January, 1995 to report a disturbing story posted by a U of M student on an internet "bulletin board," also known as a "user group," reserved for sexually oriented stories.

Twenty-year-old Jake Baker, born Abraham Jacob Alkbahaz, a sophomore from southern Ohio, had posted a story describing the torture, sexual abuse and murder of a young woman, who was given the name of a fellow student in one of his classes.[3]

The university investigated and suspended Baker, and contacted the FBI after the local prosecutor declined to take action, on the grounds that this didn't violate Michigan law. A search warrant was executed, and Baker also gave the investigators permission to search his stored e-mail messages. The messages discovered included a series of exchanges with someone in Ontario, Canada who used the name Arthur Gonda.[4] The series of emails, which began the previous fall, involve exchanging sexual fantasies about abusing women, and gradually escalated to a discussion of getting together at some point to do just that. The emails are graphic, and most readers would likely find them shocking and sickening.

"I want to do it to a really young girl first, 13 or 14," Baker wrote "Gonda," who replied approvingly "not only their innocence but their young bodies would be really fun to hurt … however, you can control any bitch with rope and gag."

Baker also sent an email saying "Just thinking about it anymore doesn't do the trick … I need TO DO IT." On February 9, 1995, he was arrested and charged with a felony under 18 U.S. Code § 875c, a 1948 federal law which states:

> *Whoever transmits in interstate or foreign commerce any communication containing any threat to kidnap any person or any threat to injure the person of another shall be fined under this title or imprisoned not more than five years, or both.*

Baker was jailed overnight. The next day, a magistrate judge ordered him detained without bond as a danger to the community. A district judge affirmed detention on Feb. 13, and Baker was placed in the Federal Correctional Institution in Milan, Michigan and eventually remained there for 29 days, although a psychiatric evaluation conducted on

---

3. Baker had posted several stories with similar themes, but only one used the real name of a student.
4. "Gonda" was never identified. The email account associated with the name was deactivated before charges had been filed against Baker. As Judge Cohn said, "he could be a ten-year-old girl, an eighty-year-old man, or a committee in a retirement community playing the role of Gonda gathered around a computer." Canadian authorities were never able to locate anyone named Arthur Gonda, other than one elderly man who did not know how to use a computer.

January 20, "concluded that Baker did not display any risk factors for potential violence."[5]

The case was assigned to Judge Avern Cohn, who at the time of the detention following Baker's indictment was on vacation and out of the country. When he returned, Baker requested pretrial release on Tuesday, March 7.

Cohn convened a hearing the next day and ordered pretrial services to promptly arrange a psychological evaluation to determine if Baker "would pose a danger to any other person or the community should he be released pending trial."

Before that, however, in an effort to eliminate Cohn's ability to release Baker, the U.S. District Attorney's office filed an emergency motion asked the U.S. Court of Appeals (Sixth Circuit) to direct that the defendant not be released on bond.

The Appeals Court declined to do so. A psychologist examined Baker on March 9th and 10th, and concluded that he "does not appear to be a person who will … act out violently," and recommended be discharged to the custody of his mother, a creative writing teacher in Boardman, Ohio.[6] Cohn did so March 10, releasing Baker and setting bond at $10,000.

Prosecutors convened a grand jury following the detention hearing, which eventually charged both Baker and "Arthur Gonda," with five counts of violating 18 U.S. Code § 875c, by transmitting threatening communications.[7] Though the initial focus and much of the media attention was on the story Baker wrote and posted on the internet, prosecutors did not charge him in connection with the stories, possibly because they realized they were clearly fiction and labeled as such.

While the FBI testified before the grand jury that the classmate named in the story was "extremely frightened and intimidated" when she found out a rape, torture and murder victim in it had been given her name, there was no evidence that Baker ever spoke to her or attempted to have any other contact with her.

Baker was arranged and pleaded not guilty on March 24. On April 26, Baker's counsel filed a motion to quash the entire superseding indictment, and the next day the American Civil Liberties Union filed an amicus curiae brief in support of dismissal.

Judge Cohn issued his decision on June 21, 1995. He began by denying Baker's motion to dismiss all the counts on the grounds that 18 U.S.C. 875c doesn't apply *per se* to email transmissions. "The First Amendment does not protect "true threats," the judge said, adding that whether a communication of any kind constitutes a true threat is normally a question

---

5. Cited by Judge Cohn in Footnote No. 5 from his decision ending the case. *U.S. v, Jake Baker and Arthur Gonda*, 890 F. Supp. 375 E.D Mich. 1995.
6. Baker did not appeal his suspension, and as far as is known, never returned to Ann Arbor. He later reportedly attended college in Pittsburgh.
7. Baker was initially indicted on Feb. 14, 1995 with violating 18 U.S.C. 875(c) on one count which referenced the offending story. On March 15, the government filed a superseding indictment, cited the exchange between Baker and "Gonda" and charged both with five counts of violating the statute. The short story that started the case was *functus officio*; i.e. no longer mentioned.

for a jury.

However, he then proceeded to examine the government's case, and each of the counts in the superseding indictment. "Because prosecution under 18 U.S.C. 875 (c) involves punishment of pure speech, it necessarily ... is limited by the First Amendment," Cohn said. "So long as the threat on its face and in the circumstances in which it is made (are) so unequivocal, immediate, and specific to the person threatened, as to convey a gravity of purpose and an imminent prospect of execution, the statute may be applied."

The requirements were the key. Cohn cited two cases, *Watts v. United States* (1969), in which the Supreme Court ruled that while the First Amendment does not protect against true threats, statements that are clearly hyperbole without any plan of action do not count as threats.[8]

Cohn also cited *U.S. v. Kelner* (1976) a case in which Russell Kelner, a member of the Jewish Defense League, appeared on television and announced that his group planned to assassinate Yasser Arafat while he was visiting New York and said "everything is planned in detail." This, the Second Circuit said in sustaining Kelner's conviction, was a true threat.

But Cohn noted that the Second Circuit ruled "that where the factual proof of a 'true threat' is 'insufficient as a matter of law,' the indictment is properly dismissed before reaching the jury."

As far as the superseding indictment against Baker went, Cohn said that the statements he made must meet the standard set in the Kelner case—the threats must be "unequivocal, unconditional, immediate and specific."

None of the counts meets this test, the judge said. "Discussion of desires, alone, is not tantamount to acting on those desires," he said in reference to one count. In dismissing another, the judge noted that "discussion of the commission of a crime is not tantamount to declaring an intention to commit the crime."

The final count in the superseding indictment charged Baker and the unknown Gonda with transmitting a threat to injure, based on Baker's statement that "I need to DO IT," and their discussion about getting together sometime. The judge ruled that Baker's statement "does not express an unequivocal intention immediately to do anything."

Cohn said that this, like all the others, failed to state a charge that could survive a First Amendment challenge. He dismissed the case, saying that "this prosecution presents the rare case in which "the language set forth is so facially insufficient that it cannot possibly amount to a true threat."

The case had, as Cohn noted "generated a good deal of public interest," and said that especially because it was not going before a jury, "it is important to assure the public that

---

8. Watts involved a Vietnam War protestor who said "If they ever make me carry a rifle, the first man I want to get in my sights is LBJ." The Supreme Court said that was not a true threat.

such a conclusion is not by fiat." Cohn then explained that even when viewed in the light most favorable to the prosecution, "there is no case for a jury because the factual proof is insufficient as a matter of law."

He noted, too, that the offending emails were not published on the internet, but only sent privately to Gonda.

The government appealed the dismissal, but a Sixth Circuit panel, in a 2-1 vote, affirmed Cohn's ruling.[9] While the majority declined to address the First Amendment issue, they concluded that the indictment "failed to set forth all the elements necessary to constitute the offense intended be punished, and must be dismissed as a matter of law."

The appellate judges also agreed with Cohn that "the communications between Baker and Gonda do not constitute 'communications containing a threat' under Section 875 (c), and in a further affirmation of Cohn's dismissal, noted that "As the Supreme Court has recognized, William Shakespeare's lines here illustrate sound legal doctrine."

His acts did not o'ertake his bad intent
And must be buried but as an intent
That perish'd by the way: thoughts are no subject
Intents but merely thoughts[10]

The Baker case is still regarded by scholars—some who agree with the ruling and some who do not—as an early milestone in the legality of the internet.

In an attempt to regulate obscenity and indecency on the internet, Congress enacted a Communications Decency Act as part of the sweeping Telecommunications Act of 1996. But the CDA was aimed at children, and a large portion was later struck down by the Supreme Court as infringing the free speech rights of adults.

Following the dismissal, Jake Baker vanished from the public eye. His current whereabouts are unknown, and indications are that he has never been in serious trouble with the law.

In the final analysis, the importance of Cohn's finding in *U.S. v. Jake Baker* may be that the same legal protections apply with the internet as elsewhere when it comes to First Amendment rights and the need for prosecutors to establish that there are adequate grounds to believe an offense has been committed before bringing a case.

Apart from that, the situation may be best summed up by the words Cohn quoted from a century-old ruling by Michigan Supreme Court Justice Thomas Cooley in dismissing a case:

"It is not the policy of the law to punish those unsuccessful threats which it is not

---

9. *U.S. v. Alkhabaz,* 104F.3d 1492 (1997)
10. *Measure for Measure*, Act 5 Scene 1

presumed would terrify ordinary people excessively, and there is so much opportunity for magnifying or misunderstanding undefined menaces that probably as much mischief would be caused by letting them be prosecuted as by refraining from it."[11]

---

11. *The People v. B.F. Jones,* 62 Mich. 304 (1886).

Immigrants and Justice: Three Cases

(Parlak v. Baker, May 20, 2005)

(United States of America v. Ali, Nazir, Mustak and Mohammed Ahmed, Sept. 20, 2018)

(United States of American v. Salah et al., terminated June 6, 2019)

Fairness is my polestar.

- Judge Avern Cohn

This book's title was inspired by something that Justice Louis Brandeis said was the heart of his judicial philosophy—you have to "think about the other fella."

That was also how Avern Cohn viewed his role during the 40 years he was on the federal bench in Detroit. He was devoted to justice, but also believed that a judge "has to have compassion, and have empathy—not sympathy," for the defendant.

Perhaps nothing shows that better than the way he dealt with cases involving immigrants, many of whom were of Muslim extraction. Nada Prouty, whose case is considered separately in this book, said that when she found that Judge Cohn had been assigned her case, "my friends told me that he was a Jewish judge, and I was in trouble. That wasn't true at all. He was extremely fair, and the one who really understood."

The following three cases are notable examples of how the judge appropriately combined compassion and empathy to further the pursuit of justice.

***

Ibrahim Parlak[1]

The case of Ibrahim Parlak, a Kurdish refugee who runs a restaurant in Southwest Michigan, has gotten national and, to some extent, international attention in the years since he appeared before Judge Cohn in 2005. U.S. Immigration and Customs Enforcement (ICE) has repeatedly tried to deport Parlak back to his native Turkey, claiming he was a former terrorist and a member of a terrorist group.

Those defending Parlak, including U.S. Rep. Fred Upton (R-MI), note that he has been a model immigrant who has now lived most of his life in Michigan; that he was granted permanent resident status before the government classified the Kurdish Workers' Party, the organization to which he belonged, as a terrorist group; and that sending him back to Turkey would likely mean torture and death for him.[2]

Parlak was granted asylum in the United States in July, 1992, and became a lawful permanent resident two years later. But when he applied to become a naturalized citizen in 1998, the government again investigated him. Parlak's application was denied, and he was arrested by ICE on July 29, 2004, and imprisoned after the government claimed he had lied on his application when asked if he had ever engaged in terrorist activity. Parlak denied that he had ever been a terrorist.

He had, however, been present when members of his group engaged in a firefight with some Turkish soldiers, two of whom were killed. He claimed that he had been open about his activities, and any mistakes on his original application for asylum were due to his barely rudimentary English language ability at the time.

The government, however, claimed that he could be returned to Turkey under a federal law[3] that specifies that "any alien who has engaged … in any terrorist activity as defined in section 1132(a)(3)(B)(iv) of this title is deportable."

The government claimed he was a flight risk, and an Immigration Judge refused to set bond. Parlak was then held in Calhoun County jail, in Battle Creek, pending deportation. After seven months, he filed a habeas corpus petition challenging his continued detention, noting he was a lawful permanent resident of the United States.

The petition was filed with the U.S. District Court of the Eastern District of Michigan, and the case was assigned by blind draw to Cohn. The government first claimed the Court

---

1. *Ibrahim Parlak v. Robin Baker, Detroit Field Office Director, U.S. Immigration and Customs Enforcement, 374 F. Supp.2d 551 (2005)*
2. Stories worth reading include "The Wasteful Case Against Ibrahim Parlak," by Evan Osnos, *The New Yorker*, Oct. 28, 2015. The *South Bend Tribune* published a recent update on his case: "Michigan restaurateur Parlak doubles down on torture fears as U.S. seeks deportation to Turkey. By Christian Sheckler and Greg Swiercz, Feb. 20, 2020. A full account of where the case stood when Avern Cohn had it can be found in the *New York Times* Magazine of March 20, 2005: "The Politics of Ibrahim Parlak," by Alex Kotlowicz.
3. 8 U.S.C. 1227(a)(4)(B)

had no jurisdiction, and that the person legally in charge was warden of the jail; i.e. the Calhoun County sheriff.

Cohn dismissed that claim, noting that in reality he was a federal prisoner, and said "it is clear that the District Director (of ICE; Robin Baker) has custodial control over the prisoner," and since the District Director's office was in the Eastern District, Parlak's petition had been filed in the correct jurisdiction.

Cohn also found that while ICE did have the discretionary authority to initially detain Parlak, keeping him locked up for an indefinite period of time "violates his constitutional rights." He concluded by saying "in sum, Petitioner is a lawful permanent resident of the United States. He has been a model immigrant … he is not a threat to anyone nor a risk of flight. He has strong ties to the community in which he resides … under these circumstances, there is simply no good reason to deny him his freedom."

Parlak was then released June 3, 2005 after posting a $50,000 bond.

The government appealed Cohn's ruling, but the appeal was dismissed by a Sixth Circuit Court of Appeals panel as moot after the Board of Immigration Appeals issued a final order of removal on Nov. 22, 2005.[4] Parlak was, however, neither detained, nor deported. Sixteen years later, Ibrahim Parlak is still running his restaurant, Café Gulistan, in Harbert, Michigan, and is still fighting government attempts to deport him.

When asked about his ordeal after Avern Cohn released him from custody, he said simply, "I'm glad that in America we have a justice system to correct mistakes."

***

The 'Food Stamp Cheat' Case[5]
Ali, Nasir, Mustak and Mohammed Ahmed, Sept. 20, 2018

To Readers: listen to us.
If you cheat on food stamps you are committing a federal crime and will be punished for doing so. We know: We have been punished for cheating on food stamps.

Ali Ahmed   Nazar Ahmed
Mustak Ahmed   Mohammed Ahmed

***

---

4. Ibrahim Parlak v. United States Immigration and Customs Enforcement, 2.05-cv-70826-AC-RSW, May 1, 2006
5. United States of America v. Ali Ahmed, Nazir Ahmed, Mustak Ahmed and Mohammed Ahmed, 16-cr-20086. (E.D., Mich,. 2018)

Avern Cohn handed down hundreds of sentences during his four decades on the federal bench, but this may have been among the most unusual. The words above appeared in both English and Bengali, in the weekly Hamtramck Review for three straight weeks in November, 2018. The Ahmed brothers had pled guilty to food stamp fraud.

According to the government, they cheated U.S. taxpayers out of more than half a million dollars by allowing customers at Deshi Bazar, a Hamtramck convenience store, to exchange their food stamps for cash, cigarettes, phone cards and other items that they knew food stamps did not cover. Two of the brothers also were charged with improperly collecting public assistance, even though they were not eligible to receive welfare.

Prosecutors said they each ought to be given a sentence of at least 24 months in prison. However, Cohn did not do that. He did sentence Ali Ahmed, the brother who owned the store, to nine months in prison. But the other three were sentenced to one day, supervised release for two years—and ordered to pay restitution.

Sending all the brothers to prison would have mainly served to destabilize their families. What had become a large and extended local Ahmed family in the area began in 1990, when Mohammed Ahmed, who was from an especially poor rural region of Bangladesh, was selected as part of a temporary visa lottery the U.S. government was running to allow more immigrants to enter the United States.

He arrived in New York; moved to Michigan in 1994, and worked hard at a variety of jobs and eventually paid to bring the rest of his family over. His presentencing report included many letters testifying to his good work in the community.

Each of the brothers was also ordered to pay restitution in amounts that totaled between $537,000 and $724,436. However, Cohn ordered them to each pay $25 a month, which meant it would take many lifetimes to pay their total debt.

They were also ordered to use their own money to place the newspaper advertisement above. Cohn, who approved the wording of the ad, said it was done primarily as a warning to other immigrants from Bangladesh, who, like the Ahmed brothers, lived in Hamtramck, and are now the largest ethnic group in that small city.

"They are good Americans," the judge said when he ordered the ad at the Ahmed brothers' sentencing. "They are good citizens, but they should be told or cautioned that if they cheat on food stamps, they are going to be punished." [6]

***

---

6. "Judge Shames 4 Bangladeshi food stamp crooks with unique sentence,: Tresa Baldas, *Detroit Free Press,* Nov. 3, 2018.

The Yemeni Money Laundering Case[7]

Throughout his career as a federal judge, Avern Cohn was not afraid to risk arousing negative opinion if he felt it necessary to do so in the interest of justice.

That was apparent in one of the last cases he decided before retiring, the case of a group of immigrants from Yemen who helped others send a total about $90 million back to their extremely poor and war-devastated home country—but did so illegally, since they failed to register as a money-transferring business or businesses.

Instead, they created a series of phony "shell" businesses with names like MJ Sports, Inc., whose real and sole purpose was to transfer money to Yemen.

After being charged, each of them pled guilty to one count of the indictment, after one defendant, Ahmed Al-Howshabi, admitted his guilt and offered to help authorities with their prosecution of the others, if necessary.

Each could have been sentenced to as much as five years in prison; the sentencing guidelines called for most of them to receive sentences of between 37 and 46 months, with prosecutors recommending no more than 23 months for Al-Howshabi.[8]

But after researching Yemeni culture and the current dire situation in Yemen, Judge Cohn startled both the prosecutors and likely the defendants by declining to send any of them to prison. "Only people without compassion would object,"[9] he told the Associated Press after the sentencing.

While the men clearly broke the law, attorneys for the men claimed there were no real victims. Experts on Yemen have said money sent from abroad is critical for merely preventing starvation; Yemen is poorer than any other Arab country and nearly any other country in the world, with a per capita GDP of $895 a year or less.

Sheila Carapico, a political scientist at the University of Richmond and an expert on Yemen, told the AP that such money transfers are "a mainstay for many households and the national economy." Cohn noted than in most Yemeni families wives do not work outside the home, and sending these men to prison could be financially devastating to their families. Noting that, he told one defendant it would be unfair to require them to "shed the traditions and practices of your homeland."

Instead of prison, the defendants were sentenced to supervised release, which is essentially equivalent to probation. Prosecutors afterwards conceded that they had no evidence that

---

7. Nine defendants were charged in a series of very similar cases, including U.S. v. Hazen Saleh and Fadhl AlHanshali; 18-cr-20625 (E.D. Mich, 2018) and U.S. v. Ahmed Al-Howshabi, Abdulkalk Pady, and Zaid Zaid,18-CR-20629 (E.D. Mich 2018).
8. Prosecutors asked for harsher sentences of as much as 53 months for Hazem Saleh and 71 months for Fahd Saha.
9. "Detroit-area men who sent millions to Yemen spared prison," by Ed White, *Associated Press*, Oct 20, 2019

the men were doing anything other than helping Yemenis send money to relatives,[10] though they did think prison time was appropriate.

However, U.S. Attorney Matthew Schneider did not seem unduly upset by the decision, saying, "Sometimes judges agree with us, and sometimes they don't."

---

10. Defendant Fahd Samaha said he charged clients only one percent to move money to Yemen, far less than the eight to ten percent Western Union, for example, charges.

United States of America v. Nada Nadim Prouty, 2008[1]

(May 13, 2008)

This is a highly unique situation … as a citizen, you served your country honorably and effectively and at times in situations which exposed you to extreme danger.

- Judge Avern Cohn

Among the many cases that came to the docket of U.S. District Judge Avern Cohn, *The United States of America v. Nada Nadim Prouty* is unique indeed. It has all the makings of a first-class real-life spy movie, full of heroism and betrayal. Though a movie hasn't yet been made,[2] the case produced national headlines, a *60 Minutes* investigation, and Prouty's own well-received book, *Uncompromised: The Rise, Fall and Redemption of an Arab-American Patriot in the CIA. (St. Martin's Press, 2011)*

Beyond that, Judge Cohn's handling of the case was exceptional, a story of judicial wisdom and an example of a judge who was not swayed by a torrent of media coverage which essentially convicted the defendant before trial.

Prouty was born in Lebanon in 1970, five years before that country began to be torn apart by a long civil war. In 1989, she fled the war, an abusive father and his plans to force her into an arranged marriage, and came to America to attend the Detroit College of Business. She was a superb student, but soon ran out of money for tuition.

---

1. Case No. 07-20156 ; *United States of America v Prouty,* (E.D. Mich. 2008)
2. According to an interview with Prouty in January 2021, a producer and director have been chosen for a movie version of her life, but the project has been put on hold because of the pandemic.

To be able to stay in America, she entered into a sham marriage with a U.S. citizen when she was barely 20, after a coworker in a restaurant told her "The American government knows about these sorts of marriages, and you will be fine so long as you contribute back to the government by paying your taxes."[3]

That, of course, was not true, and in the long run, it cost her dearly. The marriage, which was never consummated, was later dissolved by divorce. Prouty went on to get both bachelor's and masters' degrees in accounting. She then became a CPA, before joining the FBI in 1999, where she worked on international terrorism cases.

Eventually, she left the FBI and joined the CIA in 2003, where she was sent to Baghdad after the invasion of Iraq. After another brief legal marriage, she married Gordon Prouty, a U.S. foreign service officer who later went to work for the State Department in Washington. Various agents who worked with her said her service was exemplary and that her skills undoubtedly saved American lives. She worked on solving a number of famous terrorism cases for both the FBI and CIA, including the bombing of the *USS Cole* and the attack on the Khobar Towers.

Prouty continued to do dangerous undercover work on the streets of Baghdad after she became pregnant, wearing a bulletproof vest that had been modified to accommodate her condition. Though her husband encouraged her to leave Iraq, she said she felt unable to abandon those she worked with, especially because she was fluent in Arabic and there were very few American agents, especially women, who could speak the language; she was also busy learning Farsi for potential work in Iran.

Her life, however, was shattered in 2007, when the government began investigating Talal Khalil Chahin, who owned the La Shish restaurant chain in Metropolitan Detroit, and had fled the country for Lebanon after being wanted for a string of crimes ranging from tax evasion to extortion.

Chahin was married to Nada Prouty's sister, and had a close association with a Shia Muslim cleric who was regarded as the spiritual mentor of the terrorist group Hezbollah. The U.S. Department of Justice's investigation of Chahin eventually led to Prouty, and alarm bells were set off throughout the intelligence community about a possible relationship between the CIA agent and terrorists.

Prouty had never been Muslim; she had been raised in the Druze religion and later converted to Roman Catholicism. But the fact that she was born in Lebanon, worked for American intelligence services, and had a brother-in-law who had close ties to a top Hezbollah cleric made her a person of interest.

U.S intelligence services later admitted they did not find any indication that she had improperly disclosed secrets to any terrorist organization, or had improperly disclosed

---

3. Prouty, *Uncompromised,* p. 60

information to anyone, much less Hezbollah. But they did uncover the sham marriage that she entered into in 1990, which legally was immigration fraud.

The government then went after Prouty with enthusiasm, using the media, which often seemed all too willing to convict "Jihad Jane," without a trial or facts to support the conclusion that she had risked the nation's security in any way.[4]

There is a ten-year statute of limitations on bringing criminal charges on immigration fraud, which meant Prouty could not be prosecuted for the sham marriage. But the government charged her anyway on November 13, 1997 with naturalization fraud, perjury, and the unauthorized use of a government computer, which she allegedly used to look up information about a national security investigation of Hezbollah by the FBI in Detroit. The implication was that she was checking to see what they had on members of her family.

In her book, *Uncompromised*, Prouty said that before a trial could begin, she came under intense pressure to accept a plea bargain: "They noted that they were within the law to charge me with a felony for every use of my U.S. passport … so every time I had travelled internationally for the FBI and CIA was now an instance the prosecution could use to force me to my knees."

Worried by indications the government might come after her family and destroy her husband's career, and fearful that she could not afford the expense of adequately defending herself, Prouty reluctantly decided to sign a plea bargain which called for a sentence that would likely amount to only a few months in prison, and a fine of several thousand dollars, but which would also require her losing her citizenship,

Before a formal indictment was entered, she pled guilty to one count each of Conspiracy to Defraud the United States, Unauthorized Computer Access[5] and Naturalization Fraud. Under statutory provisions, Judge Cohn had the right to sentence her to up to 10 years in prison and, in addition, fine her up to $600,000.

A judge has, however, a certain amount of discretion in a case such as Prouty's. The Presentence Investigation Report prepared by the probation officer took into account a number of factors, including her glowing career record, lack of previous offenses and stable home life. The government did not object to these findings.

The report recommended a sentence of three years' probation, and a fine of $5,000 on each count. "There do not seem to be any aggravating or mitigating factors that would warrant a sentence outside of the advisory guideline system," the probation officer said in the report.

---

4. See, for example, "Jihad Jane's State of Bliss," by Susan Edelman, *New York Post*, Nov. 18, 2007, or "Fake U.S. Citizen Got FBI Secrets From Files; Hiring Missed La Shish, Terror Links," by David Ashenfelter, *Detroit Free Press*, Nov. 14, 2007.
5. Prouty still maintains that she never actually used the computer in question. There was no claim that she printed out, used or shared any information from it.

Judge Cohn disagreed, notwithstanding the government's urging for what he considered, in the circumstances, as an excessive sentence. He had received letters from the CIA testifying to Prouty's good character and heroic service, he noted.

When he imposed sentence on May 13, 2008, he went outside the guidelines to impose a fine of $750, a mandatory special assessment of $225, and neither jail nor probation time. He said "As a citizen you served your country honorably and effectively and at times in situations which exposed you to personal danger. The essential offense you committed was marriage fraud."

Cohn noted that her desire not to return to war-torn Lebanon was understandable. "Since that time, you have rendered extraordinary service to the United States as an agent of the FBI and in the employ of the CIA. At no time did you ever compromise or jeopardize the integrity of any work assignment to improper behavior or inappropriate conduct." He added, "I must also consider that there exists … mitigating circumstances of a kind or degree not adequately taken into consideration by the Sentencing Commission in promulgating the guidelines."

"This was not a matter of sympathy, of feeling sorry for the defendant," he said later, "but a matter of justifiable empathy with her circumstances."

He did revoke Prouty's citizenship as part of the plea bargain. This he did reluctantly. Cohn also sharply criticized the prosecution and the media in his sentencing remarks. "The media accounts of your case, perhaps prompted by the excessiveness of the press releases issued by the United States Attorney's Office, have grossly distorted the circumstances of your case."

"I was ecstatic that the judge had seen through the smoke to the real facts in my case," Prouty wrote in *Uncompromised*.[6] The tone of the media coverage soon began to change, and the tales of the heroic government exposing a terrorist mole soon ended, as T.S. Eliot said in his poem *The Hollow Men*, "not with a bang but a whimper."

On March 28, 2010, *60 Minutes* did a segment, "The Case Against Nada Prouty," which faulted the government and largely rehabilitated her reputation.

The CIA issued a statement exonerating Prouty in 2008, and the FBI followed suit on Nov. 12, 2009. In December, 2010, the U.S. Attorney General, the director of the CIA and the secretary of Homeland Security jointly announced they were granting Prouty Permanent Resident Alien status, which ended the threats of deportation.

Nada Nadim Prouty regained her citizenship in 2016. Today, she lives in the United Arab Emirates with her husband and two daughters, where she works as a private consultant. "Judge Cohn was very fair," she said in an interview in January 2021.

"He stood apart from the rest."

---

6. P. 266

U.S. v. City of Detroit, Michigan and the Detroit Police Department

(03-72258, 2014 WL 4384481 (E.D. Mich. Sept. 4, 2014)
(Final Ruling September 4, 2014)

Judges have a constitutional habit of the last word ... the operations of the Detroit Police Department have been fundamentally changed under the consent decree and the DPD now has in place appropriate training, supervision and accountability systems to identify and correct problems on its own.

- Judge Avern Cohn

One of the longest-running federal cases in recent years was the one known as the "Detroit Police Oversight Case," which began in 2003, and was finally closed down by U.S. District Judge Avern Cohn in March, 2016.

For most of those years, the case was overseen by Cohn's colleague, the late Judge Julian Abele Cook Jr., (1930-2017); it eventually came to Cohn after Cook retired.

The case itself had a stormy history. It began after media reports accused the police of multiple counts of bad behavior ranging from excessive use of force to illegal arrests and improper treatment of prisoners amounting to unconstitutional conduct.

Detroit then entered into two consent decrees with the U.S. Department of Justice, which required a federal monitor, paid to provide oversight and make sure the police were living up to the agreement—an arrangement that cost the city more than $15 million over the years it was in force.

Conditions gradually improved, and eventually both the city and the U.S. Department of Justice agreed the case could be closed. Cohn was perhaps an ideal judge to finish the case; born and raised in Detroit, he had also served on the Detroit Board of Police Commissioners and was familiar with the workings of the department.

When he signaled his intention to end the case, in September, 2014,[1] the city was in the process of transitioning from being run by an emergency manager following bankruptcy back to mayoral control. When he issued the order ending the "consent judgment", i.e. oversight, Cohn could have done so in mere boilerplate language.

Judge Cohn, however, was a man who not only had first-hand knowledge how the police department worked—he had a wide-ranging historical and governmental perspective. "Judges have a constitutional habit of the last word," his order began.

Then he added several hundred more well-chosen ones.

Cohn began with a concise but sweeping overview of the history of civilian oversight of the Detroit police department back to 1861. Noting the transition in process, and that Mayor Mike Duggan had reassumed authority over some other departments, Judge Cohn wrote, "to the court this suggests the first order of business is to give control of the (police) Department back to the Mayor."

Then he said "my second suggestion is for the Mayor to look at the charter provisions relating to the Board of (Police) Commissioners. The Charter states, as it did when the consent judgments were entered into, 'The Board of Police Commissioners has supervisory control and oversight of the Police Department.'"

Cohn then succinctly summed up the case. The reason that former Mayor Dennis Archer had asked the U.S. Department of Justice to "examine and look into what he saw as the gross deficiencies of police operations in Detroit was the consequences of a Board of Police Commissioners who had fallen down on the job of supervision and control."

How could a similar disaster be avoided in the future? The judge's answer: Civilian oversight. "Civilian oversight is different from civilian review," he wrote.

The Board of Police Commissioners should continue to exist, he said, but only as a civilian review body dealing with citizen complaints.

"In my view, what is needed today and for the future is a civilian head of the Department appointed by the mayor, and a chief of police who reports to the civilian head much like it was prior to 1972," Judge Cohn concluded.

Eighteen months later, the judge formally ended the transition, and Detroit's police department was once again completely under the authority of the mayor.

---

1. *Comments of Court (Revised) on Order Terminating Consent Judgment and Entering Transition Agreement* (Doc. 731), Sept. 4, 2014.

U.S. v. Matthew David Kuppe, 2017[1]

(April 11, 2017)

The fact that the Court adopts the sentencing memoranda does not mean that the Court agrees with everything that is said in it, but … judges should be part of the solution and not part of the problem.

- Judge Avern Cohn

Matthew Kuppe was a 21-year-old counselor at a Jewish Community Center day camp in West Bloomfield in August 2015, when a police investigator in Australia informed the Department of Homeland Security that Kuppe had posted naked pictures of little boys from the camp on a pornographic website in Russia.

The photographs were surreptitiously taken. They did not show the boys engaged in any sexual activity. Kuppe made little attempt to conceal his identity.[2] During a follow-up investigation he identified one child by name. The investigation disclosed that Kuppe exchanged photos and graphic fantasies about them in email conversations with the Australian investigator, who pretended to be someone interested in collecting child pornography.

Homeland Security contacted West Bloomfield police.[3] The Oakland County prosecutor declined to press charges. However, the U.S. attorney did. Judge Avern Cohn, who was assigned the case, was on vacation when the arrest was made. A grand jury indicted Kuppe on six counts of production, distribution, receipt and possession of child pornography.

---

1. No. *15-20522, (E.D. Mich., 2017)*
2. His email address was jcclockerroom@gmail.com
3. The U.S. Department of Homeland Security's involvement in the Kuppe case was unusual and never has been fully explained; the department was established after the September 11, 2001 attacks, essentially to guard America against terrorism and other external threats.

A magistrate judge ordered Kuppe detained without bond. Within days after Kuppe was arrested and arraigned and before an indictment was returned, the government posted a notice of Kuppe's arrest and description of the charges, and invited any parents whose children had attended the day camp to contact it.

This was before much was known about Kuppe as a person, or exactly what he was alleged to have done. The effect was to create the clear impression that he was a child molester.

This was reminiscent of the Jake Baker case[4] twenty years earlier, when first a magistrate judge and then another federal judge ordered Baker detained. When Cohn returned to Detroit, he ordered an immediate psychological examination, and when the psychologist reported Baker was not a threat to the community, Cohn freed him on bond after he'd spent 29 days in detention.

In Kuppe's case, something similar to what happened to Baker occurred. Three psychologists' opinions had been sought; two by the government and one by the magistrate judge. Two of their reports recommended release; the third psychologist, who recommended detention, had never interviewed Kuppe, and in his report included "circumstances that are significantly incorrect," Cohn said in vacating the detention order.[5]

Noting that there is a presumption of innocence and that pretrial release is the norm, even in sex offender cases, Cohn released Kuppe, who had been detained for 97 days, to the custody of his parents and under conditions that included a tether and Kuppe staying away from computers and off the internet.

The release set off a firestorm of criticism which was reported in the media; Cohn was portrayed as having more sympathy for a child molester than for his victims.[6] Media stories reported allegations that Kuppe had physically molested children, though no evidence was ever shown that he had touched any child.[7]

Over the next eight months, lawyers for Kuppe and the government worked out a plea bargain in which he agreed to plead guilty to count four of the indictment; distributing child pornography. The agreement stated that the other counts were to be dismissed on the plea of guilty.

As part of the plea bargain, Kuppe agreed to a ten-year sentence. This much time for distribution was not required by the statute. The recommended sentencing range under the guidelines, as Cohn noted, was between 76 and 87 months, meaning Kuppe possibly could have served less than six and a half years.

The pre-sentencing report also indicated Kuppe had been in intensive therapy since his

4. *U.S. v. Jake Baker, aka Abraham Jacob Alkhabaz.* 890 F. Supp. 1375. (E.D. Mich. 1995)
5. Memorandum and Order Vacating Order of Detention. Nov. 24, 2015.
6. "Parents blast judge who set JCC porn suspect free." By Tresa Baldas, *Detroit Free Press*, Nov. 25, 2015.
7. WDIV-TV, the NBC affiliate in Detroit, still has a huge headline on its website from Sept. 4, 2015: "Feds: Ex-West Bloomfield Counselor Likely Had Sexual Contact with Children."

arrest and had made great progress in getting his impulses under control.

But by pleading guilty, Kuppe had to serve ten years, no more and no less.[8] Why did he accept the ten years? Had he not done so, the government could have gone to trial on the *production* of child pornography charge, since he had taken the pictures of the boys and put them on an internet pornography site. If convicted of the offense of production, it meant a mandatory 15-year-sentence.

Cohn had little choice but to approve the agreement. Had he sentenced Kuppe to less time, the plea bargain could have been invalidated, and as noted the government would have been free to require Kuppe to go to trial on the production charge.

There was an uncertainty as to or whether what Kuppe did would qualify as production of pornography—or if a jury would have convicted him of this offense. But Kuppe and his family indicated they did not want to take the risk, and Cohn felt bound to accept the family's position.

"Because your lawyer and the government have agreed to what the … agreement says, the Court is not going to stand in the way of fulfilling it," Cohn said in his remarks at sentencing.

The judge went on to say that the process was deeply flawed. "It is clear to me (that) … this case does not represent one of the government's finest hours."

Cohn criticized the government for failing to consider anything about the defendant's persona. Kuppe had no prior criminal history of any kind and suffered from undiagnosed obsessive-compulsive disorder (OCD).

He further criticized the government, as reported by the *Detroit Free Press*,[9] noting that it "initiated a major effort to keep defendant under lock and key as representing a danger to the community. He (Kuppe) was being treated as a child molester, and there was no evidence then, or any evidence since, to suspect him of child molestation, and the case was investigated thoroughly."

Cohn was also unhappy that the plea bargain agreement tied his hands. "It has long been the rule in this country, repeated from time to time by the Supreme Court of the United States, that the judge's exercise of discretion is the single most important factor in sentencing. Here … the Court has had nothing to say about the length of the sentence," Cohn said, noting that the United States Sentencing Commission itself had criticized the sentencing guidelines in child pornography cases.[10]

"No rational system of sentencing, considering precisely what defendant did and defen-

---

8. Had the Court sentenced Kuppe to less than 10 years, the government had the option of withdrawing from the agreement and going to trial on any or all of the counts. If Cohn sentenced Kuppe to more than 10 years, something that was not seen as likely, he could have withdrawn from the agreement.
9. "Jewish Center camp counselor gets 10 years for child porn," Tresa Baldas, *Detroit Free Press*, April 12, 2017
10. In his sentencing memorandum, Kuppe's attorney cited another case from the Eastern District of Michigan, *U.S. v. Hoberman*, in which the defendant caused a minor to engage in deviant behavior that included a sex act with a dog, images of which were put on line. He was sentenced to 8 years and 9 months, compared to Kuppe's 10 years.

dant's particular characteristics, would impose on him imprisonment for 10 years."[11]

The Kuppe case stands out in two ways: First, as an illustration of the need for reform in the federal guidelines for sentencing for child pornography. But also as an example of a judge who insisted on doing what he determined to be the right thing regardless of pressure from the prosecution and from misguided public opinion reflected in the media.

Kuppe was sent to the Federal Correctional Facility in Elkton, Ohio. His "out date" is June, 2027.

---

11. Cohn also imposed two special assessments totaling $5,100 on Kuppe; these were required by law.

Two Notable Dissents

My experience teaches that there is nothing better than an impressive dissent …

- Justice Ruth Bader Ginsburg, 2009

Avern Cohn always said he found great satisfaction in being a U.S. district judge, and had no ambition to be appointed to an appellate court. He found the human interaction displayed in a courtroom vibrant and stimulating, involving opposing attorneys; plaintiffs and defendants; plus witnesses and evidence.

He also saw his role, and the work of the court, as contributing to a just society. District judges have to become involved in every dispute, continually making decisions, large and small. But from time to time, Cohn, like other experienced and highly regarded district judges, would sit on the U.S. Court of Appeals for the Sixth Circuit.

He was seldom reversed in a case he decided as a district judge, and usually was part of the majority in appellate cases as well. But occasionally, he dissented, or, as in one of the cases here, was part of a panel that was later overruled by the full court of appeals.

Dissents are often of no great significance. But the two which follow *are* significant because they say something about Cohn's sense of justice, and the law.

***

American Civil Liberties Union of Ohio v. Capitol Square, April 25, 2000[1]

This case stemmed from then-Ohio Gov. George Voinovich's 1996 directive to have the words, "With God, All Things Are Possible," a quotation from the New Testament[2] which had been included in Ohio's state motto since 1959, engraved and placed on a granite plaza at the west end of the statehouse in Capitol Square Plaza in Columbus.

The Capitol Square Review and Advisory Board, the body of state officials having jurisdiction over the Capitol building and the surrounding ten acres, did so.

But the following year, attorneys for the American Civil Liberties Union of Ohio filed a suit in U.S. District Court for the Southern District of Ohio, asserting that putting that language in front of the statehouse would be an unconstitutional governmental endorsement of religion.

The plaintiffs lost the first round of their challenge. U.S. District Judge James K. Graham ruled in September, 1998[3] that "an objective and reasonably informed observer would not perceive the motto as sectarian," or even Christian, and that it was merely an aphorism. The judge, however, ruled that Ohio "is permanently enjoined from attributing the words of the motto to the text of the Christian New Testament."

The ACLU appealed. The appeal was heard by a three-judge panel consisting of two Sixth Circuit appeals judges and Avern Cohn. Two of the three judges, Cohn together with Sixth Circuit Judge Gilbert Merritt, came to a starkly different conclusion.

"Simply put, they are an endorsement of the Christian religion by the state of Ohio," Cohn wrote. "No other interpretation in the context of their presence in the New Testament is possible." The motto, he said, clearly violated what is often referred to as the "establishment clause." This is the phrase that begins the First Amendment by stating "Congress shall make no law respecting an establishment of religion."

Their decision reversed the district court's ruling, and remanded the case for entry of a permanent injunction "enjoining the State of Ohio, its agents and employees from using the words 'With God All Things are Possible' as the official state motto."

Cohn and Merritt were aware that had their decision stood, it likely would cost the state millions to change everything from stationery to the granite plaque in the 1839-era Capitol building's plaza. "Finding a state's official motto unconstitutional is not something that we, as judges, do lightly," their decision concluded, noting:

---

1. *210 F. 3d 703 (2000).* This refers to the decision by a three-judge panel which included Cohn. The full name of the case was *American Civil Liberties Union of Ohio and the Rev. Matthew Peterson v. Capitol Square Review and Advisory Board.* The decision reversing the panel decision by the Sixth Circuit sitting *en banc* was reported at *243 F.3d 289 (2001)*
2. Matthew 19:26
3. *American Civ. Lib. Union v. Capitol Sq. Review, 20 F. Supp. 2d 1176 (S.D. Ohio 1998)*

"This decision should not be viewed as hostile to religion, but rather, an effort to assure government neutrality in relation to religion."

The late Sixth Circuit Judge David Nelson, the third member of the panel, filed a brief dissent, in which he said Ohio's motto was "remarkably similar" to "In God we trust," the national motto of the United States, adopted by Congress in 1956.

Nelson noted that three other federal circuit courts of appeal had upheld the constitutionality of the federal law, which he said fit with the nation's "long tradition of 'ceremonial deism.'" He said it was his belief that "both the Ohio motto and the national motto fit comfortably within that tradition."

The Sixth Circuit then agreed to rehear the case *en banc,* with all its judges taking part, thus staying the finding that the motto was unconstitutional and the order to remove it until the full court could decide.

Less than a year later, the full appeals court overruled the three-judge panel by a vote of 9 to 4. The majority opinion stated that "the motto is merely a broadly worded expression of a religious/philosophical sentiment that happens to be widely shared by the citizens of Ohio. As such, we believe the motto fits comfortably within this country's long and deeply entrenched tradition of civic piety … a tolerable acknowledgment of beliefs widely held among the people of this country."

Though this decision ended this case, since there was no appeal to the U.S. Supreme Court, it certainly did not end the legal debate over the separation of church and state in Ohio. The Sixth Circuit decision was later criticized for vagueness.

"Unfortunately, the court reached its decision without announcing practical standards with which to guide future Establishment Clause issues … consequently, darkness still prevails over Establishment Clause jurisprudence."[4]

Interestingly, the district court's ruling forbidding any state employees from revealing the origin of the words in the motto was left intact by the Sixth Circuit decision.

Regardless of whether one agrees with Cohn on this issue, two things stand out in this case: First, the detailed research and careful reasoning behind his opinion, in contrast with the ruling by the full Sixth Circuit overturning his original panel. Despite their citations, it is hard not to read the majority opinion and without concluding that they are essentially saying that "this is all right because we have always done it this way."

But it is also noteworthy that to rule that Ohio's motto was unconstitutional showed considerable courage. By ruling as he did, Cohn left himself open to being attacked as an enemy of religion, even an enemy of God.

America has always been fertile ground for religious fanaticism, and there are many

---

4. ACLU v. Capitol Square Review and Advisory Board: Is There Salvation for the Establishment Clause? "With God All Things Are Possible." By Theologos Verginis. *Akron Law Review*, July 2015.

Americans who neither understand nor accept the separation of church and state.

More than one public figure has been threatened, or worse, for actions seen as blasphemous. Whether this occurred to Cohn is not known. But what does seem clear is that all that mattered to him was the correct constitutional interpretation of the law.

***

United States of America v. Randy Graham, Dec. 17, 2001[5]

Randy Graham was by no means a model citizen. He had what you might charitably say was a checkered life.

In 1999, he was convicted by a jury of various weapons possessions and drug-related counts in U.S. District Court for the Western District of Michigan, as well as conspiracy to commit offenses against the United States. He was then sentenced to 55 years in prison—far more than he expected, after the presentencing report recommend his time be enhanced because what he did classified as aiding terrorism.

But did Graham really deserve to be classified as a terrorist?

His time was nearly doubled thanks to the trial judge's decision to apply the terrorist guidelines to Graham's crimes. Graham promptly appealed, but a majority of a Sixth Circuit panel agreed that "even though he was not convicted of any statutorily-enumerated federal crime of terrorism," it was correct to use a "domestic terrorism enhancement formula" to increase his sentence "inasmuch as his offenses were intended to promote such crimes of terrorism."[6]

However, Cohn, who was again sitting on a Sixth Circuit panel, disagreed. He did not think applying those guidelines was appropriate in Graham's case.

"Terrorism, by nature, is difficult to define," he said in his dissent, quoting a respected book.[7] "Even the government cannot agree on one single definition."

While exactly what terrorism *is* may be elusive, there was no real dispute about the facts of the case. Graham, a Battle Creek native, collaborated with a friend to illegally grow and sell marijuana, and then used some of the proceeds to buy illegal weapons and also to fund militia activities.

Graham and several others, court testimony showed, had been expelled from a militia group for advocating violence against the government. They formed a new group, the North American Militia, who were stockpiling weapons and planning a first-strike, "Armageddon"

---

5. *275 F.3d 490, 2001*
6. Ibid.
7. Philip Heymann: *Terrorism and America: A Commonsense Strategy for a Democratic Society.* MIT Press, 1998

style attack against the United States, according to the evidence at trial.

The group did stockpile weapons and make plans, but their group was infiltrated by an ATF agent, who testified at trial about Graham's words and actions. No terrorist attack or evidence of violent conduct ever materialized. Graham and two members of his cell were arrested in March 1998. One of the others, Ken Carter, took a plea bargain, and was sentenced to five years in prison, the maximum allowed under the agreement.

Graham, rather than accepting a plea bargain, went to trial, and was convicted on nearly every count with which he had been charged. His presentence report recommended his sentence be greatly enhanced "for promoting terrorism." As a result, the district judge then sentenced him on January 13, 1999 to 55 years in prison.[8]

There was no prior hint that he might be sentenced as a terrorist. Naturally, Graham appealed his sentence, as well as his conviction. The Sixth Circuit panel affirmed the verdict and the sentence in all particulars, except for a technical issue having to do with the penalty for growing marijuana.

As will be seen, Cohn did agree with the verdict—but not the enhanced sentence.

Graham argued that the lower court improperly applied the terrorism enhancement of the guidelines to increase his sentence. And despite whatever he may have discussed with his friends, he had never engaged in any violent conduct, damaged government property, or attempted to do so.

In other words, he had never actually committed a "federal crime of terrorism."

While that may have been true, the panel said that the conspiracy for which Graham was convicted was "intending to promote" a federal crime of terrorism, since the three men had talked about blowing up public and private property.

A majority of the panel affirmed the district judge's decision to dramatically increase his sentence because of a "terrorism enhancement" clause, since, the court said, his offenses were intended to promote crimes of terrorism.

However, one member disagreed: Avern Cohn.

"I respectfully dissent," he explained, in one of the longest and most carefully researched dissents of his career. "I believe it was error to apply the terrorism adjustment," he noted, something which added more than 20 years to Graham's sentence.

The chief reason this was wrong, Cohn said, was that doing so meant that "effectively, the defendant was convicted by the district court, and not by the jury, of a crime not charged in the indictment and not proved at trial."

Noting that Carter, the defendant who pled guilty, had not been charged with terrorism,

---

8. The third man charged, Bradford Metcalf, went to trial and insisted on representing himself. H was sentenced to 40 years. His crimes were similar to Graham's, though his firearms offense was more severe. Interestingly, however, Metcalf was not sentenced under the terrorism guidelines. *United States v Metcalf,* 1:98-CR-54-02

Cohn noted that "likewise, the government did not view Graham as committing "a Federal crime of terrorism" until the trial judge received the presentence report, which, Cohn noted, offered no reason to support increasing his sentence on terrorism grounds "other than simply applying it."

Doing so, Cohn concluded, "did a gross wrong to Graham."

In his dissent, Cohn wrote a sweeping review of the legislative and judicial history of domestic anti-terrorism sanctions, noting that "this history must be viewed particularly in light of the fact that, until recently, there was no federal law that makes a domestic act of terrorism a crime."

His research, which has the depth of a law review article, clearly demonstrated that the language of the federal anti-terrorism statute[9] "clearly established that its application should be limited to one of the enumerated offenses."

Applying the enhanced terrorism enhancement to Graham's marijuana-involved crimes, Cohn said, "can only be described as gratuitous."

Besides the injustice of saddling Graham with a much longer sentence for a crime of which he was neither convicted nor charged, Cohn warned that the appellate judges who sustained the terrorism-enhanced sentence were "condoning a definition of a 'Federal crime of terrorism' broader than that contemplated by the Congress." [10]

"This simply allows for a soft definition of terrorism," when the entire history of terrorist legislation clearly intended for the label to apply to certain specifically defined acts.

Despite his well-documented reasoning, Cohn did not persuade the other two judges on the panel, and Graham's terrorism-lengthened sentence was allowed to stand.

It is noteworthy that Graham's appeal was argued on Jan. 24, 2001, but was not formally decided until Dec. 17 of that year, after the September 11 terrorist attacks. In his dissent, Cohn wrote that "this dissent was substantially completed before the terrorist attacks on the World Trade Center, the Pentagon and in Pennsylvania …these horrific events involve weapons of mass destruction as instruments of terrorism and are very far outside the conspiratorial conduct of Graham as reflected in the record of this case."

Randy Graham is currently in a medium-security federal prison in Southern Illinois, and is not eligible to be released until Dec. 4, 2040.[11]

---

9. Antiterrorism and Effective Death Penalty Act of 1996. *Pub. L. No. 104-132 110 Stat 1214*
10. Contemplated by Congress when enacting the 1996 antiterrorism bill referenced above: 18 U.S.C. 2332b(g)(5).
11. When the case was returned to the district court for resentencing, as required by the appeals court, a dispute arose over the calculation of the sentence; mainly, whether the multiple counts required consecutive or concurrent sentencing. The Court of Appeals affirmed the district court's calculation that the sentence should be 50 years (not the original 55). Cohn concurred in that result. *United States of America v. Randy Graham, 327 F.3d 460 (6th Cir. 2003).*

Kimberly Altman, a career law clerk for Judge Avern Cohn from 1999 to 2020, is sworn in as a new magistrate judge for the U.S. District Court, Eastern District of Michigan in a virtual ceremony September 16, 2020.

U.S. District Judge Avern Cohn: Former Law Clerks and Key Staff Members

(1979-2020)

Avern Cohn would be the first to tell you that his work was made easier and that he was made a better judge by his law clerks and staff members who worked with him over the years. Many of his law clerks, in turn, credit him for launching their careers.

Here is an "honor roll" of those who served the judge during his forty years on the bench:

Law Clerks

1979-1980
Mary Margaret BOLDA

1979-1981
Suanne Tiberio TRIMMER

1980-1982
Marc D. BASSEWITZ

1981-1983
Clark D. CUNNINGHAM

1982-1984
Paula Lee LEVITAN

1983-1985
Paul COUENHOVEN

1984-1986
Marcie Hermelin ORLEY

1986
Kathleen Moro NESI

1985-1987
Michael J. MUELLER

1986-1988
Cynthia M. YORK

1987-1989
Kelly A. FREEMAN

1988-1990
Franklin E. FINK

1989-1991
Walter David KOENINGER

1990-1992
Andrew S. DOCTOROFF

1991-1993
Michael C. FAYZ

1992-1994
Sandra E. SHAPIRO

1993-1995
Stuart BERAHA

1994-1996 & 1998-1999
Elisa M. Angeli PALIZZI

1995-1997
Jonathan Miller STEIGER

1996-1998
Andrea M. GACKI

1997-1999
Thomas M. SCHEHR

1999-2001
Susan K. DECLERCQ

1999-2020
Kimberly G. ALTMAN [1]
Career Law Clerk

2001-2002
Angela Upchurch WILHELM

2002-2003
Katie B. FEIOCK

2003-2004
Justin T. ARBES

2004-2005
Bryan J. ANDERSON

2005-2006
Andrew LIEVENSE

---

1. Career Law Clerk Kimberly Altman became a federal magistrate judge in September 2020.

2006-2007
Lucia CHRISTOPHER

2007-2008
Adam WIENNER

2008-2009
Patsy HOLMES

2009-2010
Joel VISSER

2010-2011
Susan ASAM

2011-2012
Eric BERG (Deceased)

Jeremy BROWN
(May - August 2012)

2012-2014
Jonathan KARMO

2014-2015
Joshua RONNEBAUM

2015-2016
Brittney KOHN

2016-2017
Benjamin ABLE

2017-2018
Sarah M. CRAVENS

2018-2019
Kory STEEN

2019-2020
Sarah THOMAS

2020
Michael JERNUKIAN

***

Other Staff Members

Nancy Lippert (1979-2004)   Judicial Secretary

Lori Van Hove (2004-2020)   Judicial Secretary

Tara Villereal (2020)   Judicial Secretary

***

Judy Cassady (1979-2005)   Case Manager

Julie Owens (2005-2012)   Case Manager

Sakne Chami (2012-2015)   Case Manager

Marie Verlinde (2015-2020)   Case Manager

***

Herman Tappert (1979-1996)   Court Reporter (Deceased)

Sheri Ward (1996-2019)   Court Reporter

A Selection of Avern Cohn's Articles

CONSTITUTIONAL INTERPRETATION AND JUDICIAL TREATMENT OF BLACKS IN MICHIGAN BEFORE 1870

Avern Cohn[†]

Introduction

The invitation to write for the Open Forum offers the opportunity to emphasize the importance of the Civil War amendments to Constitutional rights.[1] Too often, proponents of the theme that reliance on the original intention of the Founding Fathers should be the centerpiece of constitutional interpretation ignore the dramatic changes the Civil War amendments made in extending the protection of individual rights by the Constitution. A particular way of illustrating this point is to examine Michigan cases involving the rights of slaves and free blacks decided between the adoption of the Constitution in 1787 and the passage of the fifteenth amendment in 1870. These decisions demonstrate that the Constitution, among other things, required that slavery be recognized in a territory where local laws prohibited its introduction, and they also demonstrate that free blacks were considered inferior persons. While the promises of the Civil War amendments have yet to be fulfilled, they certainly have wrought a considerable change from the original intent of the Founding Fathers. To argue otherwise is deceitful.

Robert M. Cover, in his study of antislavery and the judicial process, *Justice Accused*,[2] discusses two such decisions written in 1807 by Judge Augustus Woodward of the Supreme Court of the Territory of Michigan. These cases, *Denison v. Tucker*[3] and *In the Mat-*

[†] J.D., University of Michigan, 1949. Currently, United States District Judge, Eastern District of Michigan.

Judge Cohn wishes to express his appreciation to Michael Mueller, Esq. for his assistance in this effort and the editors of the Detroit College of Law Review for supplying the footnotes throughout.

1. For a more complete discussion of the general subject of this essay, see Mitchell, *From Slavery to Shelley — Michigan's Ambivalent Response to Civil Rights*, 26 WAYNE L. REV. 1 (1979).

2. R. COVER, JUSTICE ACCUSED (1975).

3. 1 W.W. BLUME, *infra* note 5, at 385.

ter of Richard Pattinson,[4] as well as several other cases involving slaves, are reported by William Wirt Blume in *Transactions of the Supreme Court of the Territory of Michigan, 1805-1814*.[5] Helen Tunnicliff Caterall describes, in *Judicial Cases Concerning American Slavery and the Negro*,[6] four such cases decided by the Michigan Supreme Court: *Hedgman v. Board of Registration*,[7] *People v. Dean*,[8] *Day v. Owen*,[9] and *Gordon v. Farrar*.[10] Caterall also describes the charge to a jury by Supreme Court Justice John McClean, sitting on circuit in Detroit, in *Giltner v. Gorham*.[11]

I. Positive Law Background

These cases must be read against the backdrop of a variety of provisions of positive law. These include the Northwest Ordinance, which, while it prohibited slavery and involuntary servitude in the "Territory of the United States northwest of the River Ohio," contained a provision requiring that persons escaping into the Territory "from whom labor or service is lawfully claimed" (meaning fugitive slaves) be "reclaimed and conveyed to the person claiming" them.[12] The Constitution of 1787 contained a number of provisions relating to slavery without particular mention of the word. It gave lesser weight to "all other Persons" in determining the number of representatives to which a state was entitled, prohibited any limitation on importation of "Such Persons as any of the States . . . shall think proper to admit" before 1808, and incorporated in substance the fugitive slave provision of the Northwest Ordinance previously described. The Fugitive Slave Act of 1793 fleshed out the Constitution by providing specific procedures for returning fugitive slaves to their masters from the states to which they escaped.[13] The Jay Treaty of 1794, by which possession of the

---

4. 1 W.W. Blume, *infra* note 5, at 414.
5. 1 W.W. Blume, Transactions of the Supreme Court of the Territory of Michigan, 1805-1814 (1935).
6. H. Caterall, Judicial Cases Concerning American Slavery and the Negro (1968).
7. 26 Mich. 51 (1872).
8. 14 Mich. 406 (1866).
9. 5 Mich. 520 (1858).
10. 2 Doug. 411 (1847).
11. 10 F. Cas. 424 (C.C.D. Mich. 1848) (No. 5,453).
12. Act of July 13, 1787, art. VI., 44 Stat. 1851, 1853.
13. Act of Feb. 12, 1793, 1 Stat. 302. When the 1793 statute proved inadequate, particularly in light of the Supreme Court decision in Prigg v. Pennsylvania, 41 U.S. (16 Pet.) 539

frontier posts in the Northwest Territory, including Detroit, were turned over to the United States, assured settlers of the "continu[ed] . . . enjoy[ment], unmolested, [of] all their property of every kind . . . ." This meant that slaves owned by British settlers in Detroit on July 11, 1796, the day possession was transferred to the United States, continued in that status.

In 1819, Congress, in authorizing the election of a delegate from the Michigan Territory, extended the right of suffrage to "free white male citizens" in the Territory. The Michigan Constitution of 1835 limited suffrage in like fashion,[14] as did the Constitution of 1850.[15] The limitation was not deleted until 1869, by an amendment to the state constitution that barely received a majority vote.[16] Likewise, the apportionment provisions of the 1835 and 1850 Constitutions regarding the House of Representatives counted only white "inhabitants." The Constitution of 1850 went even further by limiting service in the militia to white males. In contrast, the constitutions of 1835[17] and 1850[18] flatly prohibited slavery. This prohibition was reinforced by an 1827 act that made the kidnapping or the selling of slaves a misdemeanor[19] (although punishable by up to ten years hard labor) and by an 1855 act that made it unlawful for local and state officials to cooperate with federal authorities in returning fugitive slaves. Additionally, the 1827 act severely limited the rights of blacks to migrate into the Territory, and on several occasions before 1869 proposals to extend the right of suffrage to blacks were defeated.

Lord Mansfield's 1772 decision in *Somerset's Case*,[20] is also an important part of the backdrop. Lord Mansfield wrote:

> The state of slavery is of such a nature, that it is incapable of being

---

(1842), which held that state courts were not obligated to participate in returning fugitive slaves, Congress enacted the Fugitive Slave Act of 1850, which expanded the federal role in reclaiming fugitive slaves. The Fugitive Slave Act of 1850 was entitled, "An Act to amend, and supplementary to, the Act entitled, 'An Act respecting Fugitives from Justice, and persons escaping from the Service of their Masters,' approved February twelfth, one thousand seven hundred and ninety-three." Act of Sept. 18, 1850, 9 STAT. 462.

14. MICH. CONST. of 1835, art. 2, § 1.
15. MICH. CONST. of 1850, art. 7, § 1.
16. Mitchell, *supra* note 1, at 12.
17. MICH. CONST. of 1835, art. 11, § 1.
18. MICH. CONST. of 1850, art. 17, § 11.
19. Act of Apr. 13, 1827, LAWS OF THE TERRITORY OF MICH. 470-72 (1833).
20. 20 Howell's St. Tr. 1 (1816).

introduced on any reasons, moral or political, but only by positive law, which preserves its force long after the reasons, occasion, and time itself from whence it was created, is erased from memory. It is so odious, that nothing can be suffered to support it, but positive law.[21]

This rule of the common law was well known in the United States at the beginning of the nineteenth century.

II. Decisions by the Supreme Court of the Territory of Michigan

In *Denison v. Tucker*, Elizabeth Denison, James Denison, Scipio Denison, and Peter Denison, Jr., slaves belonging to Catherine Tucker, a British settler in Detroit, were denied a writ of habeas corpus on September 26, 1807 by Judge Woodward and ordered "restored to [her] possession."[22] In deciding against the Denisons, Judge Woodward noted on the authority of Lord Mansfield's decision in *Somerset* that slavery was not permitted in England.[23] Likewise, Judge Woodward noted that slavery was prohibited in Michigan and that "[t]he existence . . . of an absolute & unqualified Slavery of the human Species in the United States of America is universally and justly considered [its] greatest and deepest reproach."[24] Nevertheless, Judge Woodward went on to hold that because the Denisons had lawfully been slaves under the law of Upper Canada, which governed Detroit prior to July 11, 1796, Tucker's claim as their master had to be recognized under the Jay Treaty.[25] Moreover, because of specific provisions in the laws of Upper Canada, Judge Woodward held that all slaves living on May 31, 1793[26] and in the possession of settlers in Detroit prior to July 11, 1796 continued in such state for their lives.[27] As to the children of slaves, some continued in slavery until age twenty-five and others, depending on their date of birth, were immediately free.[28] As explained by Cover, Judge Woodward "explicitly reject[ed] the possibility of judicial officers effectuating natural law in the face of

---

21. *Id.* at 82.
22. 1 W.W. Blume, *supra* note 5, at 395.
23. *Id.* at 385-86.
24. *Id.* at 386.
25. *Id.* at 395.
26. This was the date of a Canadian statute providing for gradual emancipation.
27. 1 W.W. Blume, *supra* note 5, at 395.
28. *Id.*

positive enactments."[29]

On October 23, 1807, Judge Woodward, in *In the Matter of Richard Pattinson*, denied an application for a warrant by Richard Pattinson of Sandwich, Essex County, Upper Canada, for the arrest of Joseph and Jane Quinn, fugitive slaves who had escaped to Detroit.[30] In his opinion, Judge Woodward discussed the law of nations, principles of common law, and United States domestic law.[31] Judge Woodward stated that under the law of nations, persons accidentally found in another country could not be recognized as property, as distinguished, for example, from a horse, or ox, or sheep escaping from France into Spain.[32] The common law, he stated, simply did not recognize a property right in the human species, again citing Lord Mansfield.[33] Lastly, under domestic law Judge Woodward found that:

> a right of property in the human Species Cannot exist in this territory, excepting as to persons in the actual possession of british Setlers within this territory on [July 11, 1796], and that every other man coming into this territory is by the law of and land a freeman, unless he be a fugitive from lawfull labor & service in Some other american State or territory, and then he must be restored.[34]

Finally, Judge Woodward stated that since the laws of Upper Canada did not allow for the return of fugitive slaves who escaped to there, the Quinns need not be returned because of the absence of reciprocity.[35] Judge Woodward's decision was, as Cover points out, based on a choice-of-law rule "grounded . . . firmly in nature law"[36] and, in Woodward's words, "[c]ertainly a just principle."[37]

III. Decisions by the Michigan Supreme Court

As noted by Caterall in her introduction to the discussion of Michigan cases, "Michigan escaped the turmoil characteristic of Ohio and Wisconsin in the solution of slavery questions in the

---

29. R. Cover, *supra* note 2, at 90.
30. 1 W.W. Blume, *supra* note 5, at 414.
31. *Id. passim.*
32. *Id.* at 415.
33. *Id.* at 416.
34. *Id.* at 417 (original spelling retained).
35. *Id.*
36. R. Cover, *supra* note 2, at 91.
37. 1 W.W. Blume, *supra* note 5, at 416.

courts." Although limited in number, they offer a considerable insight into the subject at hand. The first of the four Michigan cases, *Gordon v. Farrar*[38] involved a suit against Detroit election inspectors for refusing to receive Gordon's vote in the 1844 congressional election on the ground that he was not a white person. Gordon was "partly of Saxon and partly of African descent, but the Saxon blood in him greatly predominat[ed] . . . ."[39] A circuit jury in Wayne County gave him a judgment of twelve and one-half cents subject to a determination of whether under such circumstances he should be allowed to vote, since the law governing the duties of the inspectors did not provide for testing the color or descent of electors.[40] The supreme court held that notwithstanding the limitations of the statute, the right to vote was limited to white male citizens and that the inspectors must inevitably make a determination as to qualification when "a colored person should offer his vote."[41] Because they were acting judicially, and not ministerially as claimed by Gordon, the inspectors were not liable.[42]

In *Day v. Owen*,[43] Day, "a colored person" and an abolitionist of some note, was denied the right to purchase cabin accommodations on the defendant's steamer going from Detroit to Toledo. Day offered to pay the required fare for the accommodations but was told he could travel only on the deck.[44] Day sued for the damages he suffered because of the inconvenience of having to travel overland.[45] The case came to the supreme court on Day's exception to the defendant's defenses and, in particular, on his exception to the assertion that the rule excluding "colored persons" from cabins was promulgated for the convenience of the community at large. The supreme court held that while the defendant as a common carrier was absolutely obligated to carry Day as a passenger, the reasonableness of the cabin rule was for a jury to decide.[46] The supreme court stated that "to deny [defendant] the right would be

---

38. 2 Doug. 411 (1847).
39. *Id.* at 412.
40. *Id.* at 412-13.
41. *Id.* at 414.
42. *Id.* at 416.
43. 5 Mich. 520 (1858).
44. *Id.* at 520-21.
45. *Id.* at 521.
46. *Id.* at 526-27.

an interference with a carrier's control over his own property in his own way, not necessary to the performance of his duty to the public as a carrier."[47]

People v. Dean[48] involved a prosecution for illegal voting and extended the question involved in *Gordon v. Farrar*. Dean voted in an election for Nankin Township officers and regents of the University of Michigan.[49] A Wayne County circuit court jury found Dean guilty of voting illegally after being charged by the trial judge that a person of more than one-sixteenth African blood was not a white person.[50] After an extended discussion of the history of the constitutional provision confining the franchise to white male citizens, the characteristics of the races, and the case law discussing such provisions from other states, Justices Campbell, Christiancy, and Cooley as a majority concluded that a person was white who had less than one-fourth African blood.[51] Chief Justice Martin in dissent argued that so along as white blood predominated, a man was white and entitled to vote.[52] The Chief Justice declaimed against what he considered the "arbitrary and artificial test" of a fixed percentage and accused the majority of "ursurp[ing] legislative power."[53] He noted that the Constitution declared only those who may vote, *viz.*, white males, and that "blacks and coloreds [were] not mentioned."[54] The Chief Justice was particularly critical of the examination of Dean's nose at trial, suggesting that if the majority decision established the correct rule, it would be necessary to amend the Constitution "to authorize the election or appointment of nose pullers or nose inspectors, to attend the election polls . . . to prevent illegal voting."[55] Notwithstanding his acquittal, Dean still had to resort to mandamus to register as a voter.[56]

The fourth of the Michigan state cases, *Hedgman v. Board of Registration*,[57] decided after the adoption of the fifteenth amend-

---

47. *Id.* at 527.
48. 14 Mich. 406 (1866).
49. *Id.* at 425.
50. *Id.* at 413.
51. *Id.* at 424.
52. *Id.* at 439.
53. *Id.* at 432.
54. *Id.* at 433.
55. *Id.* at 438-39.
56. *See* Dean v. Board of Registration of Nankin, 15 Mich. 155 (1866).
57. 26 Mich. 51 (1872).

ment, illuminates the legal status of slaves in prior years. Hedgman was born in Canada of a slave couple who had escaped to Canada from Virginia before the Civil War.[58] Hedgman moved to Detroit at the age of twenty and, asserting that he was a citizen, brought a mandamus action to compel his registration as a voter.[59] The application was denied on the ground that neither Hedgman nor his parents took any rights under the fourteenth and fifteenth amendments and, therefore, he had to seek United States citizenship like any British subject. The Michigan Supreme Court expressly found that *Dred Scott v. Sandford*,[60] which held, among other things, that free blacks were not citizens, was no longer good law. However, the supreme court said that notwithstanding the fact that "[s]lavery was the great ugly fact of [United States] history,"[61] it was necessary to recognize that Hedgman's parents were slaves before emancipation and, because they were never citizens of the United States prior to the adoption of the fourteenth amendment, Hedgman was not a citizen.[62] The supreme court noted that "we have abolished slavery, but we have not abolished the pre-existing slavery, and we cannot prevent the consequences following the facts recorded."[63]

IV. Federal Cases from Michigan

The only federal case from Michigan discussed by Caterall dealing with the subject of slavery and the rights of blacks involved enforcement of the Fugitive Slave Act through an action for damages. *Giltner v. Gorham*[64] is the report of Justice John McLean's jury charge in a case brought to recover the value of escaped slaves from Kentucky, first arrested by slave catchers in Marshall, then set free by the defendants.[65] McLean was well known for his antislavery views; he was later one of the dissenters in *Dred Scott*. But as can be seen from his charge, and as Cover notes, "[McLean] constantly appealed to a dichotomy between law and anarchy. He

---

58. *Id.* at 51.
59. *Id.*
60. 60 U.S. (19 How.) 393 (1857).
61. 26 Mich. at 53.
62. *Id.* at 56.
63. *Id.* at 53.
64. 10 F. Cas. 424 (C.C.D. Mich. 1848) (No. 5,453).
65. *Id.* at 425.

constantly attributed to others whatever power existed to ameliorate the situation, and he used the language of helplessness more than any other single judge."[66]

The charge first described the purposes of the Fugitive Slave Act, went on to describe the claims against the defendants, detailed the evidence at trial,[67] and continued with something akin to the boilerplate of today's civil jury instructions. McLean concluded his charge by cautioning the jury against any consideration of the "abstract principle of slavery" on the ground that it was not their duty to deal with abstractions.[68] He stated, "[w]ith the policy of the local laws of the states, we have nothing to do. However unjust and impolitic slavery may be, yet the people of Kentucky, in their sovereign capacity, have adopted it."[69] He told the jurors that they would "[v]iolate [their] oaths and show [themselves] unworthy . . . [if they adopted], as a rule of action, [their] own convictions of what the law should be, rather than what it is."[70]

The jury could not agree on a verdict after a night of deliberation and was discharged.[71] At the succeeding term of court, in a trial conducted by District Court Judge Ross Wilkins, the plaintiff received a verdict for the value of his lost slaves.[72]

Interestingly, after the events in *Glitner* but before the trials, there was a considerable embroglio in Cass County involving another effort by Kentuckians to return escaped slaves and their escape to freedom. As in *Giltner*, while the Kentuckians lost their slaves they obtained a money judgment in the United States District Court in Detroit for their value against the abolitionists who had aided their escape.[73] Though not authenticated, there is a view that the number of unsuccessful efforts to return escaped slaves to Kentucky from Michigan led Henry Clay to promote legislation leading to the Fugitive Slave Act of 1850.

---

66. R. COVER, *supra* note 2, at 249.

67. McLean's description of the evidence at trial was a textbook description of abolitionist activities.

68. 10 F. Cas. at 432.

69. *Id.*

70. *Id.* at 433.

71. *Id.*

72. For a historical narrative of *Giltner*, see Yzenbaard, *The Crosswhite Case*, 53 MICH. HIST. 131 (1969).

73. *See* Wilson, *Kentucky Kidnappers, Fugitives and Abolitionists in Antebellum Cass County, Michigan*, 60 MICH. HIST. 339 (1976).

Conclusion

This brief and unscholarly excursion in judicial history suggests the extent of the schizophrenic attitudes in Michigan towards slavery and blacks before the Civil War amendments. On the one hand slavery was deplored, while on the other hand blacks were denied many of the benefits of the Constitution and their worth as human beings. William Woodbridge, in the course of his successful campaign for governor in 1839, when solicited by A.L. Porter, Chairman of the Executive Committee of the Michigan State Antislavery Society, to answer the question whether he favored removing color as a condition of suffrage, summed up the predominant view of the children of the Founding Fathers[74] when he said:

> While I hold then, that the descendant of Africa has the same right by nature to be free, I do not hold that any correlative duty is thereby imposed upon white men, to admit him, as an integral part of their community. The world is wide: and Abram and Lot were permitted each unmolested by the other, to pursue his own path to happiness.[75]

If a child of a Founding Father as significant in Michigan history as Woodbridge could not bring himself to look upon blacks as his equal, how much more severe must have been the attitude of his father? Certainly, therefore, the intent of the Founding Fathers is of questionable assistance to us today in defining constitutional rights without referring to the intent of the Civil War amendments.

---

74. Woodbridge's father was a minuteman.
75. Letter from William Woodbridge to A.L. Porter (Oct. 14, 1839) (Burton Historical Collection, Detroit Public Library, William Woodbridge papers).

DOE V. UNIVERSITY OF MICHIGAN: A SOMEWHAT PERSONAL VIEW

Judge Avern Cohn[†]

Judge Avern Cohn's decision in Doe v. University of Michigan has become something of a benchmark in the first amendment analysis of campus policies seeking to regulate "hate speech" on campus. The following remarks on the Doe case were delivered by Judge Cohn to a gathering of the University of Michigan Law Review Alumni on October 20, 1990.

What I propose to do this evening is give you something of a personal view of *Doe v. University of Michigan*, a case I decided in September, 1989 in which I held unconstitutional a university regulation governing certain kinds of verbal behavior on campus. The decision was not appealed. The University revised the regulation. The decision, I am told, has had a good deal of influence on similar regulations around the country. In talking about *Doe*, bear in mind what a famous German legal philosopher once said about judges:

> The administration of justice has always contained a personal element in all ages. Social, political and cultural movements have necessarily exerted an influence upon him. [meaning the judge] Whether an individual judge yields more or less to such influences, whether he is more inclined to follow tradition, or rather disposed to initiate change and innovate, depends, of course, less on any theory of legal methods, than upon his own personal temperament.

And more recently in the same vein an English judge has noted:

> The law does not have the quality of a railway timetable with predetermined answers to all the questions that human life, man's wickedness and the intricacies of commerce can throw up . . . . The law, as laid down in a code, or in a

---

[†] United States District Court Judge for the Eastern District of Michigan. J.D., 1949, University of Michigan.

statute, or in a thousand eloquently reasoned opinions, is no more capable of providing all the answers than a piano is capable of providing music. The piano needs the pianist and any two pianists, even with the same score, may produce different music.

I was destined for the University of Michigan from as far back as I can remember thinking about college. I was destined to be a lawyer from as far back as I can remember thinking about my life's work.

I entered the University from the Detroit Public Schools in 1942. My undergraduate work was interrupted for 3 years in 1943 by World War II. I was a fortunate G.I. My years in the United States Army yielded enough in college credits to enable me to enter law school in 1946 without the need of an undergraduate degree.

I managed to do fairly well, but not well enough my freshman year to make Law Review. I thoroughly enjoyed my three years in school. I was able to build a good foundation. I was taught well.

There is another bit of history you should know as I talk about my views on *Doe*, and that is my long association with the American Civil Liberties Union in the years before I took the bench. ACLU furnished counsel for the plaintiff in *Doe*. When I returned to Detroit in 1950 to begin practicing law I became a cooperating attorney with the ACLU and handled several matters for it in the 1960s.

In the early 1960s the ACLU sued Wayne State University for wrongfully limiting the use of one of its community buildings to only charitable groups. Underlying the issues in the case were first amendment principles. I was successful in obtaining a revision of the policy which allowed any recognized community group, regardless of what it stood for, to use the McGregor Conference Center. In the late 1960s, I received a good deal of publicity for a speech I made castigating the Michigan State Senate for attempting to financially punish universities because of a dislike of certain campus speakers. These antecedents undoubtedly sensitized me to the tensions on college campuses regarding first amendment matters. If one believes in predestination, it is more than coincidence that *Doe v. The University of Michigan* ended up on my docket in May 1989.

Now those of you familiar with the assignment of cases in multi-judge federal district courts know that it is done strictly by

PERSONAL VIEW

blind draw. Each case as it is filed is assigned to a particular judge and there is just no hanky-panky about it. Except for extraordinary considerations, a case once assigned stays with the judge to whom it is assigned throughout its life. And no judge ever anticipates getting a particular case or is disappointed because a particular case goes elsewhere. Whatever walks in the door is handled.

As for *Doe*, its filing was preceded by several years of turmoil on campus involving various minority groups, particularly the feelings of many black students that their particular needs and desires were either not being adequately met or were being ignored. I was not personally familiar with all of the details of the turmoil. The details as expressed in the pleadings and papers in *Doe* are related in the decision. I recall from media accounts that then President Shapiro was having a rather hard time of it and the Michigan Legislature, or at least several of its members, were vocal in expressing the opinion that the University was doing an inadequate job in maintaining equal educational opportunities for all students. The press contained accounts from time-to-time of some very ugly incidents of racial harassment and verbal abuse of minorities.

President Shapiro left. Robben Fleming came back as interim president and set in motion a process leading to a policy statement by the Regents, approved April 15, 1988, entitled *Discrimination And Discriminatory Harassment By Students In The University Environment.* In the course of drafting the statement and consideration of its adoption, at no time did the Regents receive, or even ask for, a formal opinion as to its constitutionality notwithstanding campus comment critical of preliminary drafts, first as a first amendment violation and second as poor policy. In briefest terms, the policy allowed for "discrimination and discriminatory harassment" in public forums such as the "Diag," but prohibited it in educational and academic centers as well as in housing units. Discrimination and discriminating harassment were defined as:

>   1. Any behavior, verbal or physical, that stigmatizes or victimizes an individual on the basis of race, ethnicity, religion, sex, sexual orientation, creed, national origin, ancestry, age, marital status, handicap or Vietnam-era veteran status, and that:
>   a. Involves an express or implied threat to an individual's academic efforts, employment, participation in University sponsored extra-curricular activities or personal safety; or

> b. Has the purpose or reasonably foreseeable effect of interfering with an individual's academic efforts, employment participation in University sponsored extra-curricular activities or personal safety; or
>
> c. Creates an intimidating, hostile or demeaning environment for educational pursuits, employment or participation in University sponsored extracurricular activities.

The policy statement included provisions for conciliation of complaints and sanction proceedings which could, in extreme cases, lead to expulsion. In the Fall of 1988 a brochure was issued by the University's Affirmative Action Office titled *What Students Should Know About Discrimination And Discriminating Harassment By Students In The University Environment* explaining the policy, its enforcement and giving examples of violative conduct. Two examples will suffice to give you some idea of the breadth University officials gave to the policy as interpreted:

> A male student makes remarks in class like "Women just aren't as good in this field as men," thus creating a hostile learning atmosphere for female classmates.
>
> You display a confederate flag on the door of your room in the residence hall.

As one reads the policy statement and explanatory brochure as well as the "legislative history," one must conclude that somehow Jack Cade's fantasy about killing all the lawyers had come true in Ann Arbor.

From the Spring of 1988 on, opponents of the policy were obviously at work searching out a proper plaintiff for an attack on its constitutionality and fashioning legal reasons in support of such an attack. This effort culminated on May 25, 1989, with the filing of a short complaint in the United States District Court for the Eastern District of Michigan praying for a declaratory judgment that the policy was void on its face in violation of the first amendment to the Constitution of the United States, and asking for a permanent injunction enjoining its enforcement.

Briefly stated, the complaint said it was being brought under 42 U.S.C. § 1983 and that plaintiff was a graduate student in biological psychology subject to the policy. After describing the policy, the complaint went on to allege, and I paraphrase,

> The policy violates the first amendment in that it included constitutionally protected expression, is vague and over-

PERSONAL VIEW

broad and creates a chilling effect on the expression of certain ideas. Students who violate the policy are subject to disciplinary sanctions including expulsion. Plaintiff is studying a field of psychology which studies biological differences among races and sexes and attempts to explain differences in cognitive abilities between those groups. Plaintiff believes that if he expresses such ideas in class he would be subject to discipline under the policy. For this reason, plaintiff has refrained from expressing such ideas.

Attached to the complaint were copies of the policy statement and the explanatory brochure.

Ordinarily my deputy clerk would have waited for the answer to the complaint to be filed before setting up a status conference. Because of the obvious public interest in the case, its filing had received a good deal of publicity, and we sent out a notice on July 7 scheduling a status conference for the 25th of July. Once before I had been involved in a case in which the ACLU had challenged a speech regulation, then at the Detroit Metropolitan Airport. In that case, using some jawboning, I managed to get the ACLU and the Airport Authority to eventually agree on rules acceptable to both sides. My cursory review of the complaint and its attachments suggested that that approach might be beneficial here. A lunchtime conversation with two of my colleagues persuaded me I should not attempt to conciliate the parties but rather simply meet the challenge and the defense head on.

The parties eventually met with me in my chambers on August 3. The day before, the plaintiff had moved for a preliminary injunction thus accelerating the pace of the case. At the conference I asked the University's counsel to lodge with me the legislative record, as I called it, of the policy statement. It appeared to me that the record of the drafting of the policy and the Regents' considerations, before adoption, must contain the justification, if there was any, of the limitations the policy obviously imposed on campus speech. I cautioned the University's counsel against over-lawyering the case, and expressed some judicial displeasure at the defense the university was asserting—that the plaintiff lacked standing to challenge the policy. It seemed to me that the standing challenge was an effort to evade having to answer for the policy in court and unbecoming of a public institution. At the conference the University lawyer stated that the explanatory brochure had been withdrawn at a prior time. This came as a surprise to Doe's lawyer.

We set August 21 as the date for the hearing on the preliminary injunction. At that time I did not know, as the record subsequently developed, that neither Acting President Fleming nor the Regents had ever obtained a formal legal opinion that what they were doing in promulgating the policy passed constitutional muster, and what they had done, and the way they did it, by-passed established procedures for enacting a regulation governing student conduct on campus.

The papers started coming in from the parties as did a plethora of xerox copies of cases and articles. By an odd circumstance I was scheduled to hear a misdemeanor case in the Ann Arbor Federal Building on September 8, 1989, so to kill two birds with one stone, and much to the consternation of the University's lawyer, I scheduled the hearing on the preliminary injunction for August 25 in the Ann Arbor Federal Courthouse and rescheduled the misdemeanor case to follow. My senior law clerk devoted almost full time to drafting a bench memo for me. Unfortunately, it was not ready the evening of August 24 when I went home. Because of a personal situation, my mind in August 1989 was most often occupied elsewhere and I had not had the time to think extensively about the case except in my 50 minute commute each morning and evening.

Shortly before the 25th, I heard via radio that the University had withdrawn the portion of the policy statement covering participation in University sponsored extra-curricular activities. Withdrawal of a part of the policy on the eve of the first open-court hearing in the case without formal notification to the judge and the earlier informal withdrawal of the explanatory brochure suggested some uncertainty, indeed, disarray, on the part of University officials as to the constitutionality and propriety of the policy.

The early morning events of the 25th are of some interest. First, I heard a 6:00 a.m. news account of the hearing. Second, the Detroit Free Press, that morning, editorialized critically on the policy. The editorial was titled, "U-M: An effort to confront bigotry may also be working to limit the pursuit of knowledge."

My limited familiarity with the file, and my reading of the briefs the evening of the 24th, caused me to almost finally conclude that morning as I left home that the policy was unconstitutional, and that, coupled with the intense media attention to the case, suggested a prompt decision was in order. Certainly, the case should be decided, if at all possible, before Fall classes began. However, I did not yet have a satisfactory grip on the reasoning that would lead me to express that conclusion. It is a 50-minute drive from my home to the Ann Arbor courthouse. During that 50 minutes, I came to the conclusion that I should, if I could do so comfortably and articulately, decide the case that day.

PERSONAL VIEW

I arrived at the Courthouse about 8:10 a.m. and in the next hour familiarized myself with enough of the record and the major United States Supreme Court cases as reflected in the bench memo of my law clerk to feel comfortable. I would be able to deliver a reasoned decision holding the policy unconstitutional unless something in oral argument persuaded me otherwise.

At the opening of argument, the parties agreed there was no need to call witnesses; the record was complete. I then ordered the hearing on the preliminary injunction combined with the hearing on the merits. The oral argument went on for some time. The highlights for me were, first, I learned that the policy was printed in a blue covered brochure and the explanatory statement in a yellow covered brochure. Up to the hearing I had only seen both in dull grey covers as reproduced. I was struck by the symbolism of taking the maize out of the maize and blue—indeed I was shocked and so stated. The University's lawyer, being a Wayne State Law School graduate, simply could not appreciate the meaning of this split of university colors.

Second, of significance to me were two excerpts of the argument as follows:

A. (By University of Michigan Counsel): . . . [w]hat the university is saying is that you cannot harm [an] individual when [he or she] walk[s] into the classroom. . . .

Q. (By the Court): Can you offend that individual?

A. Yes, you may.

Q. Now, how do you distinguish between offending the individual and harming the individual?

A. Very carefully, Your Honor.

. . . . .

Q. (By the Court): . . . President Fleming in a communication to the executive officers of the University on December 14, 1987 said, and I quote:

> But just as an individual cannot shout 'fire' in a crowded theater and then claim immunity from prosecution for causing a riot on the basis of exercising his rights of free speech, so a great many American universities have taken the position that students in a university cannot, by speaking or writing discriminatory remarks which seriously offend many individuals beyond the immediate victim and which, therefore, detract from the necessary educational climate of a campus, claim immunity from a campus disciplinary proceeding.

I am satisfied that there is not a single decision of the Supreme Court of the United States or a writing by a recognized academic expert in first amendment law which would support that statement.

A. (By University of Michigan Counsel): I agree.

Immediately after the second question and answer, I concluded the argument and proceeded to rule that the policy was unconstitutional as violative of the first amendment in a bench opinion. I began my oral statement of reasons with a quotation from Harry Kalven:

> It must be recognized, of course, that a reason implicit in the breadth of the protection afforded speech is due to the judicial recognition of its own incapacity to make nice distinctions.

And went on to say:

> I as a judge confess to limitations and what I am about to say to the university will support that observation.

I then explained why in my view the policy was unconstitutional, because, in sum, . . . the regulation was so vague that men and woman of common intelligence must guess at the meaning, violating the first principle of constitutional law. . . . [and] A prohibition on verbal behavior that stigmatizes on the basis of race . . . (and other groups listed in the U-M policy) is so overbroad as to violate the first amendment.

The follow-up permanent injunction limited its effect to "verbal behavior and verbal conduct" and did not affect the prohibitions in the policy statement on physical behavior and physical conduct. What I ruled, I hoped, would send the Regents back to the drawing board. I did not say in my bench opinion, or in my follow-up written decision, that discriminatory speech does not harm its victims or that society has no interest in regulating such speech, or that such speech was not constitutionally regulable. Shortly after the written decision, the Regents adopted a revised policy on discriminatory harassment which continued to regulate hate speech in an educational setting, albeit in a considerably narrower way than the policy statement. This revised policy has not been challenged.

By the end of September, I followed up with a detailed opinion, in which I explained in a comprehensive fashion my view that the

PERSONAL VIEW

policy was vague and unconstitutionally overboard. In the opinion I also traced the development of the policy and exercised a good deal of restraint in the way I described, what I personally saw to be flaws in the decision making process, and obliquely, the failure to draw on the considerable resources of the law school, I said:

> Throughout this process, the Director of the Affirmative Action Office consulted with a lawyer in the Office of the University Counsel and perhaps with several university law school professors.

That comment was footnoted to a sentence which read:

> This equivocation is attributable to the fact that consultations with law professors were unaccompanied by the exchange of any formal correspondence or memoranda.

I concluded the opinion with my reasons for finding the policy as to verbal conduct vague and overbroad, discussing in some detail case law precedent, and citing examples from university life of how the policy had been consistently applied to reach protected speech.

I further concluded by suggesting that the university had apparently not looked at the experience of any other university, and then described a situation at Yale several years back which served as an exemplar of the way a claim of freedom of expression challenged as uncivil and irrational should be handled. Gratuitously perhaps, I was also severely critical of the failure of university officials to take cognizance of the values embodied in the first amendment.

In the opening of my opinion, I changed the quotation from Harry Kalven to an equally perceptive quotation from the writings of Dean Bollinger, and, in what I considered to be a bit of whimsy, concluded with a quotation from Justice Cooley in which he said some 120 years ago that even if speech

> exceeds all the proper bounds of moderation, the consolation must be that the evil likely to spring from the violent discussion will probably be less, and its correction by public sentiment more speedy, than if the terrors of the law were brought to bear to prevent the discussion.

My written decision was docketed September 22, 1989, a Friday. That day's mail brought me the August 1989 issue of the

Michigan Law Review. That evening, to my utter amazement, I read an article in it; *Public Response To Racist Speech: Considering The Victim's Story*, a paper delivered at the law school in April of 1989, shortly before the *Doe* case was filed. No one told me of the paper. I later found out that no one told the author of the article about the policy statement while she was on campus. Not only did the Regents not ask anything of the law school, clearly the law school paid little attention to the actions of the Regents. That Monday I added an addendum to the written opinion making note of the article.

As I told you earlier, the University did not appeal my decision. President Duderstadt quickly issued a revised set of standards for sanctionable verbal conduct which focused on one-to-one insulting comment. It reads in part:

> Physical acts or threats or verbal slurs, invectives or epithets referring to an individual's race, ethnicity, religion, sex, sexual orientation, creed, national origin, ancestry, age or handicap made with the purpose of injuring the person to whom the words or actions are directed and that are not made as a part of a discussion or exchange of an idea, ideology or philosophy are prohibited.

Whether any student has been charged under the new policy I do not know.

As I mentioned in my opening comments, the decision in *Doe* has received a good deal of attention nationwide. I am told by Professor Robert Sedler of Wayne State University, who represented Doe, that it sets the standards under which campus ordinances in this area are now drafted. For reasons that escape me, until tonight, it received little attention here in Ann Arbor. The Michigan Alumnus briefly mentioned it. The Law Review has ignored it. I am winning 2-to-1 in law reviews published elsewhere. The only attention the Regents have given it is to change their procedures. In the words of the Michigan Daily, which I paraphrase:

> Comments made by members of the University Board of Regents at the board's monthly meeting will no longer be reprinted verbatim in the meeting's minutes.
> . . .
> One Regent said a second Regent's verbatim comments inserted in the minutes concerning the anti-discrimination

PERSONAL VIEW

policy contributed to *Federal Court Judge Avern Cohn* striking down that policy last August.

Most of the Regents agreed with the proposal to place summaries of Regent's remarks rather than any verbatim statements and to put any prepared statement in a separate archive.

. . . .

Supporters of the motion maintained this is not a censorship issue. "This is not a question of what someone can say," a Regent said. "We are just saying what the minutes should say."

. . . .

Apparently it is better that those present at Regents' meetings should rely on memory as to what each Regent said than there be a written record. Or perhaps, a majority of the Regents prefer what they say at Regents' meetings be more easily forgotten.

JUDGING THE FIRST AMENDMENT†
Hon. Avern Cohn‡

INTRODUCTION

I am delighted to participate in celebrating the bicentennial of the Bill of Rights, particularly the First Amendment from the vantage point of a judge.

My remarks are colored by my almost twelve years as a federal trial judge in the Eastern District of Michigan—a metropolitan court much like the twenty or so such courts among the ninety-four judicial districts into which our country is divided. Moreover, my remarks are colored by my upbringing, my schooling, my associations, my experiences in politics, my law practice before I became a judge, my religious community, and the 4,000 or so cases that have come across my docket since I was invested in 1979. There are undoubtedly a host of other influences, of which I know little, that have been at work molding my thinking.

I believe all judges should take the advice of the late Judge Jerome Frank and be psychoanalyzed before beginning judicial duties.

You can learn much about me and my thinking as a judge by reading the 100 or so cases in the reports that reflect my decisions, both at the trial level and when I have sat as an appellate judge. As an English judge once said, judges are like a pianist and the piano—a "piano needs the pianist and any two pianists, even with the same score, may produce different music."[1]

I. Relationship Of Judges and the Media

As recently expressed by the National Conference of Lawyers and Representatives of the Media, it is beyond dispute that

---

† Revised remarks to the Association for Education in Journalism and Mass Communications, August 9, 1991, Boston, Massachusetts.

‡ Judge, United States District Court, Eastern District of Michigan. J.D., University of Michigan, 1949.

1. Lord McCluskey, Law, Justice and Democracy 7 (1987).

there are strained relationships between lawyers and judges on the one hand, and the media on the other. As to judges, those strains, as one commentator has put it, come from a desire by judges, indeed a requirement, for a neutral decisional environment coupled with a fear of being "burned" by inaccurate, misleading, and truncated reporting.[2] This is particularly so with regard to local electronic news programs.

The media, in turn, is driven by "the importance of getting the story" and the view that nothing is a secret or sacred. The media does not consider itself in any way responsible for the fairness of the trial process—this is of course a judge's job. Too often, in a judge's view, the media stops reading the First Amendment at the freedom of press proviso, and believes the *First*, in the First Amendment, means it was intended to outrank all of the other amendments.

Lastly, judges, being a source of news, have an insight into the fact that too often what occurs in the courtroom is not what the media reports because media organizations seldom observe standard IV of the Code of Ethics of the Society of Professional Journalists, which reads: "Journalists recognize their responsibility for offering informed analysis, comment, and editorial opinion on public events and issues. They accept the obligation to present such material by individuals whose competence, experience and judgment qualify them for it."[3] But enough media bashing.

II. Relationship of Judges To First Amendment

Judges relate to the First Amendment in two fundamental ways. First, they decide disputes in which the prohibitions of the amendment are the grounds asserted as a shield protecting conduct, or the prohibitions that are raised as a defense to conduct asserted to be unlawful. These kinds of cases, whether bottomed on the religious, speech and press, or assembly provisions, many times have a significance beyond the parties to the dispute at hand. This is why the American Civil Liberties Union and similar organizations so often ask to be heard.

---

2. Robert E. Drechsler, *Uncertain Dancers: Judges and the News Media*, 70 Judicature 264, 266 (1987).
3. Codes of Professional Responsibility 42 (R. Gorlin ed., 1986).

The second relationship is in high visibility cases, civil or criminal, in which the public through its surrogate, the media, shows an interest and reporting implicates the fair trial proviso of the Sixth Amendment and the jury trial right in civil cases of the Seventh Amendment.

Both relationships are defined by judges. Both relationships inevitably involve the personal element of judging, and at the trial level, both are more fact-bound than rule-bound, notwithstanding Anthony Lewis' concerns, recently and approvingly expressed by Michael Gartner: "The grandeur and the vitality of the First Amendment can be obscured when it is turned over to lawyers, when Judges begin drawing lines between permitted and forbidden expression."[4] First Amendment cases involve line drawing. The line that is drawn is most often dictated by the facts, and it is a judge, usually with little aid from the parties, who must find the facts.

To quote an English judge:

> At every stage in the preparation of a case, it is the facts which matter to the client, from the gathering of the evidence, which often requires imagination and insight, to the presentation of the case in court. Time and again, in my experience meticulous care in collecting and collating the facts, and correlating them with the correspondence and other external events, pays a big dividend, much bigger than preparing a careful legal argument, based on insecure foundations in fact.[5]

If there is any one great failing in lawyer's work in First Amendment cases it is the failure to fully develop the facts of the dispute.

III. Kinds of Cases in Court

What follows is a rundown of the kinds of disputes that have been heard in my courthouse and by me in recent months involving the First Amendment. Some of the disputes have been resolved, others are still in court. Importantly, they rep-

---

4. Michael Gartner, *Courts Becoming Editors, Ethicists*, Lansing St. J., July 23, 1991.
5. Sir Roger Ormond, *Judges and the Processes of Judging*, in Jubilee Lectures Celebrating the Foundation of the Faculty of Law, University of Birmingham 188-89 (1981).

resent only a small number of the total cases filed. I personally can recall only five significant cases involving First Amendment issues on which I had to spend any great amount of judicial time. Under the establishment of religion proscription, judges in the Eastern District of Michigan have dealt with Christmas and Hanukkah displays on public property, the appropriateness of a cross in the logo of a municipality, and the obligation of the state to pay Christian Science practitioners health benefits. Under the free exercise of religion proviso, they have dealt with cases involving the right of parents to home-school children and the discharge of a federal employee who attempted to justify a medical absence with a Christian Science practitioner certification.

The free speech proviso has generated the most cases. These cases involved disputes over university regulation of campus comment, municipal employees discharged or disciplined for public comment, an ethnic intimidation ordinance, telephone companies cutting-off 900 numbers, a parade regulation, and various forms of adult entertainment. There was even a case in which a prisoner claimed the telephone company, identifying his collect calls as originating in a prison, violated his First Amendment rights.

I found only two fact circumstances involving the media. There were several cases in which school authorities asserted the right to regulate non-curriculum publications, and defamation cases against newspapers defended on First Amendment grounds.

The judges rarely see cases involving the assembly proviso. One of my colleagues did deal with an effort to enforce a Labor Department subpoena to a union, which resisted on the right-to-assemble proviso.

As I mentioned earlier, I have personally decided five First Amendment cases that involved some effort. I am satisfied that in four of the cases, whoever the judge, the result would likely have been the same, although the route travelled to the decision might have been different. A case in which I held a prison regulation allowing for examination of letters to the media from prisoners in administrative segregation unconstitutional because such letters from prisoners in the general population were not so examined, might have gone differently in front of some other judge. The extent to which prison regulations are found acceptable to the Constitution varies, I believe, with the proclivities of the judge deciding. This can be explained by the differing degrees in which judges accept the authority of the state, a well-known phenomenon in judicial decision making. Precisely why this is so is not well explained in the literature. Reading the contrasting views of Justice Kennedy and Chief Justice Rehnquist in the recent Nevada bar case,[6] one can see the phenomenon at work. Or read, for example, Justice Souter's dissent in the Minnesota press case,[7] this past term.

One of my decisions involved a court officer challenging his discharge because he supported his judge's opponent in an election. I upheld the discharge on the grounds that, while the officer had the freedom to support whomever he wanted, his duties as the judge's confidential assistant did not require the judge to keep him on.

In another case, I held unconstitutional a local regulation regarding door-to-door solicitations by advocacy groups, because the regulation had severe time-of-day limitations. It simply overregulated the activity and, therefore, denied the groups their First Amendment rights. I drew a line.

In September 1989, I held unconstitutional the University of Michigan's policy on discrimination and discriminatory harassment as overbroad. Many are familiar with the policy that forbids speech that is stigmatizing or victimizing when directed to individuals or groups on the basis of race, ethnicity, religion, sex, or sexual orientation. What was important in my decision were the specific incidents of the policy's application. When the policy in action was examined, it was clear it was overbroad. Moreover, the absence of any effort by the Regents of the University to obtain a legal opinion as to the constitutionality of the policy was a persuasive factor in my decision. The most recent of my First Amendment decisions invalidated the City of Ann Arbor's vacation of a part of a street so that protestors in front of a Planned Parenthood facility would be trespassers. The city tried to justify its action on the grounds that the

---

6. Gentile v. State Bar of Nevada, 111 S. Ct. 2720 (1991).
7. Cohen v. Cowles Media Co., 111 S. Ct. 2513, 2522-23 (1991) (Souter, J., dissenting).

protestors represented a public safety problem, and that nothing short of turning the street into private property could deal with the problem. The problem, as I saw it, with Ann Arbor's position was that there was nothing in the record to establish that the police had thrown up its arms and said it was helpless to control the demonstrators.

I am satisfied that in the University of Michigan and the Planned Parenthood cases I applied conventional First Amendment free speech principles. What was important was to understand the facts of the dispute. What was disconcerting was the under-appreciation by the University and the city of the inevitability of my decisions. There was in each case a misunderstanding of the fundamental requirements of the First Amendment—i.e., when First Amendment values are at stake, trial judges tend to establish bright lines and are not much given to subtle analysis.

IV. First Amendment v. Sixth Amendment

Far more significant in the life of a federal trial judge than substantive First Amendment cases is the ongoing relationship with the media in harmonizing First Amendment free press principles with the right to a fair trial in a criminal case under the Sixth Amendment and a prejudice-free jury under the Seventh Amendment. The conflicts in this area are of a relatively recent origin. In the early years, the republic disputes between judges and the media largely pitted the efforts of judges to preserve their integrity against adverse comment by the media on the judicial process.

The conflicts today play themselves out in media coverage preceding a trial, media coverage during a trial, limitations on what can be said about a case, the extent to which part of a court proceeding can be closed, and the extent to which the media is entitled to court records. I have had experiences in all of these conflict areas.

Given the relationship between the media and judges, one would think that there would be written guidelines to define what is right and what is wrong. Such is not the case. Judges, particularly federal judges, have established standards for themselves. The media has, by and large, avoided any writings to govern its conduct, and, where there are writings, the media has assiduously avoided any adjudicatory or mediating agency to decide what is right and what is wrong.

Years ago William Allen White, chairman of a 1927 Media Ethics Committee reported: "After a year's study the Committee has no report because it has no idea of what the ethics of this business is. Old Pontius Pilate had a good idea when he asked, 'What is truth?' Then he washed his hands of the whole thing."[8]

Clearly once the media has information in its possession, there can be no restraint on its publication. One of my colleagues recently erred in issuing a restraining order against publication of a surreptitiously filmed incident of medical malpractice and was promptly reversed. There will always be a judge or two with an underappreciation of the rules.

Restraint on comment by law enforcement officers, court personnel, and lawyers on a pending case is of a different order. In our district, judges have frequently issued gag orders in high visibility cases. The judicial skill involved is in promptly issuing the order and having the fortitude to see that it is complied with. What I cannot do, however, is extend the gag order to the parties themselves.

The greatest conflict area between the media and the courts involves the issue of publicity: pretrial and trial. Judges have an abiding concern about publicity that taints a prospective juror, or a juror in the box. We do not look for jurors without opinions, but for jurors who are not so influenced as to lack the ability to set opinions aside. There is little that we can do with media because of its insensitivity to the difficulties created by reporting information in advance or during a trial that will not be available to jurors and which has a high potential of prejudice to the trial process. There are devices to minimize the prejudice, such as a questionnaire, a searching voir dire, an increase in preemptory challenges, and a change-of-locale. Also, advance representations to the media can sometimes reduce inflammatory coverage.

Another area of conflict between judges and the media that has received much attention in recent years is courtroom clo-

---

8. ALICE FOX PITTS, READ ALL ABOUT IT! 41 (1974).

has assiduously avoided any adjudicatory or mediating agency to decide what is right and what is wrong.

Years ago William Allen White, chairman of a 1927 Media Ethics Committee reported: "After a year's study the Committee has no report because it has no idea of what the ethics of this business is. Old Pontius Pilate had a good idea when he asked, 'What is truth?' Then he washed his hands of the whole thing."[8]

Clearly once the media has information in its possession, there can be no restraint on its publication. One of my colleagues recently erred in issuing a restraining order against publication of a surreptitiously filmed incident of medical malpractice and was promptly reversed. There will always be a judge or two with an underappreciation of the rules.

Restraint on comment by law enforcement officers, court personnel, and lawyers on a pending case is of a different order. In our district, judges have frequently issued gag orders in high visibility cases. The judicial skill involved is in promptly issuing the order and having the fortitude to see that it is complied with. What I cannot do, however, is extend the gag order to the parties themselves.

The greatest conflict area between the media and the courts involves the issue of publicity: pretrial and trial. Judges have an abiding concern about publicity that taints a prospective juror, or a juror in the box. We do not look for jurors without opinions, but for jurors who are not so influenced as to lack the ability to set opinions aside. There is little that we can do with media because of its insensitivity to the difficulties created by reporting information in advance or during a trial that will not be available to jurors and which has a high potential of prejudice to the trial process. There are devices to minimize the prejudice, such as a questionnaire, a searching voir dire, an increase in preemptory challenges, and a change-of-locale. Also, advance representations to the media can sometimes reduce inflammatory coverage.

Another area of conflict between judges and the media that has received much attention in recent years is courtroom clo-

---

8. ALICE FOX PITTS, READ ALL ABOUT IT! 41 (1974).

sure. The Supreme Court has made it clear that openness, not secrecy, is the rule of the day. Clearly a public trial is an important outlet for community concerns, hostility, and emotions. A public trial is a check on a judge. It assures that we are publicly responsible for what we do. A public trial promotes true and accurate findings on my part because I must work in front of a critical audience.

There are, however, limitations. I can question prospective jurors outside the confines of the courtroom. If I believe an open courtroom represents a danger, I can, after making explicit findings, close it, but to assure the propriety of the closing I have on occasion notified the media of my intentions and listened to their representations.

The last area of conflict is the extent to which the media is entitled to access court records. Let me only state the general rule, the interests of privacy may outweigh the presumptive right to access to court records as public records and, thus, a case-by-case examination is necessary. This is a developing area.

Conclusion

I have lived with the media as a judge for eleven and one-half years. I have ambivalent feelings about the relationship. I agree with Justice Brennan's view:

> There exists a fundamental and necessary interdependence of the Court and the press. The press needs the Court, if only for the simple reason that the Court is the ultimate guardian of the constitutional rights that support the press. And the Court has a concomitant need for the press, because through the press the Court receives the tacit and accumulated experience of the Nation, and—because the judgments of the Court ought also to instruct and to inspire—the Court needs the medium of the press to fulfill this task.[9]

I know that since the 1930's, when the trial of Richard Bruno Hauptman for kidnapping Charles Lindberg's baby son first nationalized the tensions between a free press and a fair

---

9. William J. Brennan, Jr., Address, 32 RUTGERS L. REV. 173, 174 (1979).

trial, the media and the courts have come a long way. One of the rules unanimously agreed upon by a 1937 American Bar Association—American Society of Newspaper Publishers joint committee was "[t]hat featuring in vaudeville of jurors or other court officers, either during or after the trial, be forbidden and . . . . That public discussion in speeches, magazine articles or newspaper interviews, by witnesses, during the progress of the litigation and covering the subject matter thereof, should be forbidden."[10]

Judges no longer think it seeming that jurors perform on stage in the evening, and reporters no longer interview witnesses.

I am satisfied, except for an occasional lapse, federal trial judges understand the common law and the constitutional rights of the media and know of their obligations in that regard. In the words of the late Professor Edmond Cahn, "[J]udges are tethered to a text."[11] In the long run there is little danger of a significant diminishment of the First Amendment rights of the media from the courts. I am less sure of the understanding of the media than of the meaning of the defendant's Sixth Amendment right to a fair trial. I see a great deal of self-righteousness and little of self-instruction. I do not find a text. I see constantly changing personnel. I see editors remote from the courtroom. I see a highly competitive environment. I find no mechanism for review or a window to receive complaints.

Perhaps one day a thoughtful editor will say: Are we of the media charging too much for our First Amendment rights? Meanwhile, all we can do as judges is continue to talk, continue to be alert to opportunities to instruct, continue to explore options when a media activity becomes oppressive, and continue to hope that one day the media will be less paranoid about its rights, more secure in its role, and a bit less competitive.

---

10. Report of the Special Committee on Cooperation Between Press, Radio and Bar, As to Publicity Interfering with Fair Trial of Judicial and Quasi-Judicial Proceedings, A.B.A. Proc. 865 (1937).

11. CONFRONTING INJUSTICE: THE EDMOND CAHN READER 114-15 (1986).

A Federal Trial Judge Looks at Academic Freedom
Avern Cohn

Introduction

Thank you for that kind introduction, Dr. Hollingsworth.

I first came to Ann Arbor as a student in January 1942. I left in March 1943, on being drafted into the U.S. Army. I returned in September 1946 to begin a three-year stint in the Law School. Neither when I entered as a freshman in the College of Literature, Science, and the Arts (LS&A) nor when I returned as a freshman in the Law School did I imagine I would one evening be speaking to the faculty as the annual Davis, Markert, Nickerson lecturer. I am humbled by the privilege.

Although I alone am responsible for what I say tonight, I must express thanks to a number of persons whom I have spoken to in recent months, including: Peggie Hollingsworth, Elsa Kircher Cole, Jon Cosovich, Thomas Moore, Tom Roach, Carl Dibble, and particularly Professor Ted St. Antoine. Professor St. Antoine came to the Law School after my time. I regret not having the opportunity to be his student.

As you know, I am not an academic. I am not a scholar. In Cass Sustein's words in his book *Legal Reasoning and Political Conflict* (1996), I am not given to high-level theoretical thinking. Rather, almost always I think low level and deal with incompletely theorized agreements.

This is unusual territory for me. Customarily I speak mostly to lawyers—some even say I mostly bark at lawyers. I also talk to judges and law students. When I go outside the profession it is to answer questions and defend judges against the accusation that we too often do dumb things—which is partially true—and have too much power—which is also partially true.

The lecture is an important event in the life of the university and the community. Its spirit is expressed in the enabling resolution:

The protection of academic and intellectual freedom requires a constant reminder of their value and vulnerability.

The Davis, Markert, Nickerson Lecture is a continual reminder of things past. Had the university authorities apologized for their sins and made amends, as some of you urged, we might not have this reminder. Apologies, even with reparations, do not undo past wrongs, as the Japanese who were interred during World War II tell us.

A third-century rabbinic sage, Reshi Lakish of the Academy of Tiberias, said:

Each generation has its own interpreters; each generation has its own teachers.

Tonight I am an interpreter and a teacher from a perspective you have not heard from before.

What I propose to do is first tell you something about me personally, not because I am particularly exciting or unique but because I believe I am the paradigm—or close to the paradigm—of a federal district court judge, one of the six hundred who regularly make decisions, many times affecting the academy, in the ninety-four judicial districts that make up the federal court system in the United States. We are real people. Then I will tell you something of the federal court system in which I operate. And I remind you there are also fifty state court systems in the United States, each with its own particular procedures and each with its own particular jurisprudence. In this connection you should know that the vast majority of the cases in which the university is a party, for whatever reason, start and finish in the state courts of Michigan and particularly the Washtenaw County Circuit Court here in Ann Arbor, as we have recently seen.

After that introduction, which I believe is an important predicate to any discussion of academic freedom in today's environment of judicialization of institutional personnel matters, as David Adamany, president of Wayne State University, has put it, I will talk about the events of the 1950s here at Ann Arbor, review briefly the prior lectures, and go on to talk about academic freedom before and since World War II, describe the university in federal court, and offer some concluding thoughts.

A Federal Trial Judge Looks at Academic Freedom

I will be speaking largely anecdotally and selectively, and I want to make three points at the beginning. First, so far as academic freedom is concerned, my inquiries tell me the university is in a generally healthy condition. This is so even in light of the concerns President Duderstadt spoke of in his farewell letter last June and even in the face of the fact that the defining quality for one of the nominations for regent at last summer's Republican state convention appears to have been the competing candidates' position on a university policy regarding distribution of condoms on campus. Second, I do not see the challenges facing the academic community today to be nearly as serious as those of the 1950s. Third, the years before World War II did not display a more hospitable environment to academic freedom than today. Until the courts began to view academic freedom through the prism of the Constitution, particularly the First and Fourteenth Amendments, the only protection of academic freedom in public universities and colleges was contractual and jawboning. And today academic freedom at private colleges and universities is still largely protected only by contract and jawboning.

My Persona

I have been a federal judge for seventeen years. I came to the bench from private practice through the confluence of several events taking place more or less at the same time. Jimmy Carter, a Democrat, was president. I had been active in the Democratic Party and in Jewish and general community affairs including bar activities. The Senate was under Democratic control. Don Riegle, in whose campaign I had been active, was the senior U.S. senator from Michigan. There were five positions open for appointment. I had strong support from the leadership of the Jewish community in Detroit and particularly those who had strongly backed Senator Riegle in his 1976 election effort. I was acceptable to organized labor even though I was a partner in a corporate law firm, and Mayor Coleman Young endorsed my candidacy. My particular skills as a lawyer or my potential for being an erudite and wise judge were certainly not as important as the factors I have just mentioned.

Now, what do I bring to the bench? What makes up my persona as a judge? These are important matters in my decision making. Ninety to ninety-five percent of all cases in federal court are likely to be decided the same way regardless of the judge. Ten percent or fewer are likely to be decided more by the persona of the judge than by their facts or rules of law because in these few cases there is no particular course laid out to follow. In a book published by the University of Michigan Press, *The Federal Judiciary and Institutional Change,* Barrow, Zuk, and Gryski (1996) discuss how alternating party control of the Congress and presidency, together with an accelerating turnover of judgeships, and what they describe as a constant acculturation of new judges through record-breaking growth, affect decision making in a system initially thought to be politically independent and stable. There are liberal judges and there are conservative judges, and these casts of mind do not come about after a judge takes the bench.

There are two quotations I am partial to in talking about the differences in the personas of judges. The first is from an English judge of the 1920s:

> The law as laid down in a code, or in a statute or in a thousand eloquently reasoned opinions, is no more capable of providing all the answers than a piano is capable of providing music. The piano needs the pianist, and any two pianists, even with the same score, may produce very different music. (McCluskey 1987, 7)

The second is from Chancellor James Kent, an early-eighteenth-century New York state judge:

> I was master of the cause & ready to decide it. I saw where justice lay and the moral sense decided the cause half the time, & I then sed [sic] down to search the authorities until I had exhausted my books, & I might once & a while be embarrassed by a technical rule, but I *most always found principles suited to my views of the case.* (Kent 1897, 210)

Now what determines the way I play the piano and the music I produce? What determined my moral sense when, for example, I looked at the facts and what I thought to be applicable in *Doe v. University of Michigan* or *United States v. Baker,* two cases with which I am sure you are familiar? Of course, my years as a judge give me a body of experience, as does my understanding of the facts and my reading of the rules. But more is involved. Had I followed the late judge Jerome Frank's advice and been psychoanalyzed when I came to the bench I might better know. I have not been psychoanalyzed, so I must speculate.

I know my life history plays a role. I come from an upper-middle-class socioeconomic background. I, like my father who practiced law for more than sixty years and graduated from the Law School in 1917, went through the Detroit Public Schools and took my law degree at Michigan. My political background is liberal Democrat. Some say I was a yellow-dog Democrat—that is, had a yellow dog been the Democratic candidate I would have voted for him or her. My religious background—Conservative Judaism—certainly has helped shape my thinking process. The three years I spent in the Army, all in the United States, give me some humility, although it may have faded with the years. My age at investiture, fifty-six, and the fact that I have life tenure and my pay cannot be reduced, and that I still worry about being right are of significance. I had street experience as a lawyer before I came to the bench. In my early years as a lawyer, I accepted criminal assignments when there was no pay. My experiences at the bar—my public service assignments—are all factors that contribute to the way I play the judicial piano.

This is the background I brought to the bench. As for what I am as a judge, it is really for others to tell you. I will tell you that when recently asked by the *Detroit Jewish News* the way I view myself as a judge, I said:

> Some judges have an imperfect heart: they are harsh, vindictive, narrow. I like to think of myself as having, not a perfect heart—but the absence of an imperfect heart.

There is a difference in persona among judges; that is a fact of life. James Boyd White (1985), in *Heracles Bow*, puts in this way:

> Of course one may properly argue against the results of particular cases and, more deeply, against a judge's institutional or political premises, and one may properly criticize technique as well. But any judge brings a set of basic values and orientations to his or her work, and it is hard to fault someone for having a different set from one's own.

The Federal Court System

There are at least fifty-one court systems in these United States. Each state has its own system, as does the federal government. Many disputes can be handled by either system. Most of the major constitutional disputes, particularly those with significance to the academy, are in the federal system. They begin in the district court and may come into court at the behest of a citizen or a taxpayer, a student, an academic, or sometimes an institution. A decision by a district judge is sometimes publicly reported but is not binding precedent. At best, it is only an authoritative statement of the law. If a party disagrees with such a decision, an appeal can be taken to one of the twelve regional courts of appeals where three judges review the case and make the decision. A decision at this level is precedential and binding on the district judges with the states comprising the region, and the law can be different among the circuits. In *United States v. Baker*, for example, the government argued that the law regarding threats is different in the Sixth Circuit—that is, in Michigan, Ohio, Kentucky, and Tennessee—than in the Second Circuit—that is, in New York, Connecticut, and Vermont. That is an issue in the appeal now pending from my decision dismissing the indictment.

The Supreme Court is the ultimate decision maker on constitutional matters, but it takes only the cases it wants to decide and frequently leaves differences among the courts of appeals unresolved.

District judges such as me are generalists. We have civil cases and criminal cases. We get our cases by blind draw. What is assigned to us we decide. As an example of the generality of my work, during a three-month period in the spring of this year cases before me ranged over the following:

- A threat to kill the president
- My approval of $1.5 million in legal fees for defense attorneys in a mammoth drug case that included five defendants potentially facing the death penalty
- An invasion of privacy claim involving Jenny Jones showing home movies of a bachelor party
- An accusation against the Internal Revenue Service of wrongful disclosure of tax information

- An alleged illegal police raid in which a television reporter was invited along

I and my colleagues are well housed and well staffed. We have strong support services. We are part of an elaborate governance structure that has at its top a group called the Judicial Conference of the United States headed by Chief Justice Rehnquist, which is composed of chief judges of the twelve courts of appeal and a district judge from each circuit. The conference operates through a multitude of committees that are also well staffed. As a think tank and for continuing teaching we have the Federal Judicial Center. Lastly, in every law school we have at least one academic and sometimes a multitude studying and writing about what we do. We do not lack for critics or critical analysis.

The Events of the 1950s at Ann Arbor

In preparation for tonight, I sought to familiarize myself with the Davis, Markert, Nickerson events. You each have, I am sure, your particular view. Ellen W. Schrecker, in her seminal work *No Ivory Tower: McCarthyism and the Universities*, described very well the environment of the early 1950s when she said:

> The academy did not fight McCarthyism. It contributed to it. The dismissals, the blacklists, and above all the most universal acceptance of the legitimacy of what the congressional committees and other official investigators were doing conferred respectability upon the most repressive elements of the anti-Communist crusade. In its collaboration with McCarthyism, the academic community behaved just like every other major institution in American life. (Schrecker 1986, 340)

The way the administration in Ann Arbor responded was consistent with its history on these matters. In 1935 President Alexander Ruthven, in response to the activities of the National Student League, a socialist organization, said, "attendance is a privilege and not a right" and to make clear the point, wrote a student, who had gained some visibility in his support of the league's views, as follows:

University of Michigan
Ann Arbor
President's Room
July 9, 1935

Mr. Daniel Cohen,
155 S. Broad Street
Trenton, New Jersey

My dear Mr. Cohen:
   It has been decided by the authorities of the University of Michigan that you should be asked not to re-enter the University. It has proved to be impossible to persuade you to refrain from interfering with the work of the University and with the work of other students.

Yours sincerely,
(Signed) Alexander Ruthven

Student Cohen was no slouch. He sued the university in the federal district court in Detroit, asserting a rather primitively phrased right of due process and denial of equal protection because of the failure to follow then-in-place procedures for expulsion. Cohen asked for a court order requiring his readmission. The university took the position that Cohen had no legal right to attend. I do not know what happened to Cohen. The court docket shows the case was dismissed by agreement shortly after the university filed its answer. Of particular interest is the fact that Cohen was one of four students, in President Ruthven's words, "of the same persuasion."

While I was in law school in the early winter of 1947, Gerhard Eisler, then reputed to be head of the Communist Party in the United States, was denied the right to speak on university property and the mayor of Ann Arbor canceled a permit for a meeting in Felch Park at which Eisler was scheduled to talk. Eisler then spoke from the steps of a house and eventually had to flee into the house when students began pelting him with snowballs. I can still recall a front-page picture in the the *Michigan Daily* of the house, faces in a window, and a large group of angry students outside.

The reaction to the Davis, Markert, and Nickerson response to the demands of East Lansing Congressman Kit Clardy to name names should have come as no surprise. Professor Davis surely should have known at the time, or at least his lawyer should have told him, that the courts were not likely to rule against the will of Congress. And the result in *Barenblatt*, the case that did him in, was predictable. Professors Markert and Nickerson should have known the weakness of the support they would get for their reliance on the Fifth Amendment. Although the outcome of the administrative process was certain, formalities were followed. The university then, and now, is dependent to a considerable extent on public money and legislative goodwill. At work were political processes; moral judgment was absent.

Prior Lectures

As I now direct my comments more particularly to academic freedom and the courts, let me recall for you the lectures that have preceded tonight's. I am the sixth in the series. All of the lectures have been printed, with the exception of Professor Metzger's. However, Professor Metzger's lecture was extensively reported in *The University Record*.

Professor Robert O'Neil gave a historical overview of academic freedom and discussed current concerns. He urged "resisting notions of what is politically correct or incorrect" and "combatting self-imposed orthodoxy as vigorously as we protested orthodoxy imposed on us from the outside."

Lee Bollinger talked of the impulse to intolerance and what can be done about it and the need to have a floor of principles. He pointed out the special role of the university. Particularly, he said:

> in these two great pulls of life, the impulse to intolerance and the need for commitment to belief, the university and its principle of academic freedom opt to overcome the former, because they live primarily in a world of the latter.

Catharine Stimpson gave a reasoned argument in support of freedom of speech and why the academy should support the absence of restrictions. She expressed concern with the antipornography movement and the ban hate speech movement.

Professor Metzger talked about the watchdog role of the American Association of University Professors (AAUP). He traced the history of the involvement of the AAUP in protecting academic freedom and noted that much of the combat zone is outside the academy. He observed that it is the AAUP's position that it is not fair for faculty members to indoctrinate students or to introduce controversial matters not related to class subject matter. He concluded by noting that academic freedom is in better shape today than in 1950 and that it would be naive to dismiss the tension between law and the academy. He said, "They aren't always pals."

Last year Linda Ray Pratt looked to the future when she spoke of the merits of uncertainty and cautioned:

> Increasingly, we shall need our academic freedom to protect the space in which to be uncertain, the space in which to hang possibilities that do not reconcile, the space in which to explore the connections that might be built between differences, the space in which to adjudicate an ethical outcome when opinions are in conflict.

Pre–World War II

Now let me get to some particulars. In the early years the difficulty in defending academic freedom—that is, in the words of the *American Heritage College Dictionary*, "Liberty to track and pursue knowledge and to discuss it openly without restriction or interference"—was the absence of support in the law for such a liberty.

The *Yale Law Journal*, in 1937, prompted by the failure to appoint a professor at its divinity school and by the dismissal of the president of the University of Wisconsin, said:

> It is extremely difficult to frame a legal action through which the courts can give relief against such unwarrantable limitations on academic freedom. Academic freedom is not a "property" right, or a constitutional privilege, or even a legal term defined by a history of judicial usages. Moreover, where a case is brought the plaintiff faces the added barrier of judicial reluctance to intervene in the internal affairs of an educational institution, an attitude which is said to limit the court to an examination of the authority, not the propriety, of adminis-

trative action. ("Academic Freedom and the Law," 1936–37, 670–71)

Many of you will recall a New York state court judge barring Bertrand Russell from a professorship at City College at the behest of a group of taxpayers because of the judge's disfavor with what he called Russell's moral character. The public, likely because of Russell's then controversial views on marriage, supported the decision. *Black's Law Dictionary* today uses the *Russell* case definition of academic freedom: "Right to teach as one sees fit—but not necessarily the right to teach evil" (Hamilton 1940–41, 778–79).

In a second article on academic freedom in the *Yale Law Journal*, commenting on the *Russell* case, there was the suggestion, the first I found, of the possibility of arguing a denial of a civil liberty implicating a violation of due process under the Fourteenth Amendment in the way Russell was treated.

Post–World War II

The difficulty before the 1960s was in the lack of appreciation of what the Constitution said about the actions of public officials at public universities and colleges. As the years went on judges began to have a deeper appreciation of what the Constitution, and particularly the First and Fourteenth Amendments, means. I do not intend to trace that history. The first time the words *academic freedom* appeared in a Supreme Court decision was 1952, and since then these words have appeared in some twenty-nine cases, the latest in 1990.

Walter Metzger, in discussing the 1940 Statement of Principles on Academic Freedom and Tenure of the AAUP explained it this way:

> Those who wrote the 1940 Statement put their words to paper long before academic freedom had entered the protective folds of the first amendment and some time before academic tenure had acquired strong advocates on the bench or many statehouse friends. Their animating assumption was that the defense of these professional goods would have to lie outside the law, in the perfection of the policies and practices of institutions of higher learning. Their aim was to elevate academic

conduct to a high uniform standard; their means—an inventory of "do's" and "don't's"—reflected their belief that, since the law allows academic institutions to be run like so many extraterritorial enclaves imposing rules of their own devising on the native population, the only way to achieve that elevation was through moral, not legal, prodding. That the words they concocted for that purpose might be used to affect the outcome of courtroom battles seems to have been furthest from their minds. (Metzger 1990, 3, 7)

The legal landscape today is far different. For example, the agenda of the American Civil Liberties Union today on issues of academic freedom covers such matters as the following:

1. Access to materials stored in libraries and archives that the donor has restricted
2. Speeches of students relating to nonacademic behavior and taking it into account in degree awarding
3. Racial and gender unrest on campuses and resulting restrictions
4. Disparity in qualification for scholarships among athletic students and other students
5. Excessive governmental intrusion into publicly financed academic activities
6. Religious control over faculty in parochial colleges and universities
7. The military presence on campus—recruiting and training
8. Relationship between tenure and discipline (nonacademic misbehavior)
9. Physical facilities and preference for racially and ethnically oriented programs

The University of Michigan in Federal Court

I would now like to talk about the university in federal court. I will not go into detail. The university is an arm of the state of Michigan and cannot be sued for damages in federal court because of the

Eleventh Amendment, which bars the federal court from exercising jurisdiction over a state. Consequently, the defendants are nominally individual officers and administrators. Also, many cases arise because the university is a rather large corporate enterprise that employs many people. Inevitably, employer-employee disputes arise outside the area of academic freedom and include claims of

- Sex discrimination
- Race discrimination
- Equal pay for equal work
- Collective bargaining disputes
- Breach of contract claims

Also, disputes sometimes arise between the university as a service provider and students as a consumer of such services, such as over tuition.

My research has located about ten cases in my court—one in the 1960s, two in the 1970s, and the rest in the 1980s—that have some particular interest as implicating principles of academic freedom. This is aside from *Doe,* which I will discuss separately.

The first case I found was a 1963 effort by Jackie Vaughn, then a student and now a state senator, to bar Governor Ross Barnett of Mississippi from speaking in Hill Auditorium because of the disrupting influence the speech would have on campus life. Vaughn was denied an injunction on the grounds he did not establish a clear and present danger from the speech and it was not the court's duty to decide who could speak on campus. The university said in opposing the injunction in words that should be remembered and bear repeating in detail:

> The function of the University is the education of the persons who attend. The most important feature of education is teaching and training the student to think so as to choose the true and reject the spurious. Education also extends to the imparting of knowledge but knowledge without the ability by thinking to weigh and choose is not of substantial consequence. It is because of the settled conviction accepted by all free peoples that by thinking, weighing, and choosing the right and the true will ultimately prevail that the great principles of free-

dom of speech, press, and religion are considered to be inalienable rights of the citizen. Every person has the right at all times and places to express his personal views and ideas on any subject. It is for the person to whose attention they come to determine whether sound or unsound. And it is only by having all such views and ideas before a person that he can acquire ability and facility to think, weigh, and choose. To that end Governor Barnett is permitted to address whosoever cares to come. (*Vaughn v. University of Michigan*, docket no. 24586 [E. D. Mich. 1963], 6)

Twice in the 1970s students challenged the denial of their right to continue in school, and twice they lost because the judges found the processes followed passed constitutional muster. In the early 1980s, an assistant professor of engineering challenged a denial of tenure on First Amendment, equal protection, and breach of contract grounds. The professor lost. The trial judge found the decision to deny tenure reasonable in light of deficient classroom performance.

Again in the 1980s, a medical student challenged his dismissal because of academic deficiencies. The student lost in the trial court. The judge said the school authorities had good reason to deny the student the right to take the examination that led to his dismissal. The court of appeals found the refusal arbitrary and capricious and ordered the student back. The Supreme Court of the United States upheld the dismissal on the grounds that university officials have a broad range of discretion in these matters and it is dubious at best to think there is a property interest in university enrollment. One justice wondered why the case was ever litigated.

Another case involved an expulsion for cheating in circumstances in which the student was denied the opportunity to have lawyer representation or a transcript of an administrative hearing. The student lost. The judge found the procedures adequate.

Still another case involved a challenge by a graduate student to the revocation of his master's degree on grounds his thesis was based on fraudulent research. The trial judge agreed, finding fault in the process followed. The court of appeals disagreed, stating that regents had the constitutional authority, to revoke a degree where fraud was involved because "upon the grant of a degree, the university certified to the world that the recipient has fulfilled the university's requirements and this certification continues until the degree is revoked."

The last two cases each involved a law student challenge to a denial of a degree on due process grounds. Neither was successful. The procedures followed, including requiring a polygraph test in one case because the student was thought to have been involved in a fire, were found to be adequate.

These cases, typical of cases from around the country, demonstrate the wide authority given to university administrators in the operation of the university and judge approval of procedures typically followed. It is a rare case in which a student is successful in challenging an academic decision against him or her and almost as rare a case in which an academic will be successful in resisting an adverse decision of a university administration.

Now, as you all know, the university lost in *Doe v. University of Michigan*. This case never should have been heard, and, to the credit of the university, that fact was recognized when it was over. The university, instead of appealing, went back to the drawing board.

I am not going to describe *Doe* to you. I am sure you all know the basics of the case. Also, I have written a somewhat personal account of the case for a 1991 issue of the *Wayne State Law Review*. There are a couple of comments I would like to make. My first inclination was to call the parties into chambers to see if their differences could be resolved. I had done that several years earlier in a case in which the American Civil Liberties Union (ACLU) challenged speech regulations at Detroit–Wayne County Metropolitan Airport. There I suggested the airport authority sit down with the ACLU and see if they could resolve their differences. The effort was successful.

However, two of my colleagues, both University of Michigan Law School graduates, persuaded me otherwise. They were of the view I should deal with the case head on. We all thought that the university, with its wealth of legal talent at the Law School, could not be that far off base. I discovered otherwise.

Second, in my written decision I used the words *academic freedom* only twice and then only obliquely. My concerns were directed to the First Amendment implication of the code in action.

Third, as I look back, what happened was not all that unusual. A political problem existed. The politicians developed a political solution, knowing if it did not work a federal judge would take care of the matter. The regents apparently believed that what they thought was good social policy would be good law. They did not stop to think that what was bad social policy was likely to be bad law. It was simply bad social policy to put civility above freedom of expression as a core value, as C. Van Woodward put it in his 1975 report on free speech at Yale.

Speech codes are still a problem. In 1995 the Court of Appeals for the Sixth Circuit held unconstitutional a speech policy at Central Michigan University. The current issue of the *Northern University of Kentucky Law Review* contains a student note "Campus Speech Codes: Whatever Happened to the 'Sticks and Stones' Doctrine?" The same issue also contains, to my dismay, a distorted description of the events of *Doe* by Lino Graglia, a law professor at the University of Texas, without so much as a mention that I held the speech code unconstitutional.

Conclusion

I am not sure how to conclude. As I told you earlier, I am one of six hundred federal district judges. In the Eastern District of Michigan a case involving the university could end up on the docket of any one of our current complement of eighteen regular and senior judges. I might not see a case involving the university for years to come. The university may not get to federal court on an academic freedom issue for years to come. However, given the complex nature of rules and regulations governing student conduct, faculty-student relationships, tenure, freedom of speech, and the like, it is more than likely that some student or academic, offended by an action taken, or some ill-thought-out administrative action ignoring what the Constitution requires, will come to my court for relief, and academic freedom issues will be part of the dispute.

As constitutional interpretation expands and contracts, so does the concept of academic freedom. Ronald Dworkin (1996) in an essay in *The Future of Academic Freedom*, notes that the phrase *academic freedom* collects different images and associations now than it did thirty or maybe even ten years ago. He says:

> We thought then about leftist teachers and McCarthyite legislators and loyalty oaths and courageous and cowardly uni-

versity presidents. Liberals and radicals were all for academic freedom. Many conservatives thought it overrated or even part of the conspiracy to paint America red. Now it is the party of reform that talks down academic freedom and conservatives who call it a bulwark of Western civilization. Now the phrase makes us think of insensitive professors and of speech codes that might protect students from their insensitivity. We wonder whether academic freedom forbids such protection, and, if so, whether academic freedom is as important as liberals once thought. (181)

Given the constantly changing landscape of constitutional rights and the scope of academic freedom, it is not safe to predict the likelihood of future cases in court or the course such cases will follow. For example, in a California case last August, setting aside discipline against a professor for having created a hostile learning environment by his sexually oriented teaching methods, the court of appeals said that the courts have yet to determine the scope of First Amendment protection to be given a public college professor's classroom speech. Just last month a district judge ordered to trial a protest by a Temple University professor that he was denied tenure because he protested conditions in a laboratory in which toxic materials were stored. The judge said the protest was protected speech on a matter of public concern and could not be the basis of adverse action. There is no mention in the decision of academic freedom. In this area the same uncertainty also obtains as to private colleges made subject to constitutional limitations in some of the states by statute as in California and by court decision as in New Jersey.

This I do know: judges will continue to differ. Justice Oliver Wendell Holmes said that the life of the law has not been logic but experience. An English judge extended that view when he said that the life of the law has not been experience but common sense. I believe that judgments ultimately are made on a commonsense basis and that most judges strive in that fashion.

I have stayed away from any discussion of the issues of multiculturalism, diversity, and affirmative action in a university setting, and for good reason. These cases have yet to come to court in any number. Thus far two decisions have gotten attention, a University of Texas Law School case and a New Jersey high school case. We are more than likely to get such a case in my court one day. I would like not to have engaged in prejudgment should it come to me. So instead of discussing the pros and cons of these issues, let me finally conclude by describing to you the decision in *Wittmer v. Peters* (681EOP.D. 4119 [7th Cir. 1996], 916) authored by Richard Posner, a noted legal scholar and chief judge of the Seventh Circuit.

The case involved a challenge by a white male to the promotion of a black male to the position of lieutenant in a boot camp for young offenders operated by the Department of Corrections of the state of Illinois. The challenger outranked the man who got the promotion in an examination for the position. The boot camp population was more than 70 percent African American. Only 69 percent of the staff was African American. Expert opinion said the camp could not achieve its goal of rehabilitation with that disparate ratio and that there was an operational need for more African Americans in supervisory positions.

Judge Posner's decision rejected the challenge and upheld the promotion. He said:

> While we may assume that a practice that is subject to the skeptical, questioning, beady-eyed scrutiny that the law requires when public officials use race to allocate burdens or benefits is not illegal per se, it can survive that intense scrutiny only if the defendants show that they are motivated by a truly powerful and worthy concern and that the racial measure that they have adopted is a plainly apt response to that concern. They must show that they had to do something and had no alternative to what they did. The concern and the response, moreover, must be substantiated and not merely asserted. (Wittmer v. Peters 1996, 918)

This is the challenge ahead. Thank you.

WORKS CITED

"Academic Freedom and the Law." *Yale Law Journal* 47 (1936–37): 670–71.

Barrow, Deborah J., Gary Zuk, and Gerald S. Gryski. *The Federal Judiciary and Institutional Change.* Ann Arbor: University of Michigan Press, 1996.

Dworkin, Ronald. "We Need a New Interpretation of Academic Freedom." In *The Future of Academic Freedom*, edited by Louis Menand, 181. Chicago: University of Chicago Press, 1996.

Hamilton, Walton H. "Trial by Ordeal, New Style." *Yale Law Journal* 50, no. 2 (1940–41): 778–79.

Kent, James Chancellor. "Unpublished Letter." *Green Bag* 9 (1897): 206, 210.

McCluskey, Lord. *Law, Justice, and Democracy.* Sweet and Maxwell: BBC Books, 1987.

Metzger, Walter P. "The 1940 Statement of Principles on Academic Freedom and Tenure." *Law and Contemporary Problems* 53 (1990): 3, 7.

Schrecker, Ellen W. *No Ivory Tower: McCarthyism and the Universities.* New York and Oxford: Oxford University Press, 1986.

Sustein, Cass. *Legal Reasoning and Political Conflict.* New York and Oxford: Oxford University Press, 1996.

Vaughn v. University of Michigan, Docket No. 24856 [E.D. Mich. 1963]:6.

White, James Boyd. *Heracles Bow: Essays on the Rhetoric and Poetics of the Law.* Madison: University of Wisconsin Press, 1985.

Joyce Cohn with President Lyndon Johnson, 1964 (*United Press International*)

A Century of Local Jews in Politics: 1850s to 1950s

By the Honorable Avern Cohn

Editor's Note: This is an abridged version of a speech delivered by Judge Cohn for the Jewish Federation of Metropolitan Detroit in Birmingham, Michigan, on October 27, 1998, celebrating the centennial of the organized Jewish community of Detroit.

Jews in Detroit have always been a small part of the voting population, and until the 1930s, there was no well-formed Jewish political agenda in Michigan as there is today. Robert Rockaway, discussing the pre-civil war history of Jews in politics, writes: "During the 1850's Detroit Jews were too busy earning a living and establishing themselves to spend much time in politics."[1] This could be said for all the years up to the 1930s. So the history I have to trace here is largely anecdotal.

Early Political Actors

The 1850s was the first decade in which we see signs of political activity in the Jewish community and a Jew holding a political office in Detroit. Between 1854 and 1861 Rabbi Leibman Adler of Temple Beth El openly declared for the Republican Party because it shared his strongly held abolitionist views. In 1857, Edward Kanter, a local banker and merchant and a member of Temple Beth El, was elected to the state legislature as a Democrat after a campaign filled with anti-Semitic attacks on him. Later, Kanter was twice a candidate for state treasurer and an activist in the Democratic Party.

In the 1880s Edward Kanter, along with Simon Heavenrich and Magnes Butzel, founders of Jewish families of note, served as officers in the Democratic Party. In those years, Jews, mostly of German descent, held a variety of civic and political positions and engaged in political activity, as Rockaway tells us, as a display of good citizenship. However, the community appeared to be splintered politically and did not vote as a bloc.

The first Jew following Kanter to hold elected office, as far as my research discloses, was Joseph Weiss, who was elected a circuit court commissioner in Wayne County in 1884 following a short stint as Chippewa County prosecutor. Weiss went on to a notable career in public office. He was elected a state

Edward Kanter

senator as a Republican in 1891, serving until 1894, and then was elected a state representative in 1907-1908. He also ran for sheriff in 1908 and circuit judge in 1918, but was defeated both times. What is important to remember about Joseph Weiss is what Rabbi Leo Franklin of Temple Beth El said in his eulogy on Weiss's death in 1936:

> He was a good American. He loved his country and all that it stood for. He was a loyal citizen of Detroit and he was a good Jew. He recognized the fact that the better Jew one is the better American he is bound to be, and conversely, the more loyal a Jew is in his American citizenship, the more faithful will he be in the service of his religion.

This dichotomy of being a Jew and an American played a large role in the late nineteenth and early twentieth century in assessing Jewish involvement in politics. Rockaway says there were admonishments regarding Jews allowing anything that appeared to segregate Jewish practices for political purposes. That would have been viewed as arousing anti-Semitism.

The German Jews felt threatened by the manner in which the newly arrived Eastern European Jews involved themselves in local politics. The latter held political rallies, formed political clubs, and bargained with politicians seeking their votes. Nonetheless, the German Jews, particularly Temple Beth El members, began to increase their involvement. The Butzel family, for example, was divided, with one brother, Fred, working for Democrats and another, Henry, for Republicans. Most Temple Beth El members identified with the Republican Party as the more respectable because it was aligned with their economic interests.

Another personality of significance was Samuel Goldwater, one-time president of the Detroit Council of Trades and an organizer of the Michigan Federation of Labor. Goldwater was an alderman in Detroit in 1891 and ran for mayor against Hazen Pingree on the Democratic ticket in 1895. Many Democrats declined to support him because he was too radical. He was reelected to the Detroit City Council in 1896, and when he died in 1898 an official day of mourning was declared.

Following Goldwater, the next Jewish politician of note was David Heineman, a Butzel family member and a lawyer. Heineman served in the state legislature in 1889 and 1890, on the Detroit City Council from 1902 to 1909, and was city controller between 1910 and 1913. He is particularly remembered as the designer of the Detroit flag and founder of the Detroit Public Library. He died in 1935. [See the Jewish Historical Society of Michigan's plaque at the Detroit Historical Museum commemorating David Heineman.]

The last Jewish political figure worthy of note in pre-World War I days is Charles Simons, who went on to be named a federal judge in Detroit in 1923, the first Jewish federal judge in Michigan. Simons was the son of

David Heineman

David W. Simons, described in a 1923 Detroit Times article as the leader in all enterprises of philanthropic and community service. "D. W." Simons was a public lighting commissioner and a member of the first nine-person city council in Detroit in 1918. I went to Sunday School in the 1930s at Shaarey Zedek in the D.W. Simons Building at Chicago Boulevard and Lawton, and attended Hebrew School in the David W. Simons Building at Tuxedo and Holmur.

Charles Simons had a long career in public life. It began with his election to the state senate in 1903. In 1905-06, he was a Wayne County circuit court commissioner and in 1908 a delegate to the state constitutional convention. In 1923 President Harding appointed him to the district court, and in 1929 President Hoover appointed him to the court of appeals. The late Philip Slomovitz, in a letter to me, described Charles Simons's appointment to the district court. He said Simons was Townsend's re-election campaign at a time when Townsend was in trouble for voting against the expulsion of Truman Newberry from the senate for excessive campaign spending. Senator Townsend recommended Simons's appointment to President Harding. I personally recall Charles Simons. Charles Levin clerked for him, and he used to lunch at the Standard Club in the Book-Cadillac Hotel, of blessed memory.

Charles Simons

Judges Take the Lead

The story following World War I up to the 1950s is largely one of successful judges and unsuccessful efforts at elective office by Jews. James I. Ellman was prominent first as a judge and then as mayor of Highland Park. His son, Erwin, is a prominent labor arbitrator in Detroit, while his son, William, is a lawyer in Detroit.

The first of the Jewish judges following Joseph Weiss was Harry Keidan, a regular in my youth at services at Shaarey Zedek. Keidan began his political career in 1912 as an assistant prosecutor in Wayne County. After leaving that position, he was twice an unsuccessful candidate for judgeship and in 1920 was appointed to the recorder's court bench. In 1927 he was appointed to the Wayne County circuit court bench, where he served until his death in 1943. He was a highly regarded trial judge. In a story of his career, a Detroit

James I. Ellman

Harry Keidan

newspaper said of him: "A fair-minded clear-thinking man whose stiff sentences to criminals were at variance with the warmth and humanity of his heart. Judge Keidan was recognized as a judge in whose hands the institution of society were safe." Judge Keidan was a deeply religious man. In the 1920s, when Saturday morning court sessions were a regular occurrence, he would walk from his home on Chicago Boulevard to and from the courthouse.

After Keidan's death, William Friedman, senior partner of Friedman Meyer & Keyes, then Detroit's pre-eminent Jewish law firm and counsel to Federation, was appointed to the Wayne circuit bench — a Jew following a Jew, clearly. Friedman was defeated when he stood for election in 1944 against Frank Ferguson, brother of Senator Homer Ferguson, in a campaign marked by overt anti-Semitism. Of particular interest is the fact that Ferguson in 1939 had defeated Charles Rubiner, then an incumbent common pleas court judge in Detroit, whom I will discuss below.

Following Keidan's ascent to the bench, Henry Butzel, then a prominent Detroit lawyer of the distinguished Butzel family, was appointed to the Michigan Supreme Court in 1929 by Governor Fred Green, where he served with distinction until 1960. While not active in politics, Justice Butzel was a Republican and what we would call today an enlightened moderate.

Henry Butzel

Political Activity Heats Up

Through the 1920s, the situation remained similar to that of the 1850s — Jews were too busy earning a living to spend much time on politics. In the 1930s, the presence of Gerald K. Smith, Father Coughlin, and of Hitler abroad began to change Jewish attitudes and actions. Roosevelt's social action programs appealed to many Jews hit particularly hard by the Depression. Political parties and candidates began to court Jews both for their votes and their contributions. Elections ads began to appear signed by "Jewish Friends" or phrases were used like "my Jewish staff members." We began to see ads and articles in the *Jewish Chronicle* endorsing candidates for office as "friends of the Jews."

The 1930s gave us two Jewish judges on the common pleas court: Charles

Charles Rubiner

Rubiner, appointed in 1931 by Governor William Brucker from his position as an assistant attorney general, and the little-known Joseph Sanders, appointed in 1933 by Governor William Comstock. Rubiner served until 1939 and, at the time of his appointment and later, was a highly respected member and worker in the Jewish community. I remember as a young child the excitement I felt when my parents told me we were going to have a judge at a dinner party at our house on Fullerton. The judge was Rubiner.

The 1930s were marked by occasions of Jewish lawyers running unsuccessfully for such offices as county clerk, state representative, and judge. However, Henry Behrendt, a member of Temple Beth El, who appeared to move between the Republican and Democratic parties with ease and who began his career in public life as chief of police in Lansing, was several times elected Wayne County sheriff.

I have located the first ad for a presidential campaign in the *Jewish Chronicle* in 1936 in the form of a pitch for Alfred Landon as a friend of the Jews in contrast to Roosevelt, paid for by the Wayne County Republican Committee. I contrast that to a story in the same paper about Harry Schumer urging the re-election of President Roosevelt in 1940. Schumer was a spokesman for the Jewish National Workers Alliance. Incidentally, William Hordes also placed a personal ad in 1940 endorsing Roosevelt. He also did this in 1942 for John Dingell for Congress and in 1954 for Philip Hart for U.S. Senate.

> **To My Friends—**
>
> **And To All Voters In The 15th Congressional District:**
>
> This is the time to show appreciation for genuine loyalty and devoted service by a great Congressman.
>
> I urge all of you to cast your ballots for Congressman John D. Dingell who should be re-elected by an overwhelming majority as a tribute for his great services to this country.
>
> Congressman Dingell is a true democrat. He is the most consistent supporter of President Roosevelt's program in Congress. He is a friend of Palestine, a defender of labor, a lover of freedom and a man with a passionate disapproval of intolerance.
>
> Please do not fail to vote on Tuesday for
>
> **Congressman**
>
> **John D. Dingell**
>
> **DEMOCRAT.   15th DISTRICT**
>
> *Sincerely yours,*
>
> **William Hordes**

A political advertisement from the *Jewish Chronicle*, October 30, 1942

Party Politics

Looking further than Jewish candidates for office, who obviously could not expect to be elected on the basis of the Jewish vote in Detroit, we began to see, as Sidney Bolkosky describes it in *Harmony & Dissonance*,[2] a coalescence of Jewish interests around parties and candidates. Between 1914 and 1926, Jewish secularists associated with the *landsmanshaften* identified with parties of the left, while Jewish establishment leaders were Republican. In 1924, the threat of a Klan mayor in Detroit resulted in a collaborative effort among blacks and ethnic groups including Jews to elect John Smith.

In the 1930s, political liberalism began to attract young people. Liberalism, one author has written, offered an answer to anti-Semitism and other problems that the Jews faced. It has been said that liberal party policies substituted for the observance of religious tradition from which Jews believed their liberal values derived. Again, more financially successful Jews assumed a politically conservative Republican image. This difference in association extends to today in my experience, with exceptions. Minutes of the organizational meetings of the Jewish Community Council in 1937 reflect a concern regarding eligibility for membership of Jewish "political groups," meaning left-leaning.

Also in the 1930s, we began to see Jewish support for candidates who opposed Nazism. For example, in 1936 George W. Welsh, Democratic candidate for governor, asked for Jewish voter support on the basis of his opposition to anti-Semitism as a legislator. In 1940, Clarence J. McLeod's reelection to Congress was urged by the Jewish War Veterans on the basis of his support for Jewish interests in Palestine. David Zack urged the election of Frank Fitzgerald in 1940 to the United States Senate on the basis of his opposition to intolerance.

Two anecdotes of significance illustrating Jewish support for friends involve Congressman John Dingell, father of the current congressman. Dingell was elected to Congress in 1934 from a district that included Northwest Detroit. He gave enormous help to those bringing Jewish family members from Eastern Europe into this country. The late Theodore Levin was then a lawyer specializing in immigration matters. Philip Slomovitz, then editor of the *Jewish Chronicle*, wrote Dingell that "an outstanding Detroit Jewish lawyer" should be appointed to a newly created federal judgeship on the grounds that "not a single Jewish appointment of importance has thus far been made in Michigan by the Democratic administration." Slomovitz then went on to recommend Levin. Dingell graciously rejected the suggestion on the grounds he had too many friends in the race and if he took a definite stand, he said, "I am afraid I would make a lot of enemies and lose friends." Dingell, in his letter, pointed out a number of Jews holding appointee positions in state government. His list included at least one person with a Jewish-sounding name whose obituary suggests he was a long-time Lutheran. Of interest to me was Dingell's statement:

> I think the chances of Mr. Levin for this appointment are very slender because there are too many men of good qualifications who have Party service records of from twenty to thirty years and the Party leaders here in Washington will certainly take that into consideration along with qualifications for Judicial service.

Things haven't changed.

Another chapter in the Dingell experience occurred in 1940 when Samuel Lieb challenged Dingell for the Democratic nomination for Congress in 1940. This caused an outrage among many Jewish leaders, including my late father, who believed Lieb betrayed the Jews of Detroit by challenging one of their champions.

In 1940 a Jew served in the legislature in the person of Charles Blondy, who was elected a state senator. Blondy is described in a biographical account as an advocate for Jewish interests in the legislature. He sponsored resolutions opposing Arab interference with the rights of Americans in Arab league countries, supporting the Jewish Tercentenary, confronting opposition to humane slaughtering legislation, providing absentee ballots for Jews unable to vote on Jewish holidays, and notice to the Hebrew Benevolent Society when a deceased person was determined to be of the Jewish faith and no one claimed the body. He came from a traditional Jewish family and served through 1964. At one time he was one of only four Democrats in the state senate. During Blondy's term in the legislature, legislators worked only part-time and were poorly paid. I remember Blondy as a Wayne County Court bailiff whose job it was to serve papers. In 1953, Alan Blondy, Charles's brother, was elected to one term in the legislature.

Charles Blondy

In 1946 Theodore Levin finally got his judgeship from President Truman, but not without a good deal of opposition from within the Democratic Party. He was accused of being a Republican. His appointment began the long and distinguished career in public office of members of the Levin family [including retired Justice Charles Levin, whose portrait was recently unveiled at the Michigan Supreme Court. See below.] Also in the 1940s, a Jew was elected circuit court commissioner in Wayne County in the person of John Schneider.

Theodore Levin

Appointments to Important Offices

The 1950s marked a change for Jews in politics. G. Mennen Williams as governor gained strong support from Jews because he was considered a liberal. There was strong support for Adlai Stevenson for president in 1952 and 1956, as you can see from ads in the *Jewish News*. Governor G. Mennen Williams appointed Jews to local judgeships: Victor Baum to the Wayne County Circuit Court and Nathan Kaufman to the Wayne County Probate Court. There is a view that Governor Williams was not all that disposed toward appointing Jewish judges, believing that they could not get elected once appointed. Kaufman's television program gave prominence to the Kaufman name and contributed to the election of Ira Kaufman to the probate court and of Charles Kaufman as common pleas court judge. The election of Charles

Kaufman in 1959 to the common pleas bench reflects the potency of the Kaufman name at the time; one of the candidates he defeated was Thomas J. Brennan, who went on to be elected to the Michigan Supreme Court. Richard Kaufman, Charles's son, served as a circuit judge from 1981 until quite recently.

Both Baum's and Kaufman's appointments by Governor Williams had their own set of difficulties. Baum's appointment was opposed by Alfred Meyers, then a powerful leader of the 17th congressional district, in which Baum lived. Victor had to move into the adjacent 15th district to get clearance so that Williams could go ahead with the appointment. Meyers, a Detroit schoolteacher, was a formative power, almost a boss, in the 1940s and 1950s. As to Kaufman, powerful UAW support enabled him to get his appointment. Nate had begun his working life in a factory where he became active in UAW affairs. He maintained that interest when he went on to law school and called on it when he sought a judgeship.

Ira Kaufman

Candidates for judgeship received extensive support from fellow Jews in the way of money, endorsements, envelope stuffing, postcard writing, and the like. In 1954, I personally recall working very hard, along with Jewish friends, to get Charles Diggs, Jr., elected to Congress from a district in Northwest Detroit. An important piece of the Jewish agenda was strongly supporting African-American aspirations for political office. We thought it the right thing to do and that it would be good for the Jews.

Leonard Kasle served on the Detroit Board of Education in the 1950s, for a time as president, the only Jew ever to hold that position on the board. In 1958 Jason Honigman ran for attorney general on the Republican ticket, and an ad supporting him in the *Jewish News* was signed by a number of Jews as the "Committee for Honigman." This brought a response from the *Jewish Daily Forward*, which was critical of "well known Jewish community leaders" who asked for votes to support Honigman because he was Jewish. The *Forward* said that this engendered religious intolerance. No similar criticism had been seen in earlier years when non-Jews asked for support because they employed Jews in the departments they headed or had "Jewish friends."

Benjamin Burdick was appointed to the Wayne County circuit bench in 1963 by Governor George Romney. Irwin, his brother, was appointed to the same bench in 1975.

No account of Jews in politics would be complete without mention of Emanuel Seidler, a Detroit lawyer who had offices in the Hammond Building. He was a friend of my father and was the father of Professor Murray Seidler of Wayne State University, a high school classmate of mine. Seidler was a socialist who did not abandon the party as did the Reuther brothers and others who supported Roosevelt in 1936. At various times Seidler was the Socialist Party nominee for governor, attorney general, and state Supreme Court justice. He was a true believer.

A Jewish Agenda Takes Shape

My years of intense involvement, the 1952, 1956, and 1960 presidential races, are reflected in the ads in the *Jewish News*, which were signed by many of us in the community. We were involved for a variety of reasons. We had partisan feelings and strong convictions. It was fun working with friends in a common cause for which we felt deeply. The cause was a better America in the form of less discrimination, more money for the poor, and important support for Israel. Beyond the association with a successful candidate, basking in the reflected glory of the office holder gave one a sense of personal satisfaction. As an example, my reward for my efforts for Lyndon Johnson in 1964 was an invitation to a state lunch, along with Mike Zeltzer, and a state dinner at the White House. These were experiences that will live with me forever, experiences that money could not buy (at least in a spiritual sense). And I must mention the fact that Stuart Hertzberg, for many years treasurer of the State Democratic Party, was the one who pushed Mike and me to the level of activities that brought us to the attention of the White House social secretary.

The 1960s began the modern era of local Jews in politics as I see it. When Sander Levin ran for governor on the Democratic ticket in 1970, when a Jew was nominated by a major political party to run for the highest political office in Michigan, it marked the point in time when Jews became fully integrated into the political life of our community. Sander, of course, ran again in 1974 and has been a Representative to Congress for some years from a largely non-Jewish district. That his brother, Carl, is now serving his fourth term as a U.S. Senator is further evidence of our complete integration. This could be the subject of a future article.

What I believe I have related to you was, in the beginning, a story of a now-and-then thing. Since 1850, a local Jew occasionally entered the political arena and had some success, mostly as a judge. Now it is a commonplace thing; a Jew contesting for political office is of no special significance and winning or losing comes from a variety of reasons, none of which relate to Jewishness.

I quoted earlier Rabbi Franklin's words in eulogizing Joseph Weiss. Let me rephrase them in concluding. It can be said of almost every Jew I have known who has gained public office, judge or legislator: He is a good American. He loves his country and all that it stands for. He is a loyal citizen and he is a good Jew. He recognizes the fact that the better a Jew one is, the better American he is bound to be, and conversely, the more loyal a Jew is in his American citizenship, the more faithful will he be in the service of the Jewish people.

Justice Charles Levin Portrait Unveiled in Supreme Court

Editor's Note: The following is excerpted from a talk given by the Hon. Avern Cohn, a colleague, friend, and cousin of retired Supreme Court Justice Charles Levin, at the unveiling of Levin's portrait at the Court in Lansing, May 6, 1999.

This occasion marks a permanent remembrance of Justice Charles Levin's twenty-four years of service as one of the justices of this high court — the final arbiter of disputes among the people of Michigan. We are here today to honor a great justice, the son of a great judge, his late father, Theodore Levin. Theodore Levin was a longtime member of the court on which I now sit, and the patriarch of the Levin family, which has contributed so much to the political life of this state.

Today also marks the sixtieth anniversary of the day Justice Charles Levin "became a man" and received his first fountain pen. It was sixty years ago today that Charles Levin of LaSalle Boulevard in Detroit became a Bar Mitzvah at Congregation Shaarey Zedek at the corner of Lawton and West Chicago. For those of you of a biblical bent, the Torah portion that day came from Leviticus, and the prophetic portion, which the Bar Mitzvah boy personally recited, came from the writings of the prophet Ezekiel. In that Torah portion, the people of Israel are commanded to keep the light continually burning in the tabernacle. It is the light of truth, shining to illuminate the darkness of injustice and discrimination. I believe there is something prophetic in the link between what was recited then and Charles Levin's career as a judge.

In his 1966 campaign to win a seat on the Michigan Court of Appeals for the First District, Levin made capital of the outstanding rating he received from the merit rating program of the Detroit Bar Association, then newly formed by the late Richard VanDusen and George Bushnell. Also noteworthy is the manner in which Levin campaigned to be elected to the Michigan Supreme Court in 1972 as the nominee of the short-lived Non-Partisan Judicial Party. By the way, Professor Maurice Kelman describes in his

Portrait of Justice Charles Levin at Supreme Court in Lansing.

article, "A Tale of Two Parties" (*Wayne Law Review*, Vol. 19, p. 253), a 1972 lawsuit in the federal court in Detroit stemming from Levin's unique efforts to gain a seat on the high court. In my opinion, Justice Levin's judicial career suggests that voters do sometimes exercise good judgment in voting in judicial elections.

From Levin's first published opinion in volume 7 of *Michigan Appeals Reports* to his last five dissents on December 30, 1996, in volume 453 of the *Michigan Reports*, he displayed scholarship, pragmatism, insight, honesty, courage, and humanity as demonstrated by his willingness to admit he has sometimes made a mistake. More importantly, on numerous occasions he voted, many times alone, in favor of review of a court of appeals decision when a majority of his colleagues turned aside the application for leave to appeal. Levin's back-of-the-volume writings merit particular attention.

Throughout his thirty years on the bench, Justice Charles Levin has demonstrated an understanding of the reality of the other fellow's predicament. This, in essence, is his contribution to the people of Michigan and will be the aura surrounding the portrait unveiled today. This portrait is a worthy addition to those already hanging in the Supreme Court, particularly in the company of the nineteenth-century greats Campbell, Graves, Cooley, and Christiancy. Justice Levin ranks with each of them.

---

1. Robert Rockaway, *The Jews of Detroit: From the Beginning, 1762-1914*. Wayne State University Press, 1986.

2. Sidney Bolkosky, *Harmony & Dissonance: Voices of Jewish Identity in Detroit, 1914-1967*. Wayne State University Press, 1991.

Further References: *Detroit Free Press. Detroit News. Detroit Times. The Jewish Chronicle. The Jewish News. Michigan Jewish History.*

The author would like to thank Judy Cantor for her research efforts; Michael Kroll, a freelance researcher at the Reuther Library, for his efforts in collecting the materials; and his secretary, Nancy Lippert, who processed many drafts of this paper.

The Honorable Avern Cohn is judge of the U.S. District Court of the Eastern District of Michigan.

The General Accounting Office Report to Congressional Committees on Sentencing Guidelines-A Reaction

More important than the publication of the General Accounting Office (GAO) Report on the Sentencing Guidelines is what Congress will do with the Report and with the December 1991 Report of the United States Sentencing Commission. Section 263 of Public Law 98-473, which mandates both reports, requires Congress to review the GAO Report to determine (1) whether the sentencing guideline system has been effective, (2) whether any changes in the system should be made, and (3) whether the parole system should be reinstated in some form and the life of the Parole Commission extended.

Congress' serious consideration in such a review is problematic since it has not exhibited any inclination up to now to revisit the guideline statute. Indeed, from all indications, and particularly from the rhetoric of the Fall campaigns, Congress seems bent on toughening existing penalties.

Most district judges agree that the guideline system is not particularly effective and that changes should be made, especially to enhance flexibility and diminish prosecutorial dominance. Courts of Appeals judges are likely of two minds-at least those who have given thought to the guideline system. More seem comfortable with the guidelines than believe that change is needed. See *United States v. Davern*, 970 F.2d 1490 (6th Cir. 1992) (*en banc*), rejecting a flexible" approach to sentencing under the guidelines, and *United States v. Silverman*, 1992 WL 230614 (6th Cir. 1992) (*en banc*), taking a broad view" of what constitutes relevant conduct under the guidelines and authorizing statute.

All who are concerned with the length of sentences and have paid attention to Sentencing Commission and Federal Judicial Center studies of mandatory minimum prison terms surely believe some sort of procedure for review during the service of a sentence is needed. The fight over continuation or change in the sentencing guidelines themselves is still to come.

The GAO Report itself has its limitations. It states (p. 27) [o]ur statutory mandate was limited to an examination of the impact of the guidelines not the desirability of the policy choices Congress and the Commission have made in enacting and implementing the guidelines." I suggest that some mention should have been made of policy choices that have been made in Court of Appeals decisions. For example, there is considerable disagreement over the standards to be applied in assessing two points for obstruction of justice by falsely testifying at trial. U.S.S.G. §3C1.1. Compare *United States v. Dunnigan*, 944 F.2d 178 (4th Cir. 1991, *cert*. granted 60 U.S.L.W. 3798 (burdens defendant's right to testify) and *United States v. Collette*, 1992 WL 257746 (3rd Cir. 1992) (the perjurious testimony must have imposed some incremental burden on the government) with *United States v. Easley*, 1992 WL 248388 (7th Cir. 1992) (sufficient that defendant testified falsely). Surely the *Dunnigan-Collette* view of §3C1.1 allows for more discretion at sentencing. I have little doubt that if Courts of Appeals judges were a bit more generous in their view of district judges' discretion Congress's evaluative job would be a lot easier.

The basic findings of the GAO should come as no surprise to district court judges, probation officers, and defense lawyers: (1) the amount of sentencing disparity has been reduced to some extent (the Report takes no position on whether that is good or bad); (2) a significant amount of unwarranted disparity in sentencing continues (that is certainly not good); and (3) judicial workload has increased (the Report does not say whether the benefits have been commensurate).

GAO's recommendations for further study by the Sentencing Commission[1] should not be an excuse to delay Congressional study even though the topics have merit. The Sentencing Commission may not be the best institution to give the answers. The bureaucratic structure of the Commission, its imperviousness to suggestions-witness the modesty of its acceptance in the 1992 round of amendments of the Judicial Conference recommendation for changes in the guidelines (admittedly the Commission's creation of the Judicial Working Group to consider amendments for 1993 may mark a change in attitude), and its primitive communication skills do not breed confidence in its ability to critically and impartially do such studies. After all, no such institution has any great desire to acknowledge its failure.

The flaws, and indeed evils, of the federal guideline system (severely limiting the extent to which an offender's characteristics and the circumstances of the crime may be taken into consideration) as required by statute, implemented by the Sentencing Commission, and interpreted by the Courts of Appeals need not be elaborated here. (There may be some easing. See *United States v. Johnson*, 964 F.2d 124 (2nd Cir. 1992), which approved a thirteen-level assistance motion. The rejection of cooperation efforts was occasioned by the defendant's exercise of his right to a preliminary hearing and a detention hearing. As a consequence, an information for enhanced penalties under 21 U.S.C. § 851 was stricken.

Regarding the instability in Court of Appeals' guideline decisions, not much has changed. The Commission noted in its December 2012 Report to Congress, *Report on the Continuing Impact of* United States v. Booker *on Federal Sentencing*:

> Finally, the courts of appeals have not promoted uniformity in sentencing to the extent the Supreme Court anticipated in *Booker*. The appellate courts lack adequate standards and uniform procedures in spite of a number of Supreme Court rulings addressing them, and the ultimate outcome of the substantive review of a sentence may depend in part on the circuit in which the appeal is brought. Additionally, only a small percentage of sentences are appealed, and usually only by the defendant. (p. 3)

In all, Judge Marvin E. Frankel's goal to rationalize the federal sentencing process as explained in his seminal book, *Criminal Sentences: Law With Order*—which stimulated the Sentencing Reform Act of 1980, thus enabling legislation for the Commission and the guidelines—has yet to be achieved. Following the recent presidential election, the promise of significant sentencing reform from Congress in the Sentencing Reform and Corrections Act of 2015 is unfortunately not likely to come to fruition. In some way, fashioning a fair sentence still involves an exercise of

> Mastering the lawless science of the law,
> That codeless myriad of precedent,
> That wilderness of single instances
> . . .
>
> — Alfred, Lord Tennyson, *Aylmer's Field* (1793)

Note

[1] See Avern Cohn, *The General Accounting Office Report to Congressional Committees—A Reaction*, 5 Fed. Sent'g Rep. 3 (Nov./Dec. 1992).

JUDGE AVERN COHN

United States District Court, Eastern District of Michigan

Reflections

The General Accounting Office Report to Congressional Committees on Sentencing Guidelines-A Reaction

My thanks to the editor of the *Federal Sentencing Reporter* for the opportunity to comment on the sentencing guidelines twenty-five years after I first went public with my views.[1] What I said in 1992 was "a reaction"; what I say today is best called a reflection.

To provide some context, prior to 1992, I had over ten years of discretion in imposing sentences, except for statutory limitations, followed by twelve years under the strictures of guideline ranges established by the U.S. Sentencing Commission. Now for the last thirteen years, I impose sentences exercising some discretion to vary as allowed under *Booker*, except for minimums mandated by law. Throughout all this time, I have also kept a wary eye out for inconsistencies in the Court of Appeals.

At the outset, it is important to note that during the last thirty years, the work of the Commission in reviewing, adding to, and amending the guidelines from time to time has played a considerable role in my sentencing work. For me, the guidelines have been a useful assist by establishing a benchmark range in imposing a sentence. The Commission's publication of statistics and reporting on various aspects of sentencing has also been a valuable asset.

In 1992, I discussed my concerns regarding what I then described as the flaws and evils in the guideline world of sentencing. Particularly, I had a concern about the limitations imposed on my discretion, the uncalled for length of sentences, the limitations in considering offender characteristics and the particulars of the conduct of the offender in front of me. I also expressed concern over mandatory minimums, as well as the failure of the sentencing process to include a periodic review of the inordinate length of time given offenders who were subject to many years of custody. Lastly, I expressed concern over the extent to which prosecutorial discretion was displacing judicial discretion in determining a fair sentence.

On reflection, I can see where some of my concerns are outside the control of the Commission. Like judges, the Commission is subject to the will of Congress. The pervasiveness of mandatory minimums, as well as the lack of periodic review of lengthy sentences—for the most part, white-collar offenses—could be obviated only by Congressional action or more restraint on the part of judges. Reform in these areas of sentencing is not, sadly to say, a likelihood.

The failures of the current system are best illustrated by examining the guidelines governing child pornography offenses. The Commission recognized the shortfalls in the child pornography guidelines in its December 2012 Report to Congress: *Federal Child Pornography Offenses*, when it called attention to the need to consider certain factors: (1) an offender's collecting behavior, (2) an offender's engagement in child pornography, and (3) an offender having a history of sexually dangerous behavior.

The Second Circuit recognized the need for discretion outside of the guidelines in fashioning a fair sentence involving food stamp fraud. In *United States v. Algahaim*, 842 F.3d 796 (2d Cir. 2016), the court of appeals found that the within-guidelines sentence was correctly calculated but required a remand because the loss adjustment required under the guidelines substantially increased the defendant's offense level. The Second Circuit explained:

> We do not rule that the sentences were imposed in error. We conclude only that a remand is appropriate to permit the sentencing judge to consider whether the significant effect of the loss enhancement, in relation to the low base offense level, should result in a non-Guidelines sentence.
> — *Alagahim*, 842 F.3d at 800

Of note in *Alagahim* is that the government has filed a petition for rehearing *en banc* contending in part that the court of appeals exceeded its statutory authority in ordering a remand.

As to cabining unwarranted prosecutorial control over the sentencing process, I am not sure what can be done. A December 2013 study by Human Rights Watch entitled *An Offer You Can't Refuse: How U.S. Federal Prosecutors Force Drug Defendants to Plead Guilty*, describes the extended role and control federal prosecutors have in the federal criminal justice system, including the sentencing process. One example of prosecutorial control in sentencing is a Rule 11 agreement that calls for a specific sentence and permits withdrawal by either side in the event the court does not abide by the sentence called for in the agreement. In such a circumstance, the sentencing decision becomes little more than a formality.

That said, courts have some ability to rein in an excess of prosecutorial discretion, which impacts sentencing. The decision in *United States v. Terrell*, 2016 WL 7197420 (N.D. Iowa Dec. 9, 2016) is an illustration. In *Terrell*, the district judge found prosecutorial vindictiveness in the refusal to allow a defendant to continue to cooperate with law enforcement with the expectation of receiving a substantial

Vignette

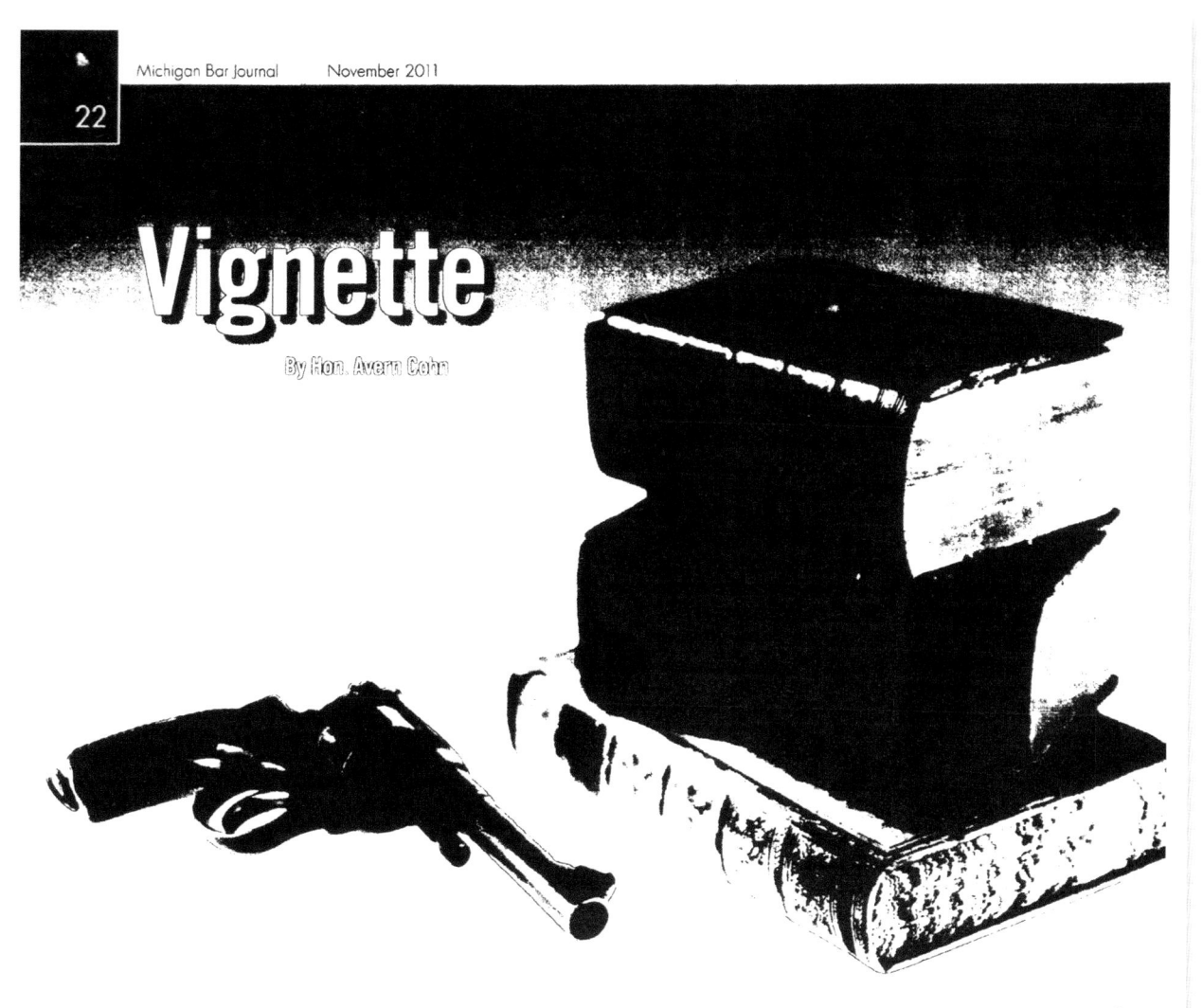

By Hon. Avern Cohn

What does an 1829 contempt proceeding before the Supreme Court of the Territory of Michigan have to do with Second Amendment jurisprudence? In *District of Columbia v Heller*, Justice Antonin Scalia's holding that the Second Amendment secured an individual's right to keep and bear arms relied in part on what the syllabus prepared for the opinion described as "[i]nterpretation of the Second Amendment by scholars, courts, and legislators, from immediately after its ratification through the late 19th century...."[1] Among the cases Justice Scalia cited was *United States v Sheldon*, a contempt action arising out of a newspaper editor's criticism of the Michigan territorial supreme court, first published in Transactions of the Supreme Court of the Territory of Michigan, edited by Professor William Wirt Blume[2] (hereinafter Blume's Transactions).

Blume's Transactions is not well known today. It consisted of a six-volume record of the decisions of the Supreme Court of the Territory of Michigan from 1805 to 1836. In the 1920s the original records of that court were found in manuscript form, stored in an obscure part of the quarters of the Michigan Supreme Court. Milo M. Quaife, director of the Detroit Public Library, described his search for the records while researching an 1821 murder trial, as well as their subsequent discovery, in a review of Blume's Transactions:

> At the State Library in Lansing [I] was firmly informed by an attendant that the territorial court records no longer existed. Insistent upon confirmation of this surprising statement, [I] was finally escorted to an elderly judge of the state supreme court, who courteously, but no less positively, repeated the information already imparted; when or why the precious records had vanished no one knew; that they had done so seemed abundantly clear, and [I] returned to [my] distant home convinced that insofar as [my] present bit of research was concerned, [I] had come to the end of the trail; yet all the time the records [I] was seeking, covering the activities of the territorial court for three decades, lay hidden away in the vaults of the very court whose officials were denying the fact of their existence.

Eventually they were rediscovered and disinterred and a decade ago were entrusted to Professor Blume of the University of Michigan Law School for editing. The resultant achievement can only be characterized as monumental, to be viewed by most historical editors with feelings of sinful envy. Provided with every scholarly facility that could be desired and laboring eight years at the task, Professor Blume now places the fruit of his toil before the reader in six massive volumes totaling over 3,600 pages, beautifully printed by the University of Michigan Press.[3]

Decided in 1829, *Sheldon* involved a contempt action filed by the territorial Attorney General against John P. Sheldon, editor of *The Detroit Gazette*. Sheldon had published an article criticizing the territorial supreme court's decision that the Wayne Circuit Court had erred in the selection of a jury in a case in which John Reed was convicted of stealing a watch from a Detroit silversmith's shop. Sheldon raised the constitutional guarantee of freedom of the press in his defense. The court rejected the defense on the ground that punishment for publishing what is "false and malicious, or of an unlawful tendency" trumps the First Amendment.[4]

While the territorial supreme court consisted of three judges, only two heard the case: Henry Chipman and William Woodbridge. (The report of the case makes no mention of the third judge, Solomon Sibley.) Both wrote lengthy and erudite opinions. It was the Chipman opinion that Justice Scalia cited in *Heller*.

Chipman was appointed to the territorial supreme court in 1827 by President John Quincy Adams. He served through 1832. A biographical sketch of him can be found on the website of the Michigan Supreme Court Historical Society.[5]

In the course of discussing the limits of freedom of speech and of the press, Chipman said:

> The constitution of the United States also grants to the citizen the right to keep and bear arms. But the grant of this privilege cannot be construed into the right in him who keeps a gun to destroy his neighbor. No rights are intended to be granted by the constitution for an unlawful or unjustifiable purpose. And although that instrument prohibits the passing of any law abridging the liberty of the press, it does not follow, that if the act of which this defendant is charged is a contempt of the authority of the court, that it is any less a contempt because it is committed through the medium of the press.[6]

Justice Scalia cited *Sheldon* twice in his opinion in *Heller*. First, in a discussion of pre-Civil War caselaw; he stated:

> An 1829 decision by the Supreme Court of Michigan said: "The constitution of the United States also grants to the citizen the right to keep and bear arms. But the grant of this privilege cannot be construed into the right in him who keeps a gun to destroy his neighbor. No rights are intended to be granted by the constitution for an unlawful or unjustifiable purpose." *United States v Sheldon*, in 5 Transactions of the Supreme Court of the Territory of Michigan, 337, 346 (W. Blume ed. 1940) (hereinafter Blume). It is not possible to read this as discussing anything other than an individual right unconnected to militia service. If it did have to do with militia service, the limitation upon it would not be any "unlawful or unjustifiable purpose," but any nonmilitary purpose whatsoever.[7]

The second reference to *Sheldon* was at the opening of a discussion on the limitations of the Second Amendment:

> Like most rights, the right secured by the Second Amendment is not unlimited. From Blackstone through the 19th-century cases, commentators and courts routinely explained that the right was not a right to keep and carry any weapon whatsoever in any manner whatsoever and for whatever purpose. See, e.g., *Sheldon*, in 5 Blume 346; [W. Rawle, A View of the Constitution of the United States of America (1825), p 123; Pomeroy, An Introduction to the Constitutional Law of the United States (1868), pp 152–153; Abbot, Judge and Jury: A Popular Explanation of the Leading Topics in the Law of the Land (1880), p 333].[8]

Seventy years after publication, Blume's Transactions was cited in an opinion of the United States Supreme Court.

There are two points of interest in Justice Scalia's citing of *Sheldon*. First, how did he come upon the case? Blume's Transactions is not a widely known set of reports. While *Sheldon* is reported in Westlaw,[9] cases reported in Blume's Transactions had been rarely cited before *Heller*, and *Sheldon* was not one of them. More than that, the Second Amendment discussion in *Sheldon* was dictum.

The answer lies in the amicus curiae briefs filed in *Heller*. *Sheldon* was discussed in an amicus curiae brief authored by C. Kevin Marshall under the following heading:

> Early American Authorities Likewise Adopted the English Focus on Directly Punishing Belligerent Uses of Arms, Rather Than Interfering With the Freedom of Individuals to Keep Them for Defense of Home and Family.

The brief stated:

> As in England, the right did not authorize breaching the peace. The Massachusetts Supreme Court in a libel case likened the freedom of the press to the "right to keep fire arms," which did not protect "him who uses them for annoyance or destruction." *Commonwealth v. Blanding*, 20 Mass. 304, 314 (1825). The Michigan Territory's Supreme Court, also in a libel case, explained that the Constitution "grants to the citizen the right to keep and bear arms. But the grant of this privilege cannot be construed into a right in him who keeps a gun to destroy his neighbor." *United States v. Sheldon*, 5 Blume Sup. Ct. Trans. 337, 1829 WL 3021 at *12.[10]

An August 24, 2004, memorandum opinion for the United States Attorney General also cited *Sheldon*:

> In an 1829 libel case, the Supreme Court of Michigan (then a territory) drew a parallel between the freedoms of speech and press and the right of the people to bear arms to explain that individual rights are not unlimited: "The constitution of the United States also grants to the citizen the right to keep and bear arms.

But the grant of this privilege cannot be construed into the right in him who keeps a gun to destroy his neighbor."[11]

C. Kevin Marshall coauthored this memo. Marshall explained his familiarity with *Sheldon* as follows:

> I used *Sheldon* in my amicus brief because I was aware of it from the [Attorney General] opinion. As to *Sheldon*'s appearance in the [Attorney General] opinion, the news is unexciting: I believe that I came across it as part of a seemingly endless series of searches through old cases on Westlaw for any scraps of reference to the right to keep and bear arms. I do not recall having seen it in the literature. *Sheldon* was instructive both because of its proximity to the Founding—predating the spike in cases on the right beginning in 1840—and because of its linking of the arms right with the freedoms of speech and of the press. The latter aspect both indicates that the arms right is an individual one (the question presented in the [Attorney General] opinion) and suggests an approach to discerning its limits (the context of the citation in the amicus brief). In all of this, *Sheldon* is complemented by *Commonwealth v. Blanding* (Mass. 1825), citing alongside *Sheldon* in both the [Attorney General] opinion and the amicus brief.[12]

The second point of interest in Justice Scalia's citation of *Sheldon* is his reliance on what was dictum from a contempt action in a libel case dealing with the First Amendment to support his conclusion about the scope of the Second Amendment. Despite the fact that both the amicus curiae brief and the Attorney General memorandum clearly stated that *Sheldon* was a libel case, Justice Scalia did not note this. Yet elsewhere in his opinion, Justice Scalia stated the subject matter of cases that discussed the Second Amendment only in dicta. For example, he referred to *Commonwealth v Blanding*[13] as "an 1825 libel case"[14] and described *Aldridge v Commonwealth*[15] as "[a] Virginia case in 1824 holding that the Constitution did not extend to free blacks...."[16] The omission is even more curious because, as Marshall notes, the analogy between the Second Amendment and the First Amendment rights of freedom of speech and freedom of the press supports the view that the right to keep and bear arms is an individual right.

More significant is the fact that Justice Scalia suggested that Judge Chipman, had he been thinking of something other than individual rights, would have said something different. In so doing, Justice Scalia ignored the likelihood that Judge Chipman's observation was no more than a throwaway observation amidst a detailed discussion of libel and the First Amendment. While Judge Chipman's observation might provide insight into early nineteenth-century views of the Second Amendment, it was not intended to advance Second Amendment jurisprudence as Justice Scalia suggests.

What is good about Justice Scalia's discussion of *Sheldon* is not its contribution to Second Amendment jurisprudence, but the fact that 70 years after publication, Blume's Transactions was cited in an opinion of the United States Supreme Court. During his tenure at the University of Michigan Law School, Professor Blume was an esteemed member of the faculty. His contributions to the early history of Michigan jurisprudence were highly regarded during his lifetime. That his Transactions continued to have relevance in 2008 is a mark of his academic achievements. ■

Avern Cohn was appointed judge of the United States District Court, Eastern District of Michigan, in 1979 by President Jimmy Carter. Before his appointment, Judge Cohn engaged in private practice in the Law Office of Irwin I. Cohn and at Honigman Miller Schwartz and Cohn. Judge Cohn is a member of several bar associations, including the Federal Bar Association and the Bar of the Supreme Court of the United States. He received his JD from the University of Michigan Law School in 1949.

FOOTNOTES

1. *District of Columbia v Heller*, 554 US 570, 571; 128 S Ct 2783; 171 L Ed 2d 637 (2008) (syllabus prepared by the Reporter of Decisions for the *United States Reports*).
2. *United States v Sheldon*, Case No. 315 (1829), in 5 Blume, ed, Transactions of the Supreme Court of the Territory of Michigan (University of Michigan Press, Ann Arbor: 1935–1940).
3. Quaife, Book Review, 47 Am Hist R 144, 145 (1942).
4. *Sheldon*, n 2 supra in 5 Blume's Transactions, p 346.
5. Michigan Supreme Court Historical Society, *Biographies: Henry Chipman* <http://www.micourthistory.org/bios.php>. All websites cited in this article were accessed October 10, 2011.
6. *Sheldon*, n 2 supra in 5 Blume's Transactions, pp 346–347.
7. *Heller*, 554 US at 612.
8. Id. at 626.
9. *United States v John P Sheldon*, Case No. 337 (1829), in 5 Blume, ed, Transactions of the Supreme Court of the Territory of Michigan (University of Michigan Press, Ann Arbor: 1935–1940).
10. Brief of the CATO Institute and History Professor Joyce Lee Malcolm as Amici Curiae Supporting Respondent, *District of Columbia v Heller*, 554 US 570, 571; 128 S Ct 2783; 171 L Ed 2d 637 (2008), available at 2008 WL 383526, p 30.
11. Bradbury, Neilson Jr. & Marshall, United States Department of Justice, Office of Legal Counsel, *Whether the Second Amendment Secures an Individual Right* 86 (2004), available at <http://www.justice.gov/olc/secondamendment2.pdf>.
12. Letter from C. Kevin Marshall to Hon. Avern Cohn (March 4, 2009) (on file with author).
13. *Commonwealth v Blanding*, 20 Mass (3 Pick) 304 (1825).
14. *Heller*, 554 US at 602.
15. *Aldridge v Commonwealth*, 4 Va (2 Va Cas) 447 (1824).
16. *Heller*, 554 US at 611.

Prosecutors and Voters Are Becoming Smart on Crime

BARBARA MCQUADE AND SALLY Q. YATES

Barbara McQuade is a professor at the University of Michigan Law School and a former U.S. attorney.
Sally Q. Yates is a partner at King & Spalding LLP and a former U.S. deputy attorney general.

How to explain the recent trend of electing reform-minded local prosecutors? It may be that voters are seeing through tough talk to embrace smarter strategies to reduce crime.

In Florida, Illinois, Massachusetts, Missouri, New York, Ohio, Pennsylvania, Texas, and Virginia, prosecutors have been elected on issues such as reducing incarceration rates, treating drug addiction as a public health issue, and eliminating cash bail.

These reform-minded attorneys include Democrats, like Eric Gonzalez in Brooklyn, and Republicans, like Melissa Jackson in Jacksonville. The mayors of 10 cities, from New York to Seattle, have signed on to a smart-on-crime initiative to reform the criminal justice system. The U.S. Congress, in gridlock over most issues, has even passed criminal justice reform legislation known as the First Step Act, signed into law by President Donald Trump. This marks a sea change from past campaigns, when prosecutors and other elected officials wooed voters with their claims of being "tough" on crime, and the worst insult a candidate could hurl at a political opponent was that he or she was "soft" on crime.

As former federal prosecutors, we have dedicated our careers to working shoulder to shoulder with law enforcement officers to hold criminals accountable for their conduct, but we see the tough-on-crime mantra as a cynical ploy that counts on voters to be uninformed. While serious crimes should be punished to protect public safety and deter others from engaging in similar conduct, not all crimes are created equal. Voters have begun to see through the tired trope that locking up all offenders for as long as possible is in society's best interest. Instead, voters are learning the facts behind the rhetoric. Various criminal justice reform efforts have advocates at institutions across the political spectrum, from the American Civil Liberties Union to Bill and Charles Koch. Criminal justice reform has appeal whether you value equal justice under law, fiscal responsibility, or limited government.

A number of reasons may explain the change in perspective on how to address crime. First, funds that are used to send someone to prison—about $30,000 a year per inmate—can be put to better uses in some cases to make our communities safer. Second, as voters are becoming more likely to know someone addicted to opioids or other drugs, they are seeing addiction as a public health issue instead of a criminal justice issue. And, perhaps most importantly, voters are recognizing that over-criminalization and over-incarceration run contrary to our nation's founding principle of liberty. Although criminals who commit serious crimes must be imprisoned to protect society, not every offender requires the heaviest hammer. So why are many voters moving toward reform-minded prosecutors?

Cost

The first reason is cost. Voters understand that allocating resources to incarceration means fewer funds are available for enforcement and prevention. When we worked at the Department of Justice (DOJ), we helped implement a program created by Attorney General Eric Holder called "Smart on Crime." The goals of the initiative were to use scarce resources to address law enforcement priorities, to seek fair and proportional sentences, to increase prevention and reentry efforts, and to surge law enforcement resources to protect vulnerable communities.

The Smart on Crime program was launched to combat an alarming trend. The number of federal prisoners in the United States had increased from 25,000 in 1980 to 219,000 in 2012, an astonishing 770 percent increase, according to the Congressional Research Service. While the United States was home to about 5 percent of the world's population, we housed 25 percent of its prisoners, the highest incarceration rate in the world. In addition to the costs of incarceration, lengthy prison terms also bring unseen costs to society, such as lost productivity to our economy and the tax revenue that it generates, forgone income for families, and harm to the welfare of the children of incarcerated parents. We saw a staggering increase each year in the portion of the DOJ budget that was going to the Bureau of Prisons to house inmates, jumping from about $330 million in 1980 to more than $6.6 billion in 2013, an increase of 1,900 percent over 33 years. By devoting so many resources to incarcerating inmates for crimes that occurred decades earlier, the DOJ had fewer resources to investigate and prosecute crimes occurring today. The math was simply unsustainable.

A significant driver of this trend was the so-called "war on drugs," which included a policy of lengthy mandatory minimum sentences for drug trafficking offenses. Mandatory minimum sentences began during the 1980s, a time when violence relating to drugs was ravaging our cities. Congress passed laws that required judges to impose mandatory minimum sentences without regard to the details of the offenses or the particular offenders. Depending on the drug quantity involved in the offense and the defendant's criminal history, these mandatory minimum sentences might require incarceration for 10 or 20 years or even life, regardless of the offender's role in the offense. Couriers were often punished as if they were drug kingpins. Each year in prison brought taxpayers the costs of incarceration, and, as inmates advanced into old age, the costs grew to include expensive medical care. As the bills have come due for a war declared decades ago, we have come to realize that it was a poor investment.

The hope was that lengthy sentences would deter people from engaging in drug trafficking and affiliated violence by severely punishing offenders. But research published by the National

Institute of Justice shows that a more effective deterrent to crime than the length of the sentence is the likelihood of getting caught. Paying for more officers on the street thus represents a more effective approach to reducing crime than devoting resources to long prison terms. This theory suggests that when individuals see police officers in their neighborhood and know that response times are short, they are less likely to commit a crime.

At the core of the Smart on Crime program was the principle of prosecutorial discretion, the idea that prosecutors should make individualized assessments about the crime and the offender to make charging decisions. The most dangerous offenders were pursued aggressively, but the use of discretion also meant that prosecutors sometimes brought less serious charges against less egregious offenders when justice so required. A guidance memo listed factors that prosecutors should consider in making decisions about whether to seek charges that brought with them mandatory minimum sentences, such as use of firearms, connections to drug cartels or gangs, significant criminal history, and other aggravating factors. Prosecutors charged the defendants who presented these aggravating factors with crimes that brought appropriately harsh penalties. They charged other defendants, who did not present any of the aggravating factors, with crimes as well, but instead of facing mandatory minimum sentences, these defendants received sentences under the federal sentencing guidelines, which govern most other cases. As an example, a defendant in his 20s involved in a drug conspiracy to distribute five kilograms of cocaine, and who had two prior convictions for delivering small quantities of drugs, would receive a sentence of 10 to 12 years under the sentencing guidelines, instead of mandatory life in prison. Taxpayers would save more than a million dollars for that single offender. The 10- to 12-year sentence likely suffices to protect the public, punish the offender, and deter crime. And the impact of a more proportional sentence on the life of the defendant and his or her family is immeasurable.

Clemency Initiative

A related effort under the Smart on Crime program was President Obama's Clemency Initiative for nonviolent drug offenders who were currently in federal prison serving sentences imposed under outdated laws and policies that were far longer than they would receive under the new Smart on Crime program. As a result of the initiative, President Obama granted 1,715 commutation petitions, including the petitions of more than 500 people serving life sentences, most of which involved defendants in drug cases serving mandatory minimum sentences.

For example, an Army veteran with a sixth-grade education was convicted of a street-level crack sale in a case that would not even have been prosecuted federally at the time of the Clemency Initiative. The defendant did not use a gun and had no history of violence. But because the defendant had two prior state convictions for selling cocaine, one case involving only one ounce, he received a mandatory life sentence. Should this individual be held accountable for his crimes? Absolutely. Should he die in prison for three small-time drug sales? Absolutely not.

The Smart on Crime initiative had an immediate impact. For the first time in decades, in its three years of operation, the federal prison population dropped from 220,000 to 190,000, a 13 percent decrease. In addition, prosecutors were able to use their scarce resources to focus on more serious offenders, resulting in a higher percentage of cases involving firearms and defendants with aggravating roles in the offense, according to a 2016 DOJ press release.

Attorney General Jeff Sessions disbanded the Smart on Crime program in the federal system upon taking office in 2017, but the same ideas that propelled the federal initiative are now sweeping across state systems. Local prosecutors can make a significant impact on the safety of their communities by implementing some of the same policies at the state level, where the prison population of 2.3 million is more than 10 times larger than that of the federal system and the annual prison costs of $75 billion dwarfs the federal budget of $6.6 billion. By seeking more proportional sentences or deferring prosecution of minor crimes altogether, prosecutors can free up resources to tackle serious crimes. These thoughtful local prosecutors recognize that taxpayers are no longer willing to pay for a system that locks up offenders long past the useful terms of incarceration. And they are demanding a criminal justice system that is fairer and imposes more proportional sentences. Voters understand that the funds being used to incarcerate prisoners for decades could instead be used to pay for officers on the street or for crucial efforts to prevent crime and reduce recidivism. Rather than mortgage our future, we can reallocate funds to reduce crime today.

Exposure to Addicts

A second reason that voters may be turning toward prosecutors with a vision for criminal justice reform is more exposure to friends and family members struggling with addiction. When the face of addiction is one you recognize, it is harder to turn your back.

There was a time when too many white voters considered drug abuse to be someone else's problem. Crack was an epidemic largely affecting victims in African American communities, making it too easy for white voters to ignore. Drug abusers were regarded as criminals, and the problem was fought with prison instead of treatment. Now that opioid abuse is affecting a largely white population, more voters view drug addiction as a public health issue, rather than a criminal justice issue, and consequently seem to care more about prevention and treatment. While society's disregard for the victims of prior drug epidemics was wrong, we should not allow our indifference in the past to prevent us from doing the right thing today.

According to the Centers for Disease Control and Prevention, 130 Americans die every day from an opioid overdose. The rate of fatal opioid overdoses is six times higher than it was in 1999. The causes of the problem are complicated and result from a combination of factors, including aggressive marketing tactics by drug manufacturers and a small percentage but large number of unscrupulous health care providers willing to exploit users by overprescribing for profit. Users who become addicted to prescription pills often turn to cheaper but more lethal alternatives like heroin or fentanyl, resulting in overdose deaths.

The opioid epidemic's costs to society have been estimated at $78 billion per year, according to the National Institute on Drug Abuse. Costs include emergency response, health care and rehabilitation costs, burdens on the criminal justice system, and lost productivity. Some users miss work or leave the workforce altogether. And abuse generates crime because people are desperate for cash to buy more drugs.

Today, there is a growing recognition that opioid users rarely receive the treatment they need in prison to avoid a relapse upon release. Reform prosecutors are seeing opportunities for drug treatment and prevention programs instead of prosecution of drug users, and they are reaching an eager audience.

The National District Attorneys Association has made prevention and treatment part of its plan to combat opioid abuse. The plan, released in October 2018, features prescription take-back programs, rules for prescribers, support for medication-assisted treatment programs, and promotion of follow-up visits after an overdose.

One model that has seen success is the use of "drug courts" in Michigan. In drug courts, offenders whose crimes are driven by addiction undergo treatment, drug testing, and intensive supervision with frequent hearings before a judge who provides incentives for success and sanctions for violations. In a system that builds assistance into accountability or that combines accountability with assistance, offenders are able to overcome their addictions and avoid becoming repeat offenders. The recidivism rate for offenders who have completed a program in Michigan's drug courts is 6.8 percent, as opposed to 30.9 percent for offenders prosecuted in the traditional criminal system, according to the Mackinac Center for Public Policy.

In addition to drug addiction, mental health issues also needlessly send people into the criminal justice system. A disproportionate number of inmates in our criminal justice system suffer from mental illness. Screening and diverting individuals to treatment instead of punishment can reduce crime and the incarceration of the mentally ill. Voters with loved ones suffering from mental illness know too well that their family members need treatment instead of punishment. Local prosecutors are embracing mental health treatment as a way to reduce incarceration and crime rates.

More prosecutors are coming to see their role as expanding beyond putting "bad guys" in jail. The new wave of prosecutors recognizes a vision that Eric Holder shared with us—that prosecutors should be not case processors but community problem solvers. Voters who have experienced the ravages of opioid abuse are seeing the wisdom of that vision.

Finally, we think that there is one other reason for the appeal of reform-minded prosecutors, an idea as old as our nation—liberty. In our increasingly connected world, the collateral consequences of a criminal conviction have made a prison sentence less a debt to society than a stain for life. For many offenders, a life-long scarlet letter is inconsistent with our values as a free society.

Ideas That Keep People Out of Jail

The effects of arrest and prosecution are hardest on indigent or minority defendants in communities with high crime rates that are heavily policed. As the DOJ found following its investigation of the 2014 shooting of Michael Brown, African Americans made up 67 percent of the population of Ferguson, Missouri, but comprised 93 percent of arrestees. This type of disparate impact tends to delegitimize the credibility of the criminal justice system by calling its credibility into question, particularly in the eyes of members of those communities, which in turn leads to a lack of respect for the law. People are less likely to comply with laws when they believe the system is unfair.

In response to these problems, prosecutors are championing ideas that keep people out of prisons and jails, such as diversion programs; alternatives to cash bail, fines, and fees; and prisoner reentry programs.

Diversion programs typically require a defendant to admit guilt and participate in intensive supervision with conditions of release. The conditions might require the defendant to participate in a program designed to position him or her for success by, for example, undergoing drug treatment or cognitive behavioral therapy. The defendant may be required to complete community service. In exchange for successful completion of the program, the defendant remains out of prison and keeps his or her record clear of a criminal conviction. This strategy allows defendants to maintain employment, a significant factor in avoiding further criminal behavior, and prevents a felony conviction from closing the door to future employment opportunities.

Prosecutors are also working to end financial burdens that create disparities, such as cash bail, fines, and fees. Cash bail has a disproportionate impact on indigent defendants, who cannot afford to pay. When defendants are unable to post bond, they remain in jail pending their trial. While in jail, they may lose their job or their place in a treatment program. Alternatives to this system exist. The bail system we used in federal court presumes release unless no reasonable conditions can ensure the person's appearance at trial or the safety of the community. In those cases, the defendant is appropriately detained pending trial. If the judge finds that the defendant is not an undue risk of danger or flight, however, the judge permits the defendant to post an unsecured bond, which the defendant pays only if he or she fails to appear or otherwise violates bond conditions. This program has been used successfully in federal court for decades.

Similarly, fines and fees, which are used to fund some state courts, have a disparate effect on indigent defendants. The inability of poor defendants to pay these penalties can result in a return to jail, making it a debtors' prison of sorts. The DOJ investigation into police practices in Ferguson found that the city's focus was on generating revenue from fines and fees rather than protecting public safety. This practice had an adverse effect on minorities, causing "deep mistrust between parts of the community and the police department, undermining law enforcement legitimacy among African Americans in particular."

One solution some state prosecutors are advocating is to use payment plans for those who cannot afford to pay in full. Another solution is to follow the lead of federal courts, where judges waive fines and fees for indigent defendants. Court costs are an essential part of a criminal justice system, but they need not be paid by defendants.

Effective prisoner reentry systems are another way to reduce crime and keep people out of prison. Citizens who have completed their sentences and return to their communities face a number of obstacles to becoming productive members of society. People with felony convictions have trouble finding jobs, qualifying for public housing, and obtaining vital documents, such as driver's licenses, among other challenges. Considering that some states report recidivist rates at more than 60 percent, helping citizens returning from prison to succeed in society is a smart bet.

Under the DOJ Smart on Crime program, prosecutors and other professionals worked to promote successful reentry in a variety of ways, such as connecting returning citizens with job training and placement programs, and finding law students and legal clinics to assist former offenders with issues relating to credit repair, license restoration, landlord-tenant disputes, and outstanding traffic tickets and warrants. State prosecutors, corrections officials, and nongovernmental organizations are doing similar work all across the country. By assisting returning citizens in establishing the basic needs of civilian life, prosecutors can help position them for success, which will, in turn, prevent them from committing new crimes. In addition to reducing crime, reentry programs keep returning citizens out of prison and in our communities, where they are able to contribute to their families, neighborhoods, and society.

Reducing our reliance on prison is not just a smart strategy to manage costs and reduce crime; it is also consistent with our fundamental notions of liberty, that all persons have an inalienable right to be free. While individuals who violate our laws need to be held accountable, that accountability must also be just and proportional. Americans believe in second chances. We should deprive individuals of their liberty only when necessary, and our institutions should adopt policies that promote liberty after a sentence is served.

> As the bills have come due for a war declared decades ago, we have come to realize that it was a poor investment.

As societies mature, norms change, but values endure. It may be that the days of "tough-on-crime" chest pounding are coming to an end with higher goals in mind. We are seeing prosecutors making smart choices about how to address the consequences of crime to protect public safety and deter misconduct, and voters are liking what they hear. When we get past overly simplistic rhetoric and understand the facts, we can see the importance of factors like cost, law enforcement priorities, and the human toll of addiction and mental illness. Innovative strategies to reduce incarceration are taking hold across the country as people begin to realize that there are real costs, both fiscal and human, that come with unnecessarily lengthy prison sentences.

And perhaps even more importantly, our views of crime and punishment are shaped by the kind of nation we want to be. Would we rather use our finite resources to lock up millions of our citizens at a rate greater than that of any country in the world, or instead use those resources to enhance public safety, reduce addiction, treat mental health issues, and provide individuals with skills that equip them to contribute to the workforce?

Not only is it a wise strategy to look for alternatives to incarceration, but it is consistent with our founding principles. For a nation that is a beacon for those who yearn to breathe free, we should work harder to live up to the closing words of our pledge of allegiance—"with liberty and justice for all." ∎

SUA SPONTE

A Judge Comments

Prosecutors and Voters Are Becoming Smart on Crime

HON. AVERN COHN

The author is a senior U.S. district judge for the Eastern District of Michigan.

Barbara McQuade and Sally Q. Yates, both senior federal prosecutors in the Obama administration, focus their attention on three goals in our criminal justice system:

- budgeting less money for sending people to jail
- using tax money for drug prosecutions and treatment programs
- reducing the number of people we send to prison

They find encouragement in achieving these goals in changes in voters' and local and state prosecutors' attitudes. And although McQuade and Yates find some hope in these changes, we cannot rely on reform at the state level alone. Reform is required at the federal level as well. My familiarity is with the federal criminal justice system. It extends almost 40 years.

A good start when considering reform is to look at the rise in the prison population, something that has been a topic of debate for decades. Indeed, in 1980, in *Imprisonment in America: Choosing the Future*, Michael Sherman and Gordon J. Hawkins raised a yellow flag when they asked, "Should we build more prisons?" In 1990, James Q. Whitman's *Harsh Justice* cautioned us against the way we managed criminal justice, pointing out that there was a widening divide between prison populations in the United States and Europe. We cannot say our system of punishment's deterioration blindsided us.

A discussion of reform at any level must take into account the elephant in the room: the current massive populations in the prisons and the ethnic and racial disparities within those populations. The Sentencing Project estimates it will take 75 years to cut the prison population in the United States to half. Malcolm C. Young says in his essay *Prisoners in 2016 and the Prospects for an End to Mass Incarceration*, published in June 2018 by the Center for Community Alternatives, that prospects for decreases in the federal population are fading. A description of Young's study can be found in the May 2019 issue of *Prison Legal News*.

Selected statistics on the number of persons held in federal prisons demonstrates why reform is a hot topic today:

Year	Prison Population	Drug Offenders	Immigration Offenders
1985	31,300	9,482 (34%)	8,650 (13%)
1995	88,000	9,400 (41%)	8,360 (14%)
2006	176,000	93,000 (53%)	19,000 (11%)
2016	167,000	79,000 (47%)	11,000 (6.5%)

State Level

Reform at the state level of criminal justice, where the prosecutors and judges are mostly elected, is a far different phenomenon than on the federal level, where judges are appointed. In the federal system, change comes through congressional action and presidential approval. At the federal level, the Sentencing Commission is also a player. Voters have almost no voice, and the U.S. attorneys across the country seem satisfied with the mandatory minimums and severe sentences that are the primary cause of high prison populations. The Judicial Conference of the United States has never said anything about reform, as far as I know. In short, with the exception of the First Step Act, which McQuade and Yates mention and is discussed below, or executive actions that risk being changed with every new administration, reform at the federal level must take a different path.

Moreover, discussion of reform at the state level is primarily directed at the pretrial level of the system. An article in the December 2018 issue of *Federal Probation* reports that a 2015 discussion, *Electronic Monitoring for Pretrial Release Report*, and a 2015 survey of jail populations found that, nationwide in the United States, two-thirds of the population of county jails are pretrial offenders.

Illustrative of the effort at reform in Michigan, the governor has appointed the Michigan Joint Task Force on Jail and Pretrial Incarceration. In her executive order appointing the commission, the governor noted a significant portion of county budgets go to justice system costs. A current story in *Bridge*, an online newspaper, is captioned "Republican Speaker Seeks Michigan Jail Reform." Optimism as to the success of the task force should be restrained. In March 2005, the Michigan Task Force on Jail and Prison Overcrowding got lost on the governor's desk. No changes have been seen in the level of jail populations in Michigan since the publication of the 2005 report and today.

The Federal Level

As to the federal criminal justice system, there is some glimmer of light on the horizon with the enactment of the First Step Act, which McQuade and Yates discuss. Another American Bar Association publication described the act as "prospectively narrow[ing] the scope of certain mandatory minimum sentences and expand[ing] the existing 'safety valve' that allows judges to use discretion in sentencing lower-level nonviolent offenders. The act also makes retroactive the reforms enacted under the Fair Sentencing Act of 2010, which had reduced the disparity between crack and powder cocaine sentences."

Judge Patti Saris, past chair of the Sentencing Commission, says that "the First Step Act is a major step for sentencing reform." Both in 2017 and 2018, Congress passed criminal justice reform legislation. The Sentencing Commission has published a detailed analysis of each act in a *Sentencing and Prison Impact Estimate Summary* covering the impact on offenders in the federal prison population. Praise, however, must be moderated. A federal defender wrote me:

I think it's probably more apt to call it the Baby Step Act. It does some good things, but it is most definitely not a sweeping reform of federal sentencing laws. And sweeping reform is what's needed—both because sentences are too harsh and because the mandatory nature of so many sentences gives prosecutors undue power to coerce pleas which has resulted in the current, abysmal trial rate of 2.5% (as compared to roughly 20% in the pre-Guidelines and mandatory minimum era).

In addition, the 2020 budget allocated only $14 million to implementing the First Step Act despite the law requiring $75 million a year over five years. Without adequate funding, implementing the reforms called for in the act will be challenging at best.

For any meaningful reform at the federal level, the Sentencing Commission must play a significant role. As we all know, the commission was created in 1984, motivated by Marvin Frankel's 1972 book, *Criminal Sentences: Law Without Order*.

Frankel was prompted to write because of what he saw as unwarranted disparities in sentencing by federal judges. It must be admitted that these disparities are coming back, as can be seen in a January 2019 Sentencing Commission study, *Intra-City Differences in Federal Sentencing Practices*, a survey of sentences imposed by federal judges in 30 major cities from 2005 to 2017.

> The fact that Congress has not acted suggests it is not interested in pursuing this avenue of reform.

The commission is sometimes alert to what it sees as flaws in the system. A good example is its recommendation in 2016 in its *Report to Congress: Career Offender Sentencing Enhancements*. In this report, the commission concluded, after a detailed explanation, that the career offender enhancement focuses on those offenders who have committed at least one "crime of violence. Notably, the commission found that drug trafficking career offenders should not categorically be subjected to the substantial increases in penalties required by the career offender enhancement. The commission again made mention of this in an August 17, 2017, policy work report for 2017–2018.

The recommendation appears again more recently in the *Public Comment on Commission's Proposed Priorities for the*

2018-2019 Amendment Cycle. In short, the commission has several times sent a message to Congress that use of the career offender enhancement for drug trafficking offenses is problematic. The fact that Congress has not acted on it suggests it is not interested in pursuing this avenue of reform.

In an April 2017 article in the *Federal Sentencing Reporter*, I reflected on what I saw in the guidelines and stated particularly:

> In 1992, I discussed my concerns regarding what I then described as the flaws and evils in the guideline world of sentencing. Particularly, I had a concern about the limitations imposed on my discretion, the uncalled for length of sentences, the limitations in considering offender characteristics and the particulars of the conduct of the offender in front of me. I also expressed concern over mandatory minimums, as well as the failure of the sentencing process to include a periodic review of the inordinate length of time given offenders who were subject to many years of custody. Lastly, I expressed concern over the extent to which prosecutorial discretion was displacing judicial discretion in determining a fair sentence.

On reflection, I can see where some of my concerns are outside the control of the Commission. Like judges, the Commission is subject to the will of Congress. The pervasiveness of mandatory minimums, as well as the lack of periodic review of lengthy sentences—for the most part, white collar offenses—could be obviated only by Congressional action or more restraint on the part of judges. Reform in these areas of sentencing is not, sadly to say, a likelihood.

In addition to being subject to the will of Congress, the Sentencing Commission can act only if the vacancies in its numbers can be filled and it formally approves pending recommendations. As of this writing, the commission lacks a quorum. The currently pending proposed amendments to the Sentencing Guidelines cannot be acted on because of vacancies in the commission. The vacancies stall progress.

Another aspect that impedes reform is in the federal response to the opioid crisis. While McQuade and Yates see hope in voters recognizing it as more of a public health issue than a criminal issue, federal prosecutors have not. Instead, they have increasingly charged individuals with distribution of heroin resulting in death, a crime that carries a mandatory 20-year minimum sentence. One case illustrates the excessiveness of the government's approach. A 23-year-old woman was charged with a heroin-related death after leaving behind her friend, then 20, after they both used heroin in a public restaurant. Her friend died from an overdose. Both were struggling with their addiction. The woman will now spend 20 years in federal prison.

In the discussions on reform, I have seen only one realistic suggestion on how it can be achieved. In an essay entitled "Dramatically Reduce the Incarcerated" (in the Brennan Center for Justice's *Ending Mass Incarceration: Ideas from Today's Leaders*), Inimai Chettiar and Priya Raghavan urge ending imprisonment for lower-level crimes and reducing overly long sentences for other crimes. This is a bold suggestion and can be achieved only by congressional action and presidential approval. In sum, what is needed is reverse reform—having the prison door swing outward instead of inward. If McQuade and Yates are correct, the public appetite may be ready.

Three epigraphs come to mind in thinking about the state of reform of the criminal justice system:

First, as to mistakes of the past, Justice Frankfurter, in a dissent acknowledging he had been wrong in an earlier decision, said, "Wisdom too often never comes, and so one ought not to reject it merely because it comes late."

Second, reform moves slowly. As an ancient Greek once said, "One swallow does not a summer make."

Third, there is a Chinese saying that we must be patient: "The journey of a thousand miles begins with a single step." ∎

Illustration by Saman Sarheng

My Passion for History

Editor's Note: Native Detroiter Avern Cohn is best known for the more than forty years he spent as a U.S. District Court Judge for the Eastern District of Michigan, but he has also had a lifelong fascination with history, and has been a member of the Historical Society of Michigan, which he joined in 1942, longer than anyone now alive. This narrative is adapted from a conversation with Jack Lessenberry, then president of the Historical Society of Michigan, on March 24, 2018.

Recently I was asked how I first became interested in history. I had never thought about it. I explored the answer to the question. I thought back to when I was in elementary school in Detroit. Starting then, I developed an addiction that has lasted my entire life—an addiction to the written word.

Early on, I was a book reader. I was also an avid reader of newspapers. My late father read three newspapers every day—the *Detroit Free Press*, the *Detroit News* and the *Detroit Times*[1]. I also developed a fascination with current events.

I can remember 1938. I had become an avid listener to radio, particularly H.P. Kaltenborn[2], who was describing the events leading up to the Munich Peace Conference, when British Prime Minister Neville Chamberlain said we had achieved "Peace in Our Time." World War II began the next year.

The most significant book that really set me off was *The New American History*, by W.E. Woodward.[3] From it, I discovered that George Washington in fact never cut down a cherry tree and never threw a coin across the Potomac or even the Rappahannock River.

That was the beginning of my skepticism, delving into what happened in the past. An example of why history is so important: About fifteen years ago, the Judicial Conference of the United States asked Congress to authorize expenditures for court history. There's now a history office in the administrative office of the U.S. Courts.

---

1. The Detroit Times was a Hearst newspaper that ceased publication on Nov. 7, 1960.
2. Kaltenborn (1888-1965) was a pioneering radio news commentator for CBS and later NBC.
3. Faber & Faber, 1938.   Not to be confused with a newer work with the same title by Eric Foner,

In their resolution, the judicial conference said that knowing how things came to be contributes substantially to any assessment of current effectiveness and to appreciating the promise of proposals for change. George Santayana[4] famously said that, if you don't know the past, you are condemned to repeat it.

For us the knowledge of history has a very practical effect. You cannot understand what is going on in the Middle East and particularly the significance of moving the capital of Israel to Jerusalem unless you understand what happened after World War I when the allied powers carved up the old Turkish (Ottoman) empire.

We are still living with the consequences of this action. You have to go back at least to the First World War (1914-1918) and its aftermath to understand the rivalries among the countries of the Middle East. For example, the West Bank—which, while now controlled by Israel is not part of Israel. This can be traced to the breakup of Palestine and Turkey, formerly the Ottoman Empire, after World War I when the Middle East was divided up, primarily by Great Britain and France. No one wanted what is now Palestine.

To solve that dilemma, the British took control of it, reporting to the League of Nations. The League of Nations was dissolved at the end of World War II, and was succeeded by the United Nations. The West Bank is in some sense an orphan because of this history, which is still influencing what is happening there today.

How people learn history is important. Today they learn, or think they have learned, from television, from the internet, from the movies. Lawyers, for example, are usually poor historians. Hence their recommendations can create more problems than they solve.

You cannot get an adequate understanding of history from the Internet or from iPhones or a Kindle. You have to read hard copy and importantly, you have to read the footnotes. Without footnotes, there's no justification for what the author is saying. When I read a book I read the footnotes. The footnotes link you to original sources, and that's where you really learn history. Also read print newspapers. You cannot get a full account of the news by reading a newspaper online, even the *New York Times*, because you have to be selective as you scroll. You end up skipping stuff on line. However, when you read a newspaper copy, you go page by page by page.

This morning, I read in hard copy *The Detroit News*, *The Detroit Free Press*, the *Oakland Press*, *The New York Times* and *The Wall Street Journal*. Eventually, I hope soon they will all be on line in a searchable database. Some are; most aren't yet.

Lewis Cass[5] was the first governor of Michigan Territory. He went on to become U.S. Senator, Secretary of State and ran for President. Recently I wanted to find out what the *New York Times* said about his death in 1866. My librarian soon had a hard copy of the obituary on

---

4. Philosopher George Santayana, (1863-1952)
5. Lewis Cass (1782-1866) was the most important political figure in early Michigan history.

my desk. Newspapers, of course, have been famously called the "first rough draft" of history.

My life and legal career—I was admitted to the bar in 1949—have coincided with some fascinating years in this state, as well as the nation. I've come to the conclusion there were six major figures in my lifetime who reached an amazing level of competency, feeling, compassion, understanding, skill and achievement.

They are worth mentioning because if you look at the public officials of today, at whatever level, from established to aspiring, I do not think you can find any one of their caliber.

Two of those on my list are brothers and happen to be my cousins, and so I suppose I risk being accused of nepotism: Carl Levin and Sander Levin, each of whom served 36 years in Congress, Carl in the Senate and Sandy in the House.[6]

There was G. Mennen Williams, who was elected governor six times, a record.[7] There was George Romney, who was a great governor and a great public servant. Because he told the truth, he killed himself politically when he was running for the Republican nomination for President in 1968. He said on a popular television show that he had been brainwashed when he went to Vietnam. He was telling the truth, but sometimes the truth can hurt you.[8]

Romney was followed by Bill Milliken,[9] who was as fine a governor as ever there was. These last two were Republicans, but they helped my career. Romney put me on to the Michigan Social Welfare Commission because he was required to appoint a Democrat. He didn't know me, but someone told me I him I was a good Democrat and would do a good job.

Milliken then appointed me to the Michigan Civil Rights Commission because it was a seat traditionally reserved for a Jew.

The sixth was Detroit Mayor Coleman Young.[10] Those are the ones who stand out as exceptional for me, whose personalities, character and actions were especially memorable.

The federal court in Michigan also has a long and interesting history. When I was appointed in 1979, I was the 38th federal judge to sit in the Eastern District. The first federal judge, Ross Wilkins, was appointed by Andrew Jackson in 1837 when we became a state.

Wilkins was our state's only federal judge until 1863, when Congress divided Michigan into the Eastern and Western districts; Wilkins stayed on as the Eastern District judge till 1870.

---

6. Carl Levin (1934- served in the Senate from 1979 to 2015. Sandy Levin (1931- served in the House from 1983 to 2019.
7. Williams (1911-1995), who was usually known by his nickname, "Soapy," was governor 1949-1961. Gubernatorial terms, now four years, were two years then.
8. Romney (1907-1995) was governor from 1963-69, when he resigned to become Secretary of Housing and Urban Development. His bid for the GOP presidential nomination in 1968 was derailed when he said he had gone to Vietnam and gotten "the greatest brainwashing" from generals who wanted to convince him the war was being won, when it was not.
9. Milliken (1922-2019), a Republican, was governor from 1969 to 1983, the longest tenure of any governor in Michigan history. He was known for his strong environmental policies and willingness to help Detroit.
10. Young (1918-1997) was Detroit's first black mayor, and served from 1974 to 1994.

Parenthetically, I'm a member of the Michigan Supreme Court Historical Society. Things have changed, historically, with my court. When I came to the federal bench, we had a broad mixture of cases, criminal and civil. We have many fewer today. Important or significant cases do not come before us as frequently as they did because there are more alternatives on the civil side to resolving disputes.

On the criminal side, the war on drugs has predominated, and because of reasons that are too difficult to describe, a majority of these end up in guilty pleas. We once had many more trials.

Yet the fundamental nature of the role of the federal judge continues, and it is essential to our democracy. It is true, however, that the federal courts can default. Take slavery, for example. The courts could not deal with the issue. So we ended up with the Civil War. Politics and government have also fundamentally changed. There is less give and take.

Years ago in Michigan, there were more shenanigans and more scandal. Legislators used to only serve part-time, and were paid very poorly. That led to a huge bribery scandal during World War II. Ingham County Circuit Judge Leland Carr exposed much of this when he headed a one-man grand jury in 1945.

State Senator Warren Hooper was assassinated, likely by organized crime, on his way to testify. Another state senator was found dead in his garage two days after he testified.

Hooper's murder was never completely solved, though three people were convicted of conspiracy to commit his murder. Judge Carr ended up being elevated to the Michigan Supreme Court. The special prosecutor for the grand jury, Kim Sigler, was elected governor the next year, 1946, but lost to Mennen Williams two years later.

There were also scandals in Detroit and Wayne County—councilmen, policemen, the sheriff and the prosecuting attorney went to jail. Homer Ferguson as a one-man grand jury sent a mayor of Detroit, Richard Reading, to prison in 1941. Ferguson, a Republican, was later elected to the U.S. Senate.

These cases were all resolved thanks to local authorities investigating. Today, however, we have had a whole host of scandals. However, you don't see local initiative to investigate them.

Today, I suggest that what stands between us and anarchy is the Public Integrity Section of the Federal Bureau of Investigation. Corruption in Macomb County, for example, has been exposed as a consequence of the Public Integrity Section working with the United States Attorney's Office.

The Flint water crisis has ended up being completely politicized. There has been a rather drastic change, I believe, in the way the state approaches problem solving. I don't see any prospect for change, and we have the same problems on the national level.

Our leadership is following the laws of politics. The first law of politics is to preserve your position in the party. That takes precedence over acting in the public interest.

Back to history: I am having a map made to show Alexis de Tocqueville's travels in

Michigan. He was a French political philosopher who traveled in 1831 with his friend Beaumont through this country to study our prison system. He ended up writing *Democracy in America.*[11]

His observations were important. When you look at speeches in the United Nations about America, he is probably quoted more than anyone else. As part of that trip, he came to Michigan.

We were still a territory and Michigan was still largely unsettled. He took a boat from Buffalo to Detroit and then went by horse and foot to Saginaw Bay because he was wanted to see the natives, the Indians. After he went from Detroit to Saginaw and back, he wrote an essay called *Two Weeks in the Wilderness.*

He describes details on that trip, including the journey from Buffalo to Detroit and the one from Detroit to Saginaw.

Tocqueville also kept a diary. If you read the essay and the diary, you can track the path he took from Detroit. He stopped for lunch, in what was then called Troy Corners, and went on to Pontiac.

Then he crossed the Flint River, went to Saginaw Bay, which was regarded as pretty much the end of civilization at that time, turned around, and came back by a slightly different route that ended up on what is now Orchard Lake Road.

He went down Orchard Lake to what is now Farmington. There's a point where he said he could see the little lakes of Orchard and Pine. I once had a cottage across Pine Lake. One night I was reading the diary, and realized that I was right across the lake from where Tocqueville had been when he described his travels.

Years ago there was an essay in the *New York Times* by Richard Reeves, the political journalist who retraced Tocqueville's route and wrote a book about what someone would see if they were to travel this route.[12] The current views came out second best.

So I found a writer and a cartographer, gave them all this material and am making a map, which will be at Central Michigan University in Mount Pleasant and in a traveling exhibit.

Early Michigan history is endlessly fascinating.

I have another map in progress displaying the early route from Detroit to Montreal. The travel involved a seven-mile portage along the Niagara River—they had to carry their canoes that far to avoid the falls. They had to carry their food, their equipment.

Detroit was all French from 1701 to 1763. The only sign of that today is in the names of the streets. Then the French were beaten by the British in 1763 and withdrew from North America.

---

11. Alexis De Tocqueville (1805-1859) spent eight months traveling in America with his friend Gustave de Beaumont in 1831, ostensibly to study the U.S. penal system. But he was interested in all aspects of life in America, especially its budding democracy, which led to the publication in 1835 of his famous book.
12. *American Journey*, By Richard Reeves. Simon and Schuster, 1982

The British took over. And the British in Quebec let the people maintain their language and customs—which may have been the right thing to do, but gave them a real headache.

What is interesting is that even though the Treaty of Paris in 1783 gave Detroit to the United States, the British kept control till they finally agreed to leave all their forts in the Northwest Territories under the Jay Treaty, signed in 1795.

The British garrison finally left Detroit on July 11, 1796.

I've found these events fascinating all my life.

Three Frenchmen
Three Centuries
Across Michigan

Michigan History Foundation

Introduction

**Maps invest information with meaning by translating it into visual form.
- Susan Schulten,**
Introduction to America in 100 Maps

It is one thing to read of early travels across Michigan. It is quite another to see the routes taken: René-Robert Cavelier, Sieur de La Salle crossing Michigan to get back to Montreal; Antoine de la Mothe Cadillac leaving Montreal, going up the Ottawa and French Rivers to Georgian Bay, and then down Lake Huron to what is now Detroit; Alexis De Tocqueville traveling from Detroit to Saginaw Bay, to see what he was told was the edge of civilization.

The maps that follow display the routes taken superimposed on current maps of the areas traversed. These maps are a fascinating display of the arduous travels undertaken by three different Frenchmen in three different centuries.

After completing this work, together with Wendy Bice as writer, Laurie Blume as graphic artist and Larry Wyckoff as cartographer, I decided the best home for these maps is the Michigan History Foundation. Dedicated to preserving Michigan's rich history and culture for future generations, and the preservation and utilization of Michigan's historical resources as cultural, economic and educational assets, the Michigan History Foundation has the ability to use these materials in its educational programming and as a way to raise funds for its work.

See, learn and enjoy the visual presentation which follows.

- Avern Cohn, Author 2020

Synopsis of Explorers

1. 1680 La Salle
In August 1679, the great French explorer René-Robert Cavelier, Sieur de La Salle, known simply as "La Salle," set sail with his crew from Niagara, Canada, on the *Le Griffon*. Their goal was to explore the great Mississippi to seek out new territories for the French. It took them just three days to reach the port of what would later become known as Detroit, and they then continued up Lake Huron to Michilimackinac. After a delay, the explorers proceeded down the western shore of Lake Michigan to the mouth of Green Bay, where they left their ship. Various events led La Salle to abandon his plans for the Mississippi and instead return to Niagara. La Salle's six-week trek across the wilds of lower Michigan is believed to be the first such journey made by a white man.

2. 1701 Cadillac
Nearly a half century after La Salle's journey across Michigan, another French explorer, Antoine de la Mothe Cadillac, had begun charting the lands and waters of the territory of Michigan. In 1700, authorized by the King of France to build a fort, Cadillac departed the northern shore of the St. Lawrence River with a flotilla of 25 canoes, 100 Frenchmen and 100 natives. Their arduous 300-mile journey to *le Detroit* involved traversing rivers, crossing great lakes and making dozens of difficult portages before they finally reached their destination: a spot along a river that was resplendent with tall conifers and giant maple and oak trees.

3. 1831 de Tocqueville
Born into the French aristocracy, Alexis de Tocqueville, along with his friend and fellow explorer Gustave de Beaumont, petitioned the French minister of the interior to approve a journey to the democratic United States to study its prison system, though their real intent was to discover "untouched wilderness" and "unspoiled Indians." Their journey through the state of New York left them disappointed as they encountered more settlements than wilderness, so they traveled to Michigan where they found lands rich in silver lakes, deep forests, fields of wildflowers and friendly Native Americans.

René-Robert Cavelier, Sieur de La Salle
1680

1. 1680 La Salle

René-Robert Cavelier, Sieur de La Salle (b. November 22, 1643), in a flotilla of eight canoes, traveled south and west from Wisconsin, seeking a river or access point to the great Mississippi and the Gulf of Mexico. Numerous obstacles, ranging from lack of supplies to incursions with the Native American tribes, forced La Salle to abandon his plans. On March 1, 1680, La Salle departed on the Illinois River, from near what is now Peoria. Twenty-two days later, they arrived at the western shore of Lake Michigan. Assessing their options on how best to reach Niagara, La Salle, along with four Frenchmen and an Indian guide, proceeded across lower Michigan . . . on foot.

Although his journal did not reveal exact geographical detail, descriptions provided allowed historians to determine that La Salle's general path was a route that took him from the Benton Harbor area, through the city we now know as Kalamazoo, and through the swamps of Calhoun County near Duck Lake. In what was described as a cold and rainy spring, they traveled about 40 miles a day. Upon finding the Huron River, they knew they would soon reach Lake Erie. They stopped to build a canoe and then spent five slow days traveling past Ann Arbor and Ypsilanti to finally reach what we now call the Detroit River, then Lake Erie and home.

La Salle carefully chronicled his observations: " . . . we found the forest more open and began to enjoy better cheer, since we encountered a great many animals, [which] were subsequently so plentiful that we no longer carried provisions with us. . . ." He shared tales and tactics of survival: "The ends of the bark must be bent in and sewn together, along the full length of either side must be bound a timer half as thick as a man's arm." After nearly six weeks of travel, their journey concluded on Easter Monday, April 22, in Niagara.

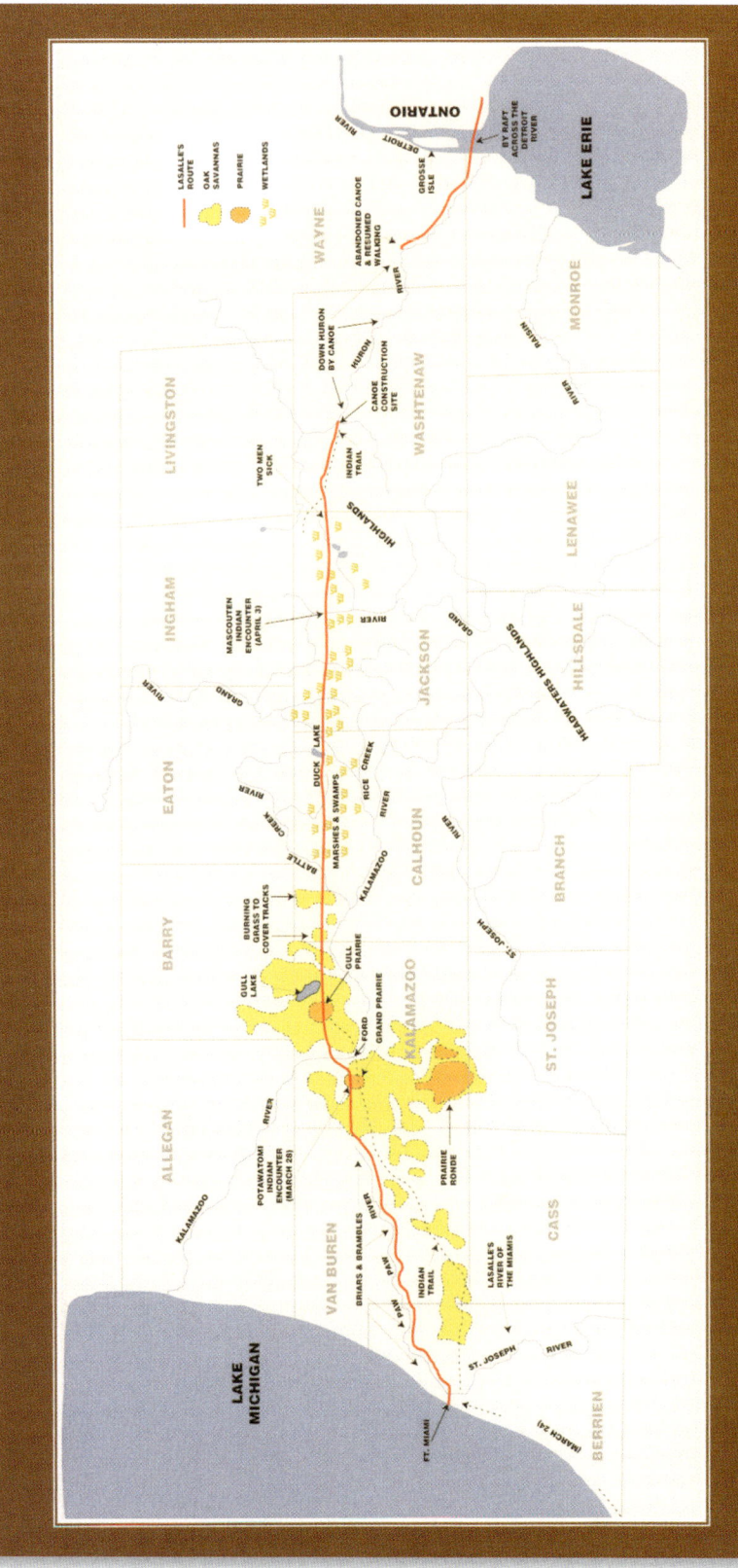

Journey of René-Robert Cavelier, Sieur de La Salle, from St. Joseph, Michigan, to the Detroit River, 1680

Antoine de la Mothe Cadillac
1701

2. 1701 Cadillac

As a commander in the French military, Antoine de la Mothe Cadillac (b. March 5, 1658) oversaw all trading in the "upper countries" (from Louisiana through the Ohio Valley and the Great Lakes) controlled by the French. In 1695, Cadillac left Fort de Buade or Michilimackinac to chart the Great Lakes with the intention of erecting a fort somewhere between lakes Erie and Huron. The project was abandoned when Cadillac was called back to Montreal in 1697. In 1700, he received authorization to undertake the two-month, 600-mile journey (including 30 portages), which concluded with the establishment of Fort Pontchartrain du Detroit and the parish of Sainte-Anne on July 25, 1701. The fort was named in honor of Cadillac's ally, the French minister of marine.

For many years prior, the waters connecting lakes Huron and Erie were referred to as *Le Détroit*, which translates to "the strait." In 1751, the Fort became known as *Fort du Détroit*, and eventually was shortened simply to *Detroit*. Detroit remained a French territory until 1783, when the British conquered the area and, in a treaty, allowed Detroit to become a part of the U.S. Northwest Territory.

Cadillac, who rose from a modest beginning in Acadia in 1683 as an explorer, trapper and trader of alcohol and furs, served as commandant of the fort at Mackinac, appointed as such by French Governor Louis de Buade, Comte de Frontenac. Despite being recognized as a prescient negotiator and mediator between the many various native tribes and the French, Cadillac did not achieve his positions of political importance without controversy. He was, on at least one occasion, accused of supplying alcohol to the Indians (a crime under French law) and of gross mistreatment of prisoners (including Native Americans) at the fort, and at other times he defied the king's orders in search of new business and territorial opportunities.

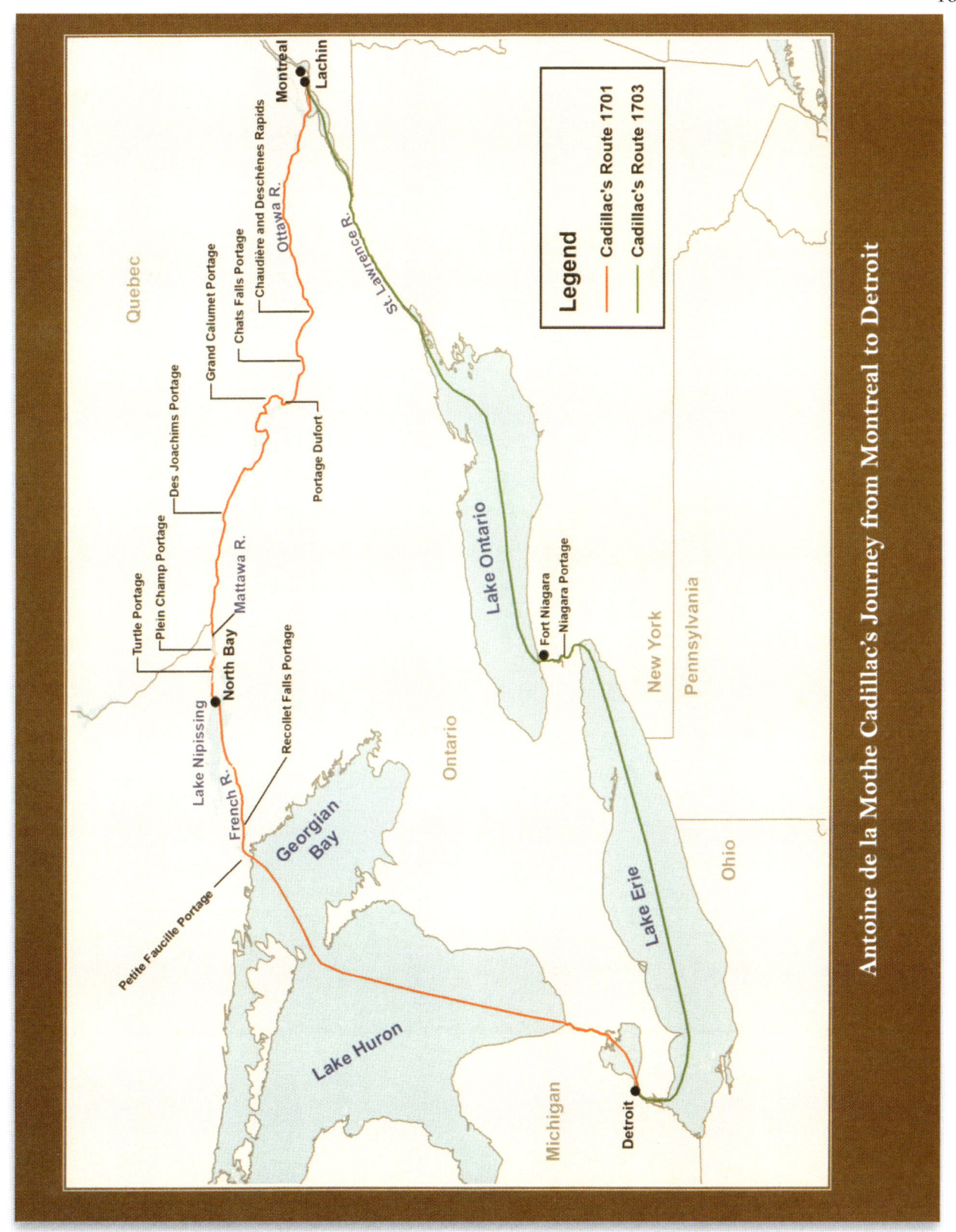

Antoine de la Mothe Cadillac's Journey from Montreal to Detroit

170

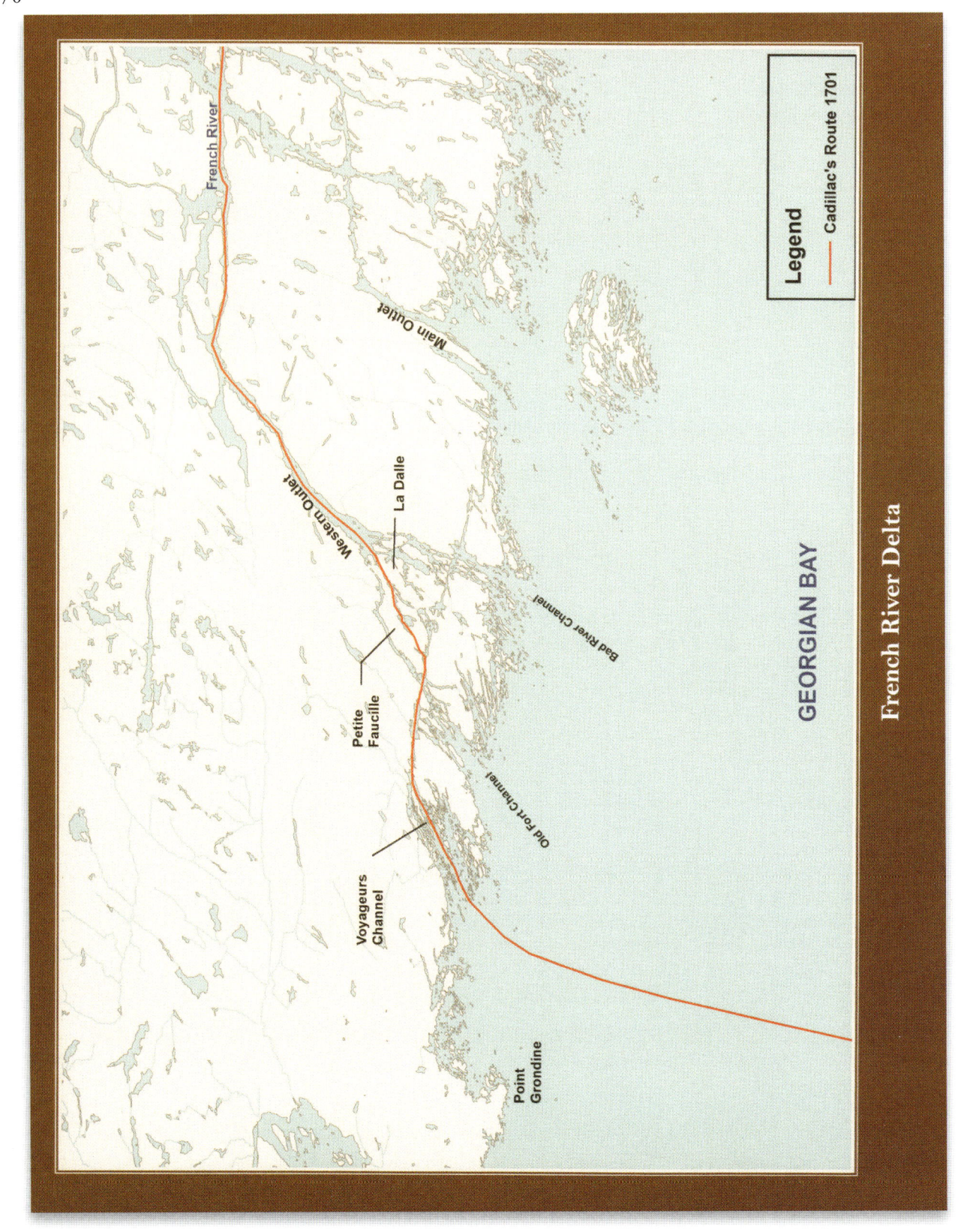

French River Delta

Lachine – Start of the Fur Trade Route to the West

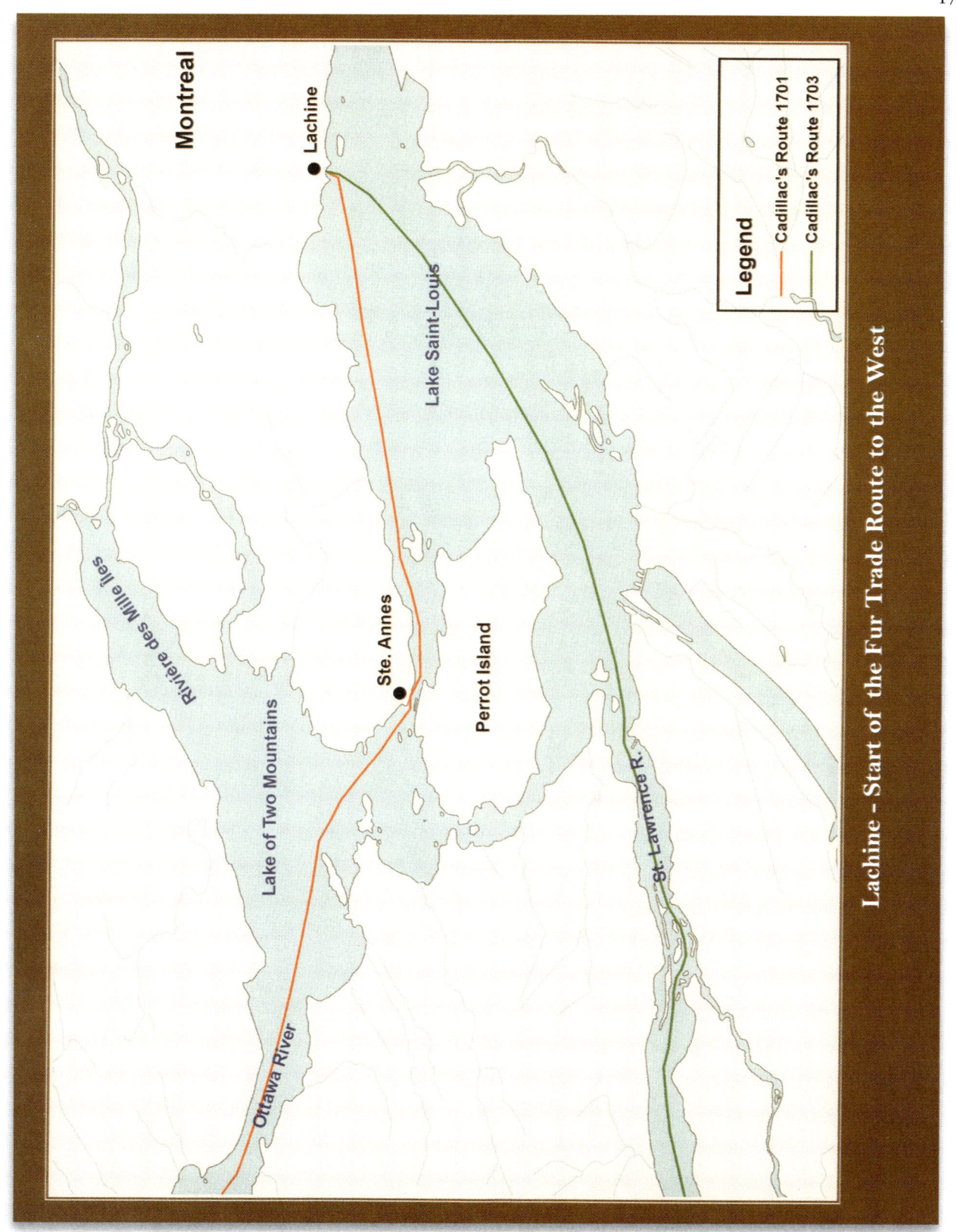

Junction of Ottawa and Mattawa Rivers

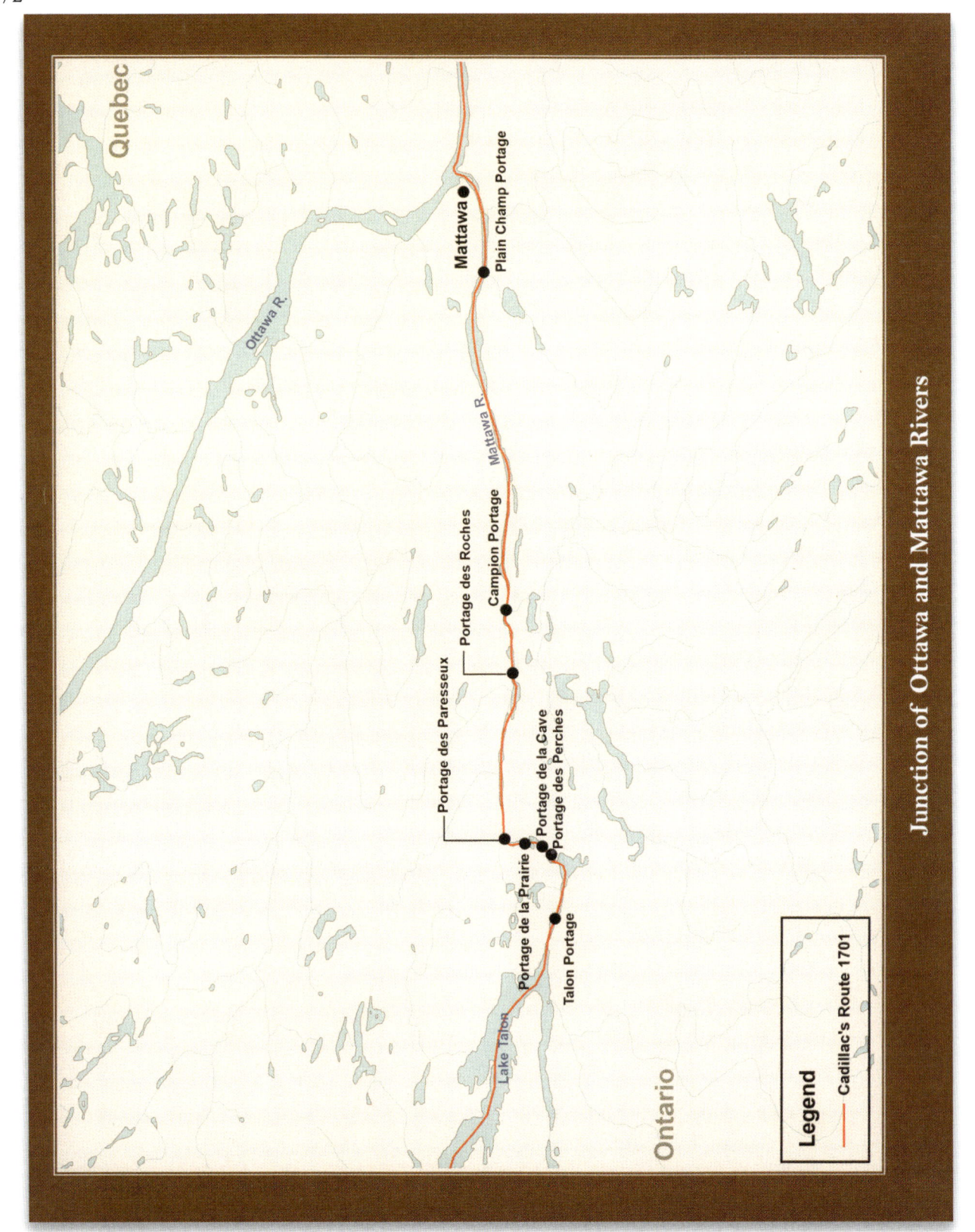

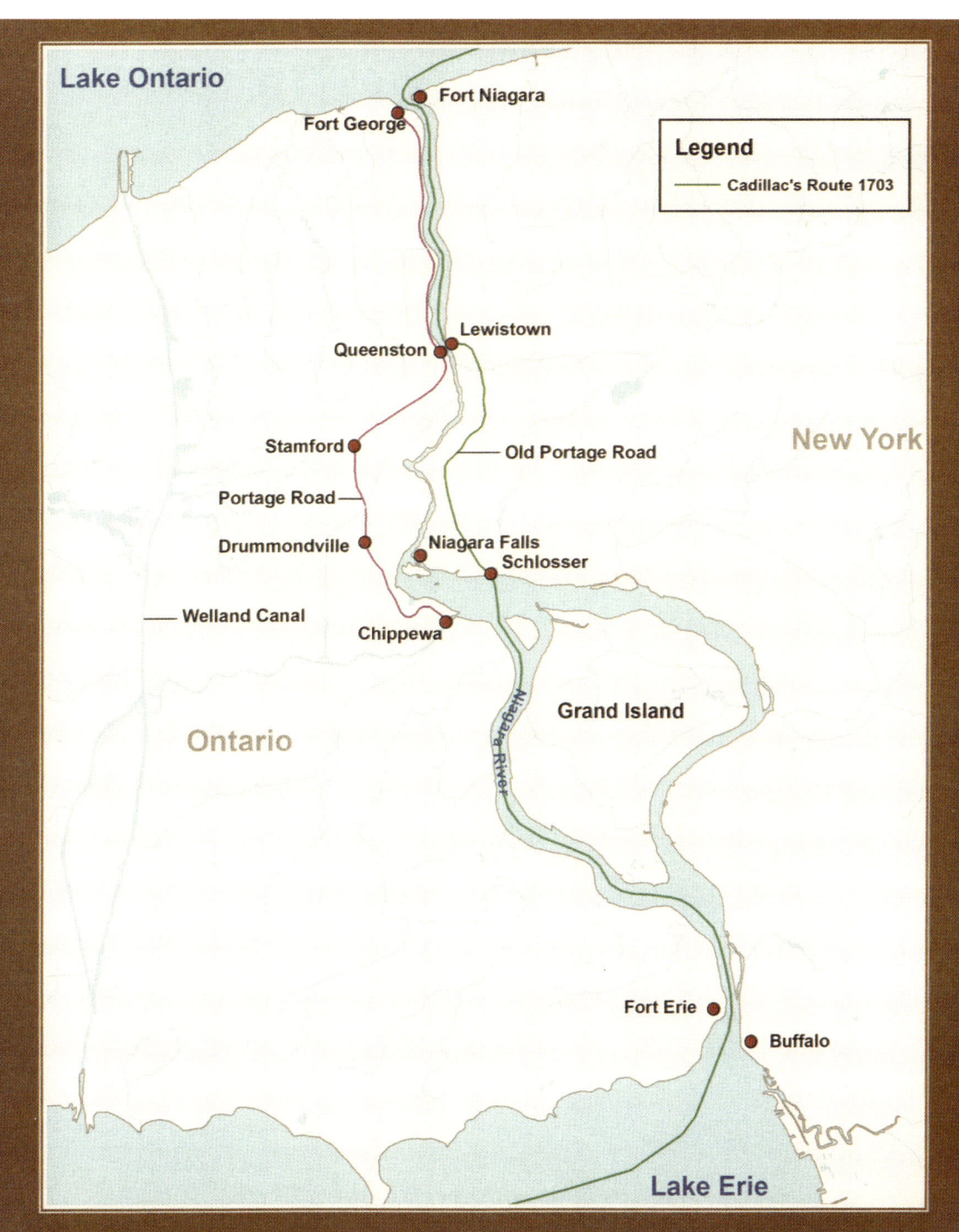

Niagara River Portage

This map depicts an alternate route between Montreal and Detroit used in the early years after Cadillac's explorations. The route became less often traveled because of the impediment of Niagara Falls and the hostility of the Indians at the Ontario end of the Niagara River. The construction of the Welland Canal in the early 1800s eased the way from Detroit to Montreal and back.

Alexis de Tocqueville
1831

Gustave de Beaumont, French magistrate, prison reformer and travel companion to Alexis de Tocqueville, made this sketch of Frenchman Island in New York State's Lake Oneida when he and Tocqueville (doubtless depicted in the lower left corner) explored it in July 1831.

(Yale Tocqueville Manuscripts. General Collection, Beinecke Rare Book and Manuscripts Library, Yale University)

3. 1831 de Tocqueville

The writings of Alexis de Tocqueville (b. July 29, 1805) have given modern-day Michiganders an invaluable timestamp. In 1831, this pioneering explorer lamented the diminishing virgin forests of the Michigan territory while marveling at the transformative agricultural revolution in the area's southeast corner.

Tocqueville and his partner, Gustave de Beaumont (b. February 6, 1802), began their exploration of American prisons and asylums in Newport, Rhode Island, then traveled to New York City and Albany. While traveling from Albany to Auburn, the pair glimpsed lush forests with "... treetops undulating in the wind like ocean waves, as far as the eye can see." Although the Michigan territories had not been on their agenda, on July 19, in Buffalo, Tocqueville and Beaumont boarded the Ohio and steamed across Lake Erie, arriving in Detroit on July 22. Despite their high hopes, no virgin lands greeted them. Instead they found a booming settlement that, in 1831, welcomed nearly 5,000 new emigrants who found ample farmland and agricultural opportunities.

After several failed attempts to find routes out of the settlement and into the wilds, Tocqueville and Beaumont, presenting themselves as prospective land seekers, were shown a map pointing to the northwest, to the area surrounding Saginaw Bay. With the map came a stern warning: Venture no farther than Pontiac! "The territory is blanketed by virtually impenetrable forest . . . and out that way you'll find nothing but wild animals and Indians."

That was the ticket they had been waiting for! A path untraveled, a route not disparaged by the floods of Europeans daily arriving who, in creating a new homeland, were trampling acres of trees.

On horseback, Tocqueville and Beaumont left Detroit, loaded with brandy, sugar, ammunition, mosquito nets, a compass and two straw hats. Tocqueville, something of a romantic, kept a detailed diary of his travels. After the journey ended, while on board the steamship Superior, he authored a manuscript, *Two Weeks in the Wilderness*. Considered a poetic and environmental masterpiece, *Two Weeks* was published in French in 1860, a year after his death. Beaumont captured much of the journey in drawings.

As they traveled north from Detroit to Troy Corners and then to Pontiac, Tocqueville observed an environment in conflict: from flat and swampy terrain, to the "signs of destruction" man was leaving in his wake as settlements were erected through forested lands. He met settlers at odds with their new environs, "like rich people who have decided to spend a season in a hunting lodge."

They left Pontiac, the "edge of civilization," on July 24. Despite the forewarning tales of "savages," the white settlers they met on the trail told vastly different stories. They spoke of the Chippewa who were fair trading partners, and of Indians who were kind and generous. As the duo came to the end of what is now northwest Oakland County, they crossed paths with an Indian who greeted them with a warm smile. The three traded goods and set off. The Indian, perhaps to protect them, trailed them for miles, "hurdling bushes and landing without a sound."

Tocqueville exquisitely describes Michigan's environment: silvery lakes, lush forests filled with lofty trees that rose "as straight as a ship's mast," the majesty of "the order above" and chaos of the grounds below: "trunks have collapsed . . . Others, buffeted by the wind, have been hurled to the ground." He marvels at stillness so complete "that all the forces of nature seem paralyzed." He bemoans, just as future settlers will, relentless mosquitos. Tocqueville also shares a gloomy forecast: "This savage natural grandeur is about to meet its end, and the idea of it mingles in the mind with the superb images to which the triumphant march of civilization gives rise."

Tocqueville and Beaumont reached the barely cultivated society of Saginaw on July 26. Sadly, Tocqueville noted that, despite living together in this most rugged of terrains, the 30 citizens – including persons of different skin color, race and affluence, regarded one another with hatred and suspicion. The travelers spent a day in the area, exploring its woods and waters, then headed back to Detroit. They completed their journey on July 31, just days after Tocqueville's 26th birthday.

The narrative for this section is an abridged version of Aristocracy on the Saginaw Trail: Alexis de Tocqueville In Michigan, *by John Fierst.*

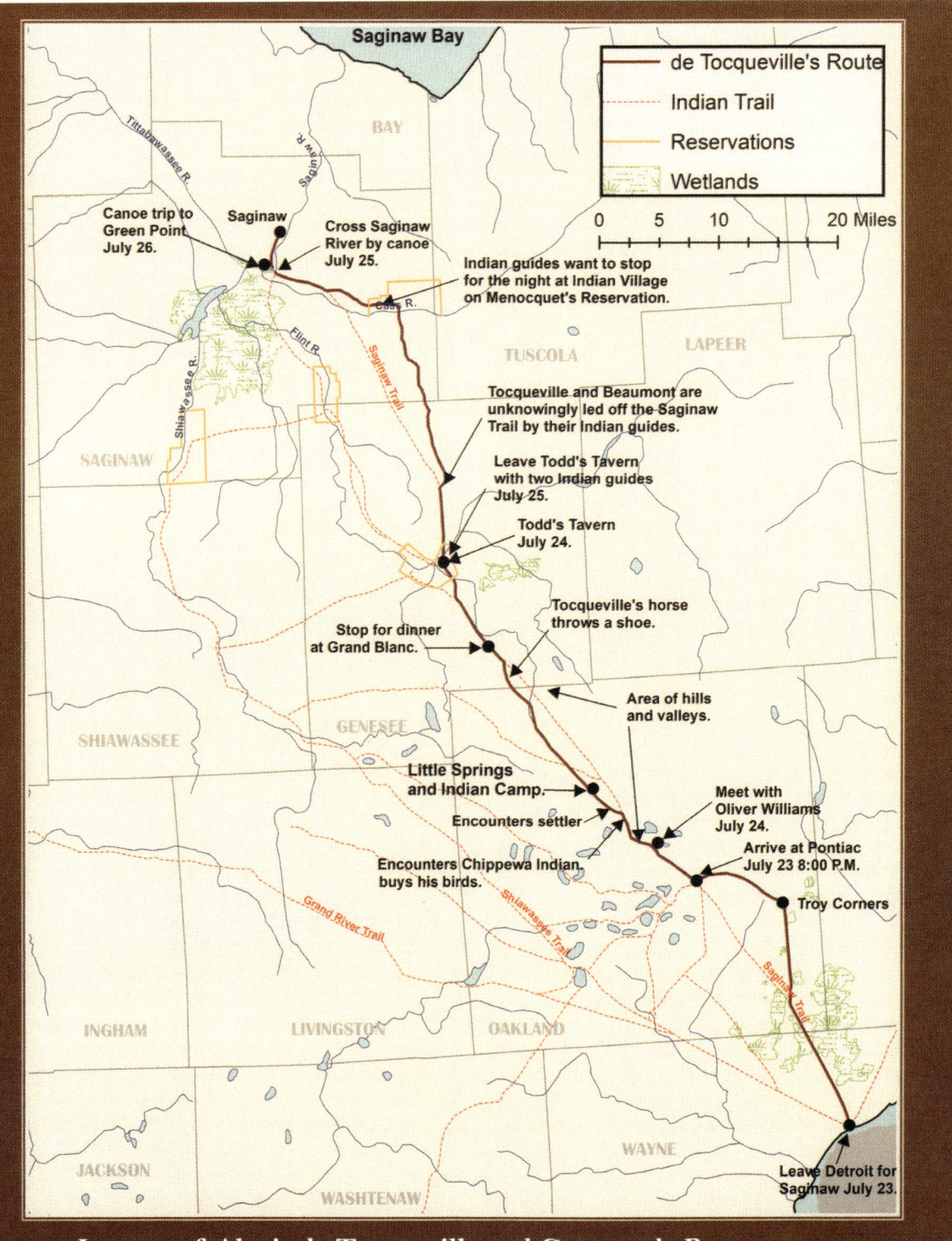

Journey of Alexis de Tocqueville and Gustave de Beaumont from Detroit to Saginaw, 1831

Pontiac and Orchard Lake Area

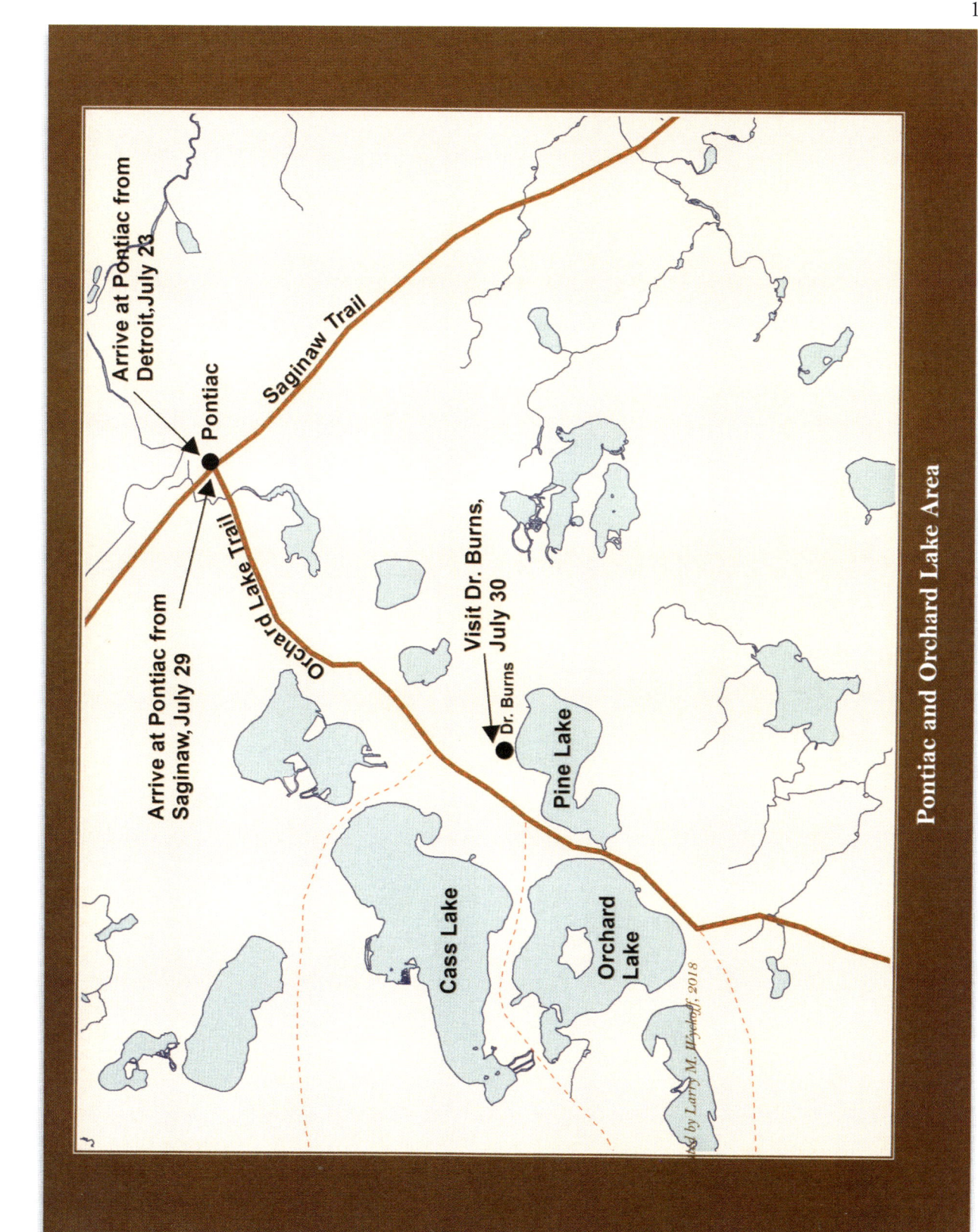

Flint River Area

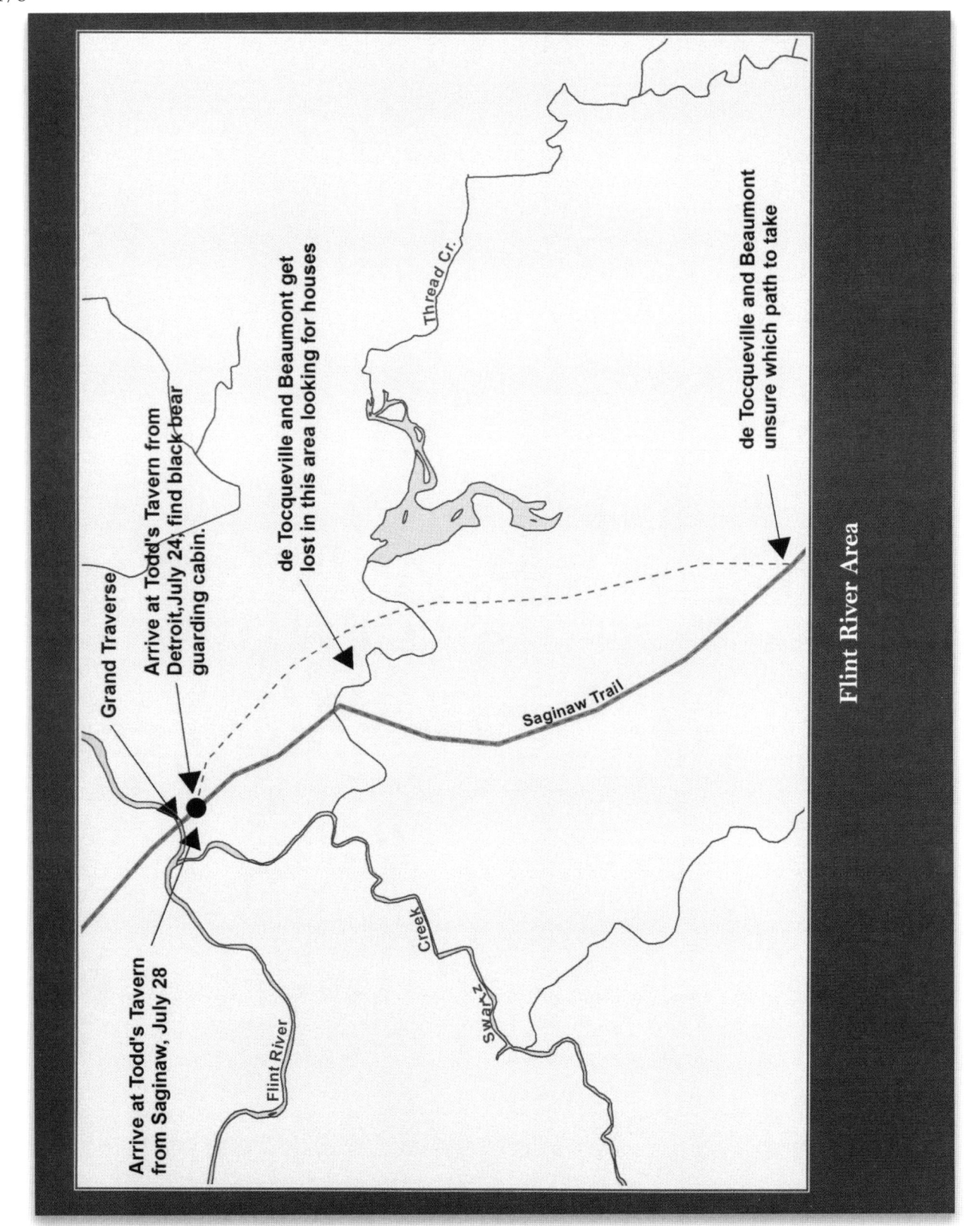

179

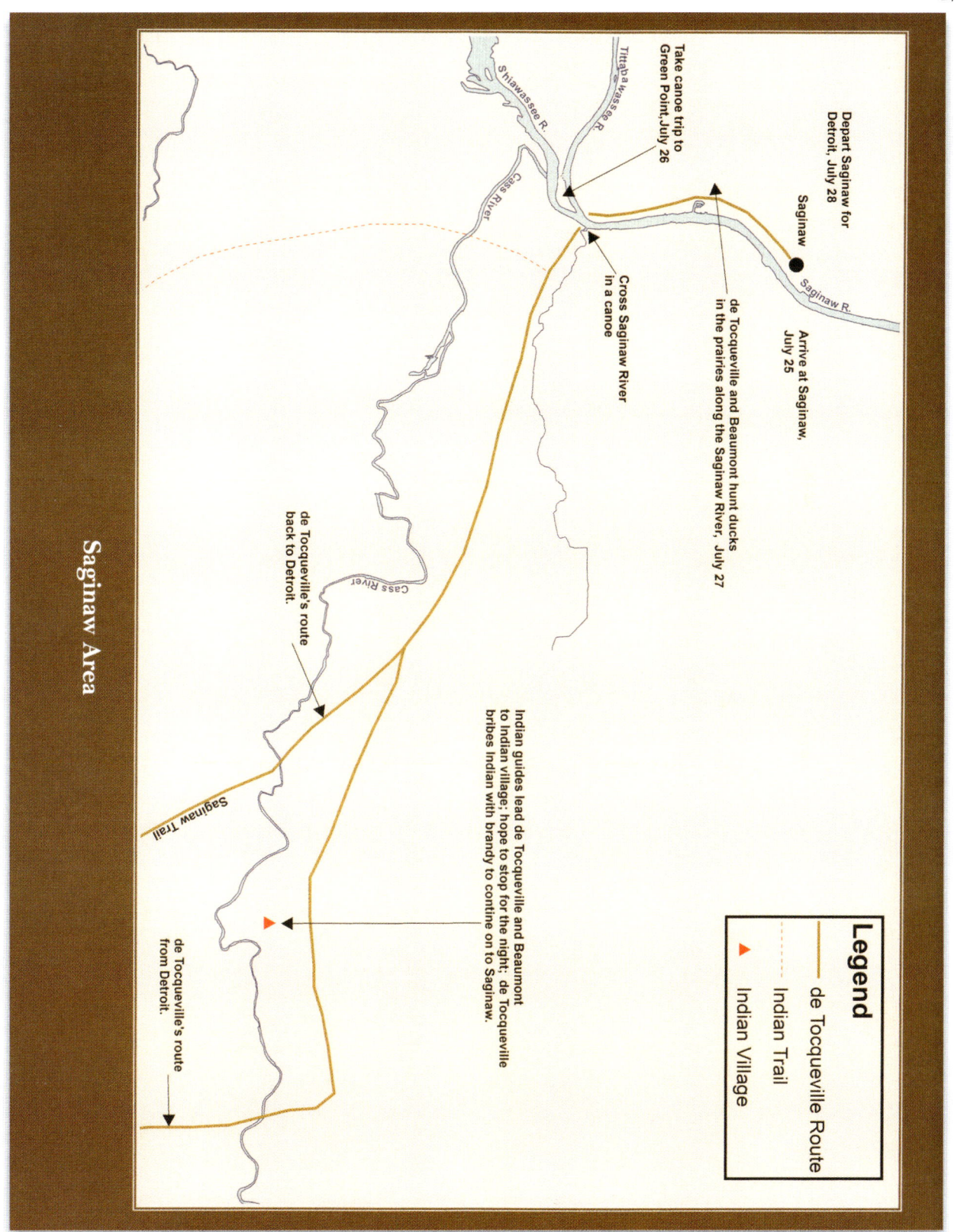

Saginaw Area

Depart Saginaw for Detroit, July 28

Take canoe trip to Green Point, July 26

Arrive at Saginaw, July 25

de Tocqueville and Beaumont hunt ducks in the prairies along the Saginaw River, July 27

Cross Saginaw River in a canoe

de Tocqueville's route back to Detroit.

Indian guides lead de Tocqueville and Beaumont to Indian village; hope to stop for the night; de Tocqueville bribes Indian with brandy to continue on to Saginaw.

de Tocqueville's route from Detroit.

Shiawassee R.
Tittabawassee R.
Saginaw R.
Cass River
Saginaw Trail

Legend
— de Tocqueville Route
··· Indian Trail
▲ Indian Village

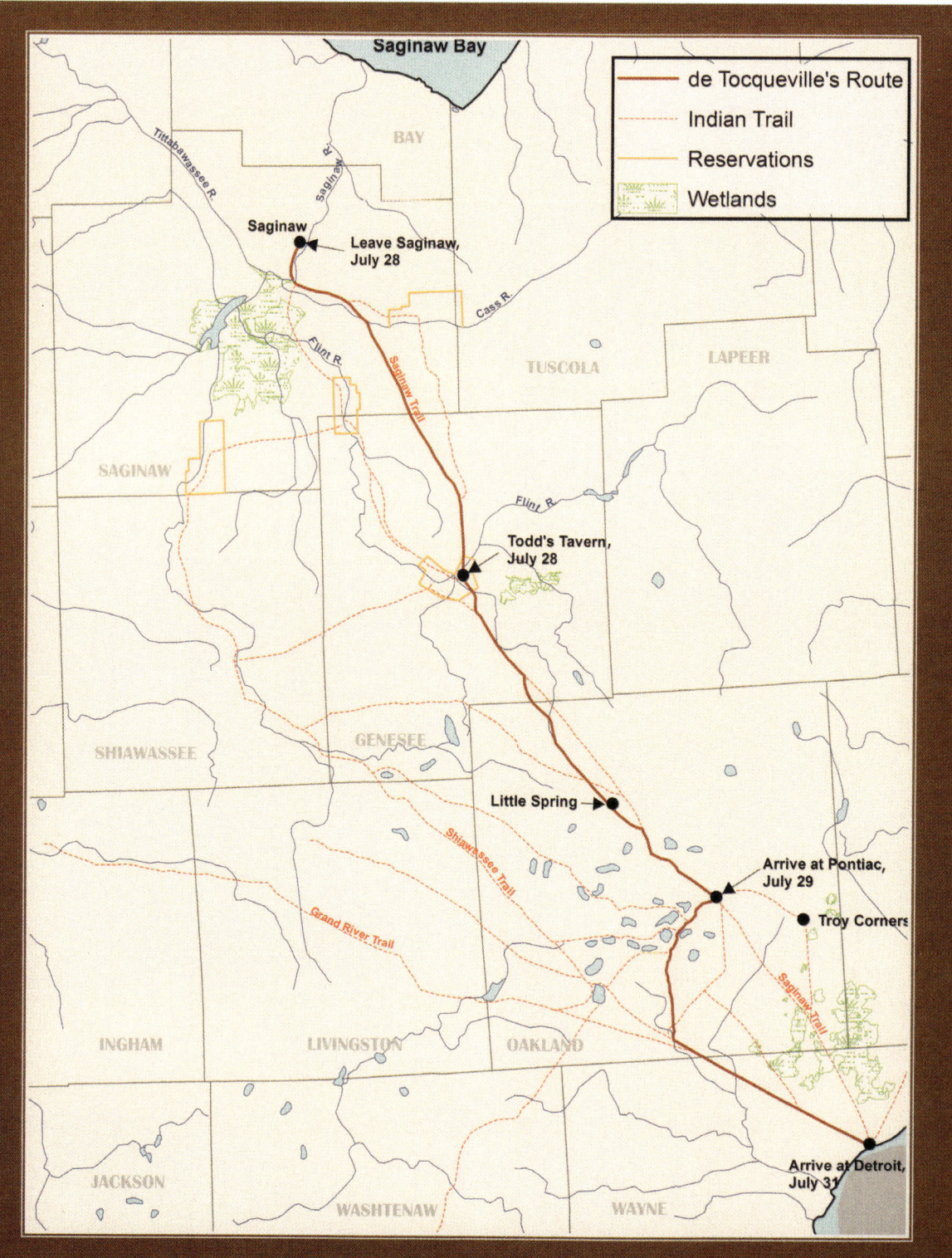

Tocqueville and Beaumont's Return Trip from Saginaw to Detroit, 1831

181

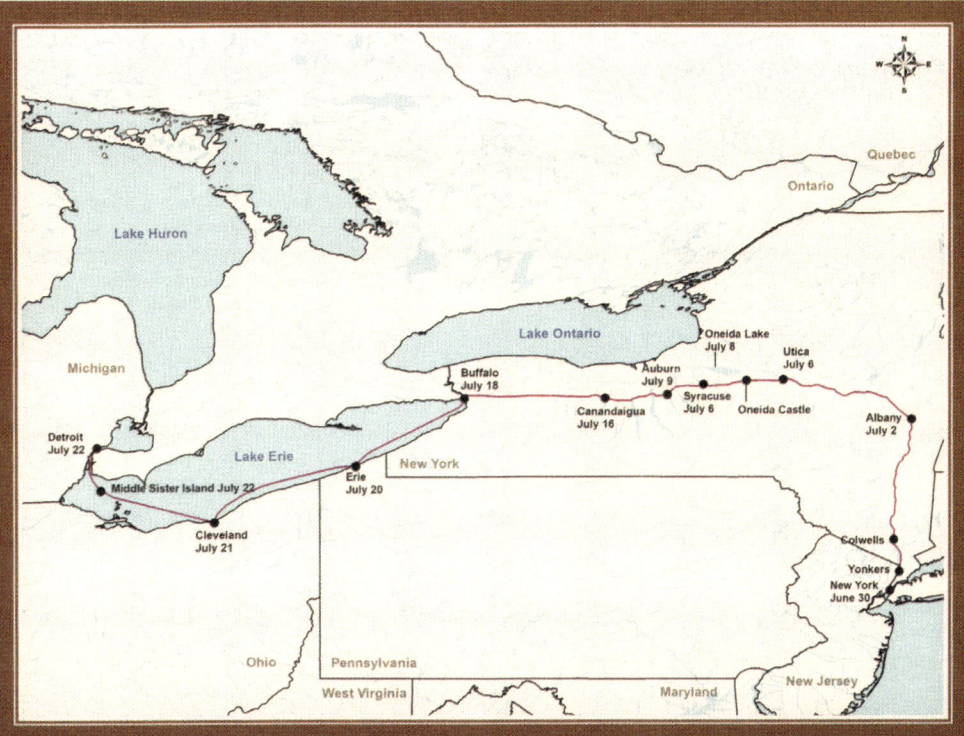

Journey from New York to Michigan

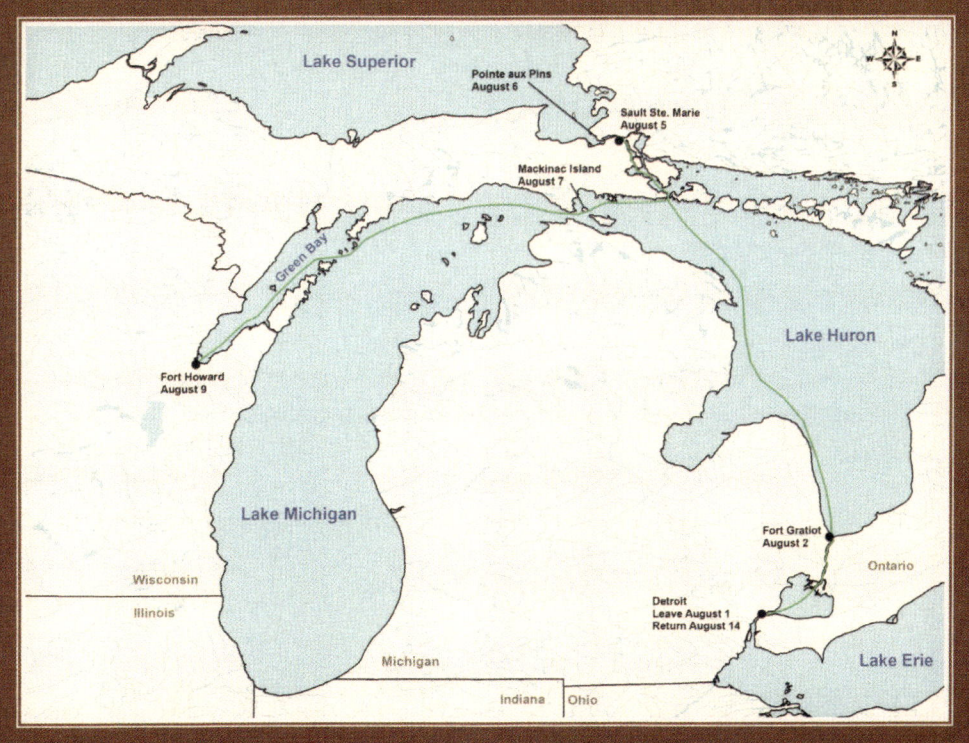

Detroit to Green Bay

THE DETROIT BANKING CRISES OF 1933

Editor's Note: Avern Cohn is perhaps as much a careful student of history as a legal scholar, and he has wide-ranging interests, as demonstrated by this short, never-previously published article on a dramatic and too-little-known episode in history.

In looking for cases in the District Court for the Eastern District of Michigan having an historical bent, I came across several books on the closing of all the banks in Michigan on Feb. 14, 1933 by the governor, William Comstock, who did so because of their precarious financial state. This momentous event was called a "Bank Holiday."

Its effect was to deny depositors access to their accounts. As one scholar put it:

> *The circumstances leading to Detroit's banking crisis in 1933 were not the result of sudden or dramatic events. The financial conditions in Detroit banks had been precarious for a period of some years before they became matters of public concern. The Detroit banks in the early 1930s had been subjected to forces similar to those which had weakened commercial banks throughout the country. Falling prices, output, and employment had decreased the value of bank assets and impaired their marketability. In addition the contraction of deposits as a result of an unfavorable regional balance of payments had drained the banks of their more liquid assets and thus increased their vulnerability should withdrawals continue.*
>
> *Unfortunately, the policies and practices of the Detroit banks prior to the 1930s had reduced their capacity to withstand a prolonged siege of this type.*[1]

---

1. McKenzie, Patricia O'Donnell: *Some Aspects of the Detroit Bank Crisis of 1933.* Page 10. Unpublished Ph.D thesis, Dec. 15, 1963. Purdy-Kresge Library, Wayne State University.

Soon thereafter, on March 6, 1933, two days after taking office, new President Franklin D. Roosevelt closed all the banks in the United States. Most of the closed banks soon recovered and reopened. However, the two major banks in Detroit, the First National Bank of Detroit and the Guardian Bank of Commerce did not. Two new banks were organized in their place, the National Bank of Detroit and the Manufacturers National Bank. The closed banks during the course of their receivership eventually paid their depositors 100 cents on the dollar. The closings and liquidations were conducted under state law. Aside from periodic examinations by the Comptroller of the Currency, there was very little federal involvement in the regulation and supervision of state banks. The closings, however, were based on the federal bank examinations which found the banks insolvent.

While a number of federal and state cases came to court on the closings, none of them dealt with the merits. For the most part, the cases involved issues relating to the assessment of stockholders of amounts related to the value of their stocks before the closings.[2] Such assessments are no longer possible these days.

As one of the many political responses to the closings, particularly the suspicion that management misbehavior was behind the insolvencies, a one-man grand jury was appointed on petition of the Michigan Attorney General, then one Patrick O' Brien, and charged with examining the management of the two failed banks.

The grand jury was held in Wayne County Circuit Court. Then Chief Circuit Judge Harry B. Keidan was appointed the grand juror. Harry S. Toy, Wayne County's Prosecuting Attorney, was counsel. A June 9, 1933 *Detroit News* headline said "Judge Keidan Fitted by Experience for Job."

The investigation extended over four months, from May to September, 1933.

Keidan's inquiry was pushed by Senator James Couzens (R-Mich.), a former partner of Henry Ford and a former Mayor of Detroit. Couzens had been appointed a Senator in 1921 to fill the position vacated by Truman H. Newberry, who defeated Ford for the position in 1918. Newberry resigned following his conviction (later reversed) for violation of the Corrupt Practices Act in regard to financing his election. Couzens accused the management of the two banks of being criminally responsible for their collapse. The bankers in turn accused Couzens of impeding federal assistance to the two banks to make up their shortfalls in capital funds.

The Keidan grand jury proceedings were unlike that of today. Now, a one-man grand jury conducts its proceedings in secret. The Keidan inquiry was open to the public. Also, unlike the truncated media reports of court proceedings today, the testimony of almost every witness called to testify in front of Keidan was published word for word in the *Detroit Free Press*.[3]

---

2. See *Barbour et al v. Thomas et al*, 7 F. Supp 271 (E.D. Mich. 1933), aff'd *Barbour. et. al. v. Thomas et al*, 86 F.2d 510 (6th Cir, 1936) which held that shareholders could not stop a receiver from enforcing the assessments.
3. The *Detroit Free Press* also published, in full, Judge Keidan's remarks at the end of the grand jury process, under the headline, "The Conclusion" on Sept. 19, 1933.

Through the magnificent efforts of Elise Keller, librarian of the Ralph M. Freeman Memorial Library of the Eastern District, I obtained and perused the daily accounts of the Keidan grand jury.[4] Scores of witnesses testified. Each was examined by Toy.

Keidan announced his findings on the evening of Sept. 18, 1933 after listening to Couzens testify that morning. The pertinent parts of Keidan's decision:

- No evidence has been found to support charges of criminality in the National Bank of Detroit.
- No evidence of 'smart money' withdrawn before the holiday has been presented.
- Testimony in the Grand Jury investigation led to the "constrained" conclusion that the First National Bank and the Guardian National Bank of Commerce were solvent.

Particularly interesting, and admirable about the grand jury proceedings:

- The speed with which the Grand Jury was convened
- The speed with which the Grand Jury inquiry was conducted and concluded
- The openness of the Grand Jury inquiry
- The completeness of the Grand Jury proceedings

In the end, one scholar's concluding comments summarize an important lesson from the "Bank Holiday" in Detroit. Her words from more than fifty years ago still hold truths for today: "The Detroit banking crisis is an important caveat to practitioners of monetary policy: Intangible political and psychological factors may sometimes become critical even when the problem at hand seems to depend almost entirely on well-known economic and financial considerations."[5]

For a full account of the closing of the banks, see Darwyn H. Lumley, *Breaking the Banks in Motor City,* McFarland and Co. (2009) and Susan Estabrook Kinney, *The Banking Crisis of 1933.* (University Press of Kentucky, 1973).

- Avern Cohn, February 2017

---

4. The grand jury's minutes are not available; they were destroyed in a fire.
5. O'Donnell, op. cit. p. 215

A Jewish Judge—Or a Judge Who Is Jewish?

Editor's Note: *U.S. District Judge Avern Cohn spent forty years (1979-2019) on the bench in Detroit. This article is adapted from a speech he gave to the Cardozo Society in Seattle, Washington in July, 2002.*

I have been a federal judge for many years. Throughout that time, I have thought much about the decision-making process, and particularly, whether my being Jewish has played a role in the way I consider a decision, and the decision itself.

I know that judges differ, and that there is a subjective quality in decision- making. In about 90 percent of the decisions, nearly all judges will likely come to the same conclusion. But for the other ten percent, there are a range of justifiable choices.

This is what we call *judicial discretion.*

For example, in procedural matters:

- Whether or not to grant an adjournment when the reasons are rather thin.
- Whether to waive the application of a rule that sets time limits, when there is clearly no substantive harm in doing so.
- Which of two instructions to give a jury when the evidence tilts slightly in favor of one of the parties—particularly a defendant in a criminal case.
- In sentencing, whether or not to go to the higher end of a prescribed range of months or years in prison.
- Finally, whether or not to release a pretrial defendant on bond when there is a slight risk he or she may abscond.

These are the types of decisions where judges are likely to differ. Now, at this time there are seven Jewish judges out of 15 in regular service for the U.S. District Court in

Detroit. Until recently, there were three more now retired, including myself.

I know my colleagues well enough to tell you some of us likely would often differ in the decision I have briefly described above.

The question is why this is—and whether our varying Jewish backgrounds would play any role in how we decide?

In the book, *Jews in American Politics*[1] there is a section called "Jewish Distinctiveness and its Explanation," where the author says:

> *In making sense of Jewish political patterns, one should start with the recognition that nothing is inevitable about the political alignment of American Jews. Although many Jews feel their community's liberal political slant is nothing more than applied Judaism, the facts tell a different story.*

For me, the key words here are **applied Judaism.**

I have long thought how being Jewish plays a role in how I go about making decisions. When I have discussed this before, I have laid some emphasis on the fact that I am Jewish, and in particular, on having grown up in Detroit's "golden ghetto" from the late 1920s to the early 40s. The Cardozo Society in Detroit is an organization of young Jewish lawyers sponsored by our federation[2]. When I spoke to them some years ago, I recounted my life history in detail, emphasizing the importance of my relationship to my Jewish classmates, to synagogue life and community associations as I went through school—more on this later in this essay.

Once, in a dinner speech to the Federal Circuit Bar Association in Washington, D.C, I described my decision-making process in general terms. I recalled what an English judge said in the 1920s:

> *The law as laid down in a code, in a statute or in a thousand eloquently reasoned opinions, is no more capable of providing all the answers than a piano is of playing music. The piano needs the pianist, and any two pianists, even with the same score, may produce very different music.*[3]

As for myself, I operate much as Chancellor James Kent (1763-1847) New York's leading judge in the early 19th century, put it.

---

1. *Jews in American Politics,* By Louis Sandy Maisel, Rowan and Littlefield, 2001
2. The Jewish Federation of Metropolitan Detroit
3. From McCluskey, *Lord Law, Justice and Democracy.* BBC Books, 1987

He said his method was to make himself fully familiar with the facts of the case. After that:

> *I was master of the cause and ready to decide it. I saw where justice lay, and the moral sense decided the cause half the time, and I then sat down to search the authorities until I had exhausted my books, and I might once (in) a while be embarrassed by a technical rule, but I most always found principles suited to my view of the case.*[4]

As for my own 'piano playing' (I don't want to sound immodest)—my view of where justice lies has these elements:

- A social conscience.
- A concern for the less fortunate among us
- A view that courts have an obligation to view the law as something for the 'have-nots', given that the 'haves' usually can take care of themselves.

Several years ago, when a Michigan Supreme Court justice left the bench and retired, I said that he may not have had a perfect heart—but that he did not have an imperfect heart. I like to think that someone will say that of me someday.

I know that being Jewish and being liberal are not necessarily synonymous, despite the cultural stereotype. There are lists worth reviewing at the end of Maisel's *Jews in American Politics.*

They contain the names of all the Jewish federal judges down through the years, not just on the U.S. Supreme Court, but also on the various appellate courts and the district courts, along with the names of the Presidents who appointed them.

These judges span the spectrum of judicial thought, from radicals at one end to conservatives at the other. Some were appointed by Republican presidents; some by Democratic presidents.

We can see this by looking at the Jewish judges who have been appointed to the U.S. Supreme Court. I do not know whether any study has been made of the judicial philosophies of judges on the courts of appeals or district courts.

But a lot has been written about the thinking of those on the Supreme Court, particularly Louis Brandeis, Benjamin Cardozo, Felix Frankfurter, Arthur Goldberg and Abe Fortas. Another Jewish justice, Ruth Bader Ginsburg, spoke in 1995 to an American Jewish

---

4. Letter to Thomas Washington, cited in *Safeguards of Liberty: Or Liberty Protected by Laws,* by William Bentley Sweeney, Oxford University Press, 1920, pp. 84-85. I have slightly modernized Kent's spelling and grammar.

Committee dinner about these justices.

What she said then bears repeating in some detail:

> *... as it evolved in the United States, law also became a bulwark against the kind of oppression Jews had endured throughout history. Thus, Jews in large numbers became lawyers in the United States, and some eventually became judges. The best of those lawyers and judges used the law not only for personal gain, but to secure justice for others.*

That's exactly the way it was with these first five Jewish justices:

Louis Brandeis (1856-1941) was on the court from 1916 till he retired in 1939. Prior to joining the court, He was known as the "People' s Attorney," and had fought trusts and monopolies and was active in the great social and economic reform movements of his day.

Benjamin Cardozo (1870-1938) was on the court from 1932 until his death in 1938. He didn't have a long tenure, but he is best remembered for using his fine and brilliant mind to adjust the common law to meet the needs of modern society.

Felix Frankfurter (1882-1965) was on the court from 1939 to 1962. Prior to the bench, he had become famous as an ardent advocate of labor's right to organize, and was a founder of the American Civil Liberties Union. He also had called loudly for a new trial for Sacco and Vanzetti, two immigrant Italian anarchists who were later executed on robbery and murder charges.

Arthur Goldberg (1908-1990) succeeded Frankfurter, but was on the court only three years (1962-1965) before leaving to become the U.S. Ambassador to the United Nations. He had previously been an attorney for labor unions, steelworkers and newspaper men in an era when strikers were often attacked by armed thugs.

Abe Fortas (1910-1982) was on the court from 1965 to 1969. Though he is remembered today for having to resign under a cloud because of financial issues, he was also a courageous lawyer who defended Owen Lattimore against smear charges by U.S. Sen. Joseph R. McCarthy. He was also the appointed attorney for the plaintiff in *Gideon v. Wainwright,* the case that established that the states are required to provide lawyers for defendants who cannot afford one.

Ruth Bader Ginsburg (1993-2020) scarcely needs any introduction; she has become a folk hero and a cultural icon for her efforts to use the law to fight gender discrimination prior to joining the U.S. Court of Appeals in 1980. She served on the court longer than any other Jewish justice in our history.

The two Supreme Court justices who are Jewish today also have had distinguished careers prior to joining the court:

Stephen Breyer, who was appointed in 1994, also was elevated to the Court of Appeals in 1980. Prior to that, he was a Harvard law professor whose writing thinking on administrative law and deregulation were highly influential on a generation of lawyers.

Elena Kagan, appointed in 2010, had previously held many impressive positions, including White House counsel, U.S. Solicitor General and the first female dean of Harvard Law School, where she won high praise for her ability to build consensus—and for her efforts to fight discrimination based on sexual orientation.

What is evident in the careers of all these men and women is the concept of law as the protector of the oppressed, the poor, the minority, the loner. They are all tied together by a common strand, the commandment in the Torah, "Justice, Justice thou shalt pursue." [5]

It has been said that a judge's judicial philosophy is shaped by two principal forces: Their personal history, and their world view—what the Germans call *Weltanschauung*.

So let me briefly recount my background:

Earlier, I referred to having grown up in Detroit's "golden ghetto." By that, I meant that until I was graduated from high school that I lived in middle class neighborhoods with a large Jewish component, in an era when the city was approaching its zenith in terms of population and prosperity.

I attended a high school in which at least 80 percent of the student body was Jewish. I regularly attended synagogue. My father was a successful lawyer whose clients were largely Jewish. My paternal grandparents were observant Jews who both died a few months apart when I was twelve years old.

Next I went to the University of Michigan, where I immediately joined a Jewish fraternity. The United States had just been drawn into World War II, and a year later, at the age of 18, I went into the U.S. Army. That, incidentally, was the first time I had any non-Jewish friends. When I got out of service in 1946, I returned to the University of Michigan and then its law school, where once again most of my friends were Jewish.

What were my politics?

---

5. Deuteronomy 16:20

To illustrate the answer, let me cite two incidents. When Franklin D. Roosevelt died in 1945, I literally cried myself to sleep.

Three years later, in 1948, I stayed up all election night, believing my cheerleading efforts would somehow help Harry Truman win the upset of the century over Thomas Dewey.

(Evidently, I might say with tongue in cheek … it worked.)

When I began practicing law with my father in 1949, I almost immediately became active in the lower reaches of federation life in Detroit, an activity that eventually led to my election as the president of the Jewish Welfare Federation of Metropolitan Detroit.

Politically, I began pushing doorbells for Adlai Stevenson in 1952, and stayed active, working in and on many Democratic Party campaigns, until I was appointed to the federal bench.

I was also involved in many bar association activities, and did service for the general community. I eventually spent time serving as a member of the Michigan Civil Rights Commission, the Michigan Social Welfare Commission and of the Detroit Board of Police Commissions, which I eventually chaired.

How did I end up a U.S. District Court judge in 1979? There were several factors involved. They included:

- Jimmy Carter, who I had supported for the Democratic nomination, was President of the United States.
- Democrats controlled both houses of Congress, making my confirmation much easier. U.S. Sen. Donald Riegle was a Democrat and our senior senator. He decided who to recommend for appointment.
- Three new federal judgeships had been created for the Eastern District of Michigan, increasing my odds—and at that time, there were not any Jews on Detroit's federal district bench—and historically, there long had been at least one "Jewish seat."
- Additionally, I had the strong support of that part of the Jewish establishment which, apart from labor, had a major role in funding Riegle's hotly contested election three years before—and I had worked for the senator's campaign.
- United Auto Workers' President Douglas Fraser supported my appointment, and Detroit Mayor Coleman A. Young, then in his second term, thought I was a good choice, because of my strong support of affirmative action.

As I recall, the one main barrier to my appointment was Riegle's concern that I lacked proper judicial temperament—and I have to admit, there may have been something to that.

But in the end, he was satisfied.

Because of retirements and the new seats, he had five people to recommend for appointment to the federal bench. He settled on two white women; two African-Americans, and two Jews. One was a judge in his hometown of Flint … and the other was me. I was confirmed by the U.S. Senate, and began my judicial career.

Finally—was I a Jewish judge or just a judge who happened to be Jewish? That is not for me to decide.

I do know that my Jewish values, values of compassion and the need to seek justice, inform the way I see the world and the law.

This is all the answer I can provide.

∗∗

Addendum: I cannot close, however, without taking note of the three Jewish judges who preceded me on my court, the Eastern District of Michigan. If you trace the careers of each prior to their appointments, as well as while on the bench, they confirm my view that there are judges who are deeply affected by being Jewish.

Each of them had a public career of service, mostly in Jewish organizations, and as judges exhaled Jewish values—compassion and the need to seek justice in their work and on the bench.

The first was Charles Simons (1876-1964) who served on the Eastern District from 1923 to 1932, and then was elevated to the U.S. Court of Appeals in 1932, and remained there till he died.

His father had been a member of Detroit City Council, and Judge Simons had served the people as a state senator, county commissioner, and delegate to the 1908 Constitutional convention.

The second was Theodore Levin (1897-1970) who was appointed to the Eastern District by President Harry Truman in 1946, and remained on the court till he died on the last day of the year.

He was not only a leader in philanthropic activities, especially but not only in Jewish circles, but successfully campaigned for criminal sentencing reform on the district court. He was so admired by his peers that the federal courthouse was later named for him.

Lawrence Gubow (1919-1978) was on the court for less than ten years before being felled by diabetes. He was widely respected by the attorneys who appeared before him for fairness on the bench, was a veteran of infantry combat in World War II, and was extremely active in both Jewish philanthropic and veterans groups.

These men all led careers of public service, and without going into more detail, it is my view that their work as judges was strongly influenced by the fact that they were Jewish.

More letters, etc: Judge Cohn's Journalism, 2015-2020

LETTERS

Avern Cohn has been a prolific letter writer all his life, especially to newspapers; many examples of his acute observations may be found in *Letters, etc.* the book Elizabeth Zerwekh edited and published in 2015. Here are a few more which may be of interest:

***

But first, let's look at a couple on interesting letters *about* the judge:

The novelist Ann Beattie created a stir in some legal circles when she reviewed Elmore Leonard's novel Mr. Paradise in the Sunday New York Times book review section on Feb. 1, 2004 in a piece titled *First, Let's Kill the Lawyer.*

What got people upset was her reference to "the very house where the murder was committed, presided over by Satan, in the guise of a merely totally corrupt lawyer named Avern Cohn." That prompted the following amusing exchange:

The New York Times

Name That Shyster

February 22, 2004

To the Editor:

In her review of Elmore Leonard's "Mr. Paradise" (Feb. 1), Ann Beattie compliments the author on his sense of humor and goes on to say, "He's hip and has the ability to keep readers involved, even if some miss an 'in' joke or have no idea there's a literary allusion."

An "in" joke that Beattie apparently missed is Leonard's giving his "totally corrupt lawyer" character the name Avern Cohn. Of course Beattie, being a professor of literature at the University of Virginia, would have no way of knowing that Avern Cohn is a universally respected judge at Elmore Leonard's hometown United States District Court for the Eastern District of Michigan.

Norm Gottlieb

Los Angeles

The Good Avern Cohn, The Bad Avern Cohn

March 28, 2004

To the Editor:

Regarding Ann Beattie's review of Elmore Leonard's novel "Mr. Paradise," which features a corrupt lawyer named Avern Cohn, Norm Gottlieb wrote, "Beattie, being a professor of literature at the University of Virginia, would have no way of knowing that Avern Cohn is a universally respected judge at Elmore Leonard's hometown United States District Court for the Eastern District of Michigan" (Letters, Feb. 22). In fact, Judge Cohn was the winning bidder in a Michigan Opera Theater charity auction for the privilege of having his name used in a Leonard novel. It seems that neither Beattie nor Gottlieb was in on the joke.

Sharon Thomas

New York

A version of this article appears in print on , Section 7, Page 2 of the National edition with the headline: The Good Avern Cohn, The Bad Avern Cohn

***

The Green Bag: An Entertaining Journal of Law (second series) is a quarterly legal journal dedicated to publishing 'good writing' about the law; it was started in 1997, partially as a revival of a Progressive-era publication also called the *Green Bag,* which flourished from 1889 to 1914.

Avern Cohn has been a faithful and frequent contributor to the *Bag*.

TO THE BAG

PEREMPTORY CALLS

To the *Bag*:

I suggest that Professor Pizzi is far too generous with the trial judge in *Shane v. Commonwealth*, 243 S.W. 3d 336 (Ky. 2008), in suggesting that the failure to strike Juror 138 for cause, thereby requiring the defendant to use a peremptory challenge to excuse an obviously ineligible juror (the juror would have given more weight to a police officer witness' testimony than an ordinary witness), was effectively harmless error. William T. Pizzi, *"Makeup Calls" in Sports & Courts*, 11 GREEN BAG 2D 333, 338. He ignores what the Kentucky Supreme Court said about the error:

> The language to the trial court is mandatory. RCr 9.40 gives a defendant eight peremptory challenges plus one if alternates are seated. This Court, in its rule-making capacity, has recognized that this is beyond question a valuable right going to the defendant's peace of mind and the public's view of fairness. It is fundamentally inconsistent for the Court to give with one hand and take away with the other, a position that does not invite public trust in the integrity of the judicial system.

I suggest, to use another sports analogy, what the Kentucky Supreme Court said was that the trial judge's error was so egregious as to call for a forfeiture rather than the sophisticated analysis necessary to an assessment of whether or not "the error may have been balanced out by other rulings."

Avern Cohn
U.S. District Judge

TO THE BAG

THE ROOT OF THE THOUGHT

To the *Bag*:

It is not often we get an insight into the outside reading of the justices of the Supreme Court. Chief Justice Roberts gives us an insight into what he has been reading in the last sentence of his dissent in *Spears v. United States*, 2009 WL 129044 (2009), when he said, of the haste with which a majority of his colleagues were enlarging the discretion of district judges in sentencing:

> As has been said a plant cannot grow if you constantly yank it out of the ground to see if its roots are healthy.

Philip K. Howard, a well-known advocate for the proposition that "modern law under[mines] our freedom," as described in his new book, *Life Without Lawyers*, concludes his philippic with the observation:

> Plants don't flourish when we pull them up too often to check how their roots are growing.

Howard's observation was not an original thought; he was quoting from Lecture One of the BBC's Reith Lecture, 2002 by Onora O'Neil, President of the British Academy (www.bbc.co.uk/print/radio4/reith2002/lecture1.shtml?print), where she said in her conclusion:

> Plants don't flourish when we pull them up too often to check how their roots are growing: political institutional and professional life too may not go well if we constantly uproot them to demonstrate that everything is transparent and trustworthy.

Since the aphorism has yet to make Google (last visited February 1, 2009), it would have been better had the Chief Justice told us the source.

Avern Cohn
U.S. District Judge
U.S. District Court for the Eastern District of Michigan

To the Bag

Shelley's Tourist Attraction

To the *Bag*:

John V. Orth's removal of the mystery surrounding the Rule in Shelley's Case (7 Green Bag 2d 45 (2003)), recalls to the mind the answer the late Senator Burton K. Wheeler of Montana, a leading isolationist of the World War II era, gave when asked in a University of Michigan Law School class in the early 1900's: What is the rule in Shelley's Case?

After a moment of thought, Wheeler is said to have responded, "Sir the Rule in Shelley's case is the same as the rule in any other man's case! The law brooks no favorites!"

Incidentally, a Google search on the Rule discloses that Section 28 of the Northern Territory Law of Property Act 2000 abolished the Rule effective 1 December 2000. The Hon. Austin Asche ACQC, in a funeral oration at a wake to memorialize its demise, said:

> There was some talk of preserving it as a tourist attraction and SPAR (the Society for the Preservation of Ancient Relics) felt that it could be housed in the Museum.
>
> However, sterner views prevailed and a jury presided over by Mildren J in his capacity as President of the Law Reform Committee found the Rule guilty of incomprehensibility, senility and dry rot. The death sentence was pronounced and carried out in December 2000 by the new improved *Law of Property Act*.

Hinc illae lacrimae.

See Alternate Law Journal, Vol 26. No.3, June 2001 p.14.

Yours Truly,
Avern Cohn
District Judge
United States District Court
Eastern District of Michigan

Tragedy and Mercy
in Puerto Rico

To the *Bag*:

Professor Stephen R. McAllister's account of *Kentucky v. Dennison* ("A *Marbury v. Madison* Moment On The Eve Of The Civil War," 14 GREEN BAG 2D 405), is an excellent read. However, his account of *Puerto Rico v. Branstad*, which overruled *Dennison*, is too summary.

What did the Governor of Iowa do when he was told by the Supreme Court he had to honor the request of the Governor of Puerto Rico to return Ronald M. Calder, the object of the extradition effort, to the Commonwealth to face trial on charges of murder and attempted murder, whatever the Governor's views were of its justice system? And, what happened to Calder upon his return? What follows is that history gleaned from court dockets and newspapers of the day with help from an assiduous librarian.

As described in part in *Branstad*, Calder, then a civilian air traffic controller, faced charges in Puerto Rico for killing a woman eight months pregnant by running her over in a shopping center parking lot. Calder contended he accidentally ran over the woman in an attempt to get away from her husband, with whom Calder had an argument after their cars collided in the parking lot. After being arraigned on a charge of involuntary manslaughter and being released on bail, Calder fled to his home state of Iowa. Calder's lawyer, who was suspicious of Puerto Rican justice, said Calder ran away from Puerto Rico because, as a resident of the continental United States, with no ties to the Spanish-speaking Commonwealth, he could not receive a fair trial. After Calder fled, the charges were increased to first-degree murder and attempted murder.

Both Governor Robert Ray and his successor, Governor Terry Branstad, declined to sign the necessary papers for extradition, with Governor Ray stating that in the absence of a "change to a more realistic charge," the request for extradition would be denied. This resulted in an approximately six-year effort by the Puerto Rican authorities to get Calder back to Puerto Rico to stand trial.

To the Bag

Well, Governor Branstad's case was made easy by Calder; he voluntarily returned to Puerto Rico to stand trial. His wife, Jeanne, is quoted in an *Associated Press* account as saying to reporters that Calder returned so "we can put all this behind us." Upon his return, Calder was released on bond pending trial.

Calder went to trial in late January, 1988 on murder and attempted murder charges. On the second day of trial, Calder pled guilty to reduced charges of voluntary manslaughter and attempted manslaughter. He received a 15-year suspended sentence. He was allowed to return to Iowa to serve his 15 years of probation.

An interesting end of the story is the effort of Puerto Rico to get Calder to pay the $172,216.00 it cost to bring him back from Iowa. The trial judge said "no." However, the judge did require Calder to pay the husband of the victim $10,000.00 to cover the cost of his wife's funeral.

In the end, Calder's fears of the Puerto Rican justice system proved unfounded. Judges with a merciful heart can speak many languages.

Avern Cohn
U.S. District Court for the
Eastern District of Michigan

GB

***

There is also one letter to the Detroit Legal News which needs no annotation

> **Letter to the Editor**
>
> **To the Editor:**
> U.S. District Judge James Churchill was the very essence of what a federal judge should be: fair, firm, knowledgeable, and compassionate.
>
> As an example of how good of a judge he was, in the Detroit School case he had what was a truly original thought.
>
> He recommended to his colleagues as a replacement to Judge DeMascio when DeMascio recused himself from the case a non-statutory three-judge court. My colleagues had a concern that his replacement would have a tough road to follow in dealing with a pending motion to bring into the case the suburban school districts. Three judges could better absorb the public abuse likely to follow the decisional process in considering the motion. Three judges took over the case. As it so happened the motion was never pursued.
>
> *Avern Cohn*
> *Retired U.S. District Court Judge*
>
> The Detroit Legal News,
> Friday, July 24, 2020

***

Even after he had retired from the bench, Avern Cohn remained deeply interested in civic affairs. In 2021, just short of his 97th birthday, he helped spur debate on a proposed revision of the city of Detroit's charter, something that had been largely neglected by the media. This letter to the editor ran in the *Detroit Free Press* on Sunday, June 13, 2021 under a large headline:

Charter Commission Hasn't Made Case for Proposed Changes

Free Press columnist Nancy Kaffer's laudatory appraisal of the revised city of Detroit charter ("Don't ignore issues raised by Charter Commission, Free Press, June 6") is seriously flawed.

First, the full text of the revised charter including the changes that followed the Governor's veto has not been accessible to the public.

Second, the charter commission's analyses of the financial impact of the revised charter have not been posted on the internet.

Third, Kaffer focuses on Mayor Duggan's conduct of Detroit affairs, completely ignoring the City Council's role.

The Charter Commission has written a completely new charter for Detroit without finding that the changes from the present charter could be accomplished by City Council actions and the mayor's approval. Legislating through charter changes is bad public policy.

There is no good reason for the citizens of Detroit to adopt a completely new charter. A no vote is in order.

- Avern Cohn
Birmingham
(The author is a retired U.S. District judge in he Eastern District of Michigan.)

***

Avern Cohn always has cared very much about how government works, especially as far as anything having to do with the judiciary; he also has been acutely aware of the sometimes hidden potential of suggested reforms. In this letter, which was regrettably never published, he shows his deep understanding of Michigan's one-man grand jury system.

Letter to the Editor
The Detroit News
March 5, 2021

While your editorial "Michigan should scrap one-man grand juries" (March 4) has some merit, it fails to discuss the misuse of the Flint one-man grand jury and the need for reform in the grand jury process. The indictment in the Flint one-man grand jury reflects the jurisprudential parochialism in the judges in Genesee County.

Particularly, in petition for a one-man grand jury.

The late Robert Scigliano, a political science professor at Michigan State University, made it clear in his writings that the use of the one-man grand jury should be limited to cases of political corruption and conspiracies. In these kinds of cases an inquisition may be necessary in investigating criminal situations. Certainly, that is not the case in Flint. The Flint defendants have been subject to several investigations including one by former Michigan Attorney General Bill Schuette, who found no basis for criminal charges.

The defendants in the Flint case have been unfairly treated by denial of access to the evidence on which the juror found probable cause. They have no information as to the basis of the indictments, particularly the evidence to support a finding of probable cause.

I suggest that you should have concluded your editorial with a recommendation that the proceedings should be moved out of Genesee County and take place in front of judges not subject to the clamor of Genesee County voters. They also should be conducted by a special prosecutor who would not be motivated by a desire for political approval. Your editorial should also have included a recommendation for a study of the current one-man grand jury process and the need for legislative reform.

Thank you,
Avern Cohn

Judge Avern Cohn Awards and Honoraria

1949

Juris Doctorate—University of Michigan
"In recognition of the satisfactory fulfilment of the requirements pertaining to this degree"

- June 11, 1949

1962

Oath of Office—Emergency Interim Successor as Attorney General
"I do solemnly swear that I will support the Constitution of the United States and the Constitution of their states and that I will faithfully discharge the duties of the office of Emergency Interim Successor as Attorney General under the provisions of Act 202, Public Acts of 1952, according to the best of my ability."

- March 1, 1962

1975

Thank You Plaque—Michigan Civil Rights Commission
For the "outstanding contribution . . . made to the people of this State as a Member and Chairperson of the Civil Rights Commission."

- 1972-1975

Michigan Civil Rights Commission Membership—Michigan Executive Department
"Reposing special trust and confidence in the integrity and ability of Avern Cohn."

- February 13, 1975

Certificate of Appointment—Member of the Board of Police Commissioners
"Member of the Board of Police Commissioners."

- October 23, 1975

1978

Roberts P. Hudson Award—State Bar of Michigan
"In recognition and appreciation of special services performed on behalf of the Bar and the People of Michigan."

- 1978

1979

National Agencies Division Chairman 1976-1978—Jewish Welfare Federation of Detroit
"Your exemplary leadership and achievements of this major committee have strengthened Jewish life in our community."

- January 23, 1979

Presidential Appointment to the Bench—President
"I have nominated and by and with the advice and consent of the Senate do appoint him United States District Judge for the Eastern District of Michigan."

- September 26, 1979

Thank You Plaque—Board of Police Commissioners
"In grateful appreciation for your interest, concern, insight, and leadership in guiding and developing the staff of the Board of Police Commissioners. Your presence will be missed but your work will not be forgotten."

- October 4, 1979

1980

Board of Directors Recognition—Spirit of Detroit

- 1978-1980

1985

Thank You Plaque—Oakland Parks Foundation
"In appreciation of the Irwin and Sadie Cohn Family for their contributions to the Oakland Parks Foundation Independence Oaks County Park."

- 1985

1987

Distinguished Presenter—The Museum of African American History and the University of Michigan—Dearborn
Distinguished presenter of "The U.S. Constitution and its impact on African Americans."

- June 19, 1987

Thank You Letter—Jerry L. Bass
"Thank you immensely for the order you rendered on 9.22.87 granting my motion to reduce my sentence to time served."

- September 27, 1987

The Justice Louis D. Brandeis Award—Zionist Organization of America
"In recognition of exemplary service on behalf of the State of Israel and the American Jewish Community"

- November 1, 1987

1988

Eleanor Roosevelt Humanities Award—State of Israel Bonds
"For outstanding service to humanity and devoted friendship and support for Israel in the spirit of Eleanor Roosevelt."

- May 11, 1988

Distinguished Brief Judge Plaque—Thomas M. Cooley Law Review
Distinguished Brief Judge

- 1988

Fred M. Butzel Memorial Award—The Jewish Welfare Federation of Detroit
"In recognition of: length and service to the Jewish Community; service to the total Jewish Community as well as its constituent parts; service as a representative of the Jewish Community in the organized general community; character and integrity in communal affairs."

- 1988

1989

Thank You Plaque—Oakland County Bar Association
"In grateful recognition of forty years of service to the legal profession."

- December 12, 1989

Stage & Co. Award—Children's Leukemia Foundation of Michigan
"In appreciation for outstanding service, support and volunteer commitment."

- 1989

Commemorative Plaque—Detroit Zoological Society
Member of the Renaissance Circle.

- 1989-1990

1990

Special Tribute—Senator Jack Faxon & the State of Michigan
"Special tribute as he is feted at the sixtieth anniversary dinner of the Council of Orthodox Rabbis of Greater Detroit for his many contributions to the State of Michigan. May he know the high esteem in which he is held by the people of the Great Lake State."

- May 21, 1990

Honorary Shofar—Council of Orthodox Rabbis
"As a token of appreciation for upholding the principles of justice and peace as an eminent jurist and dedicated leader of the community, and for his selfless devotion to the Council of Orthodox Rabbis"

- 60th Anniversary Dinner, May 22, 1990

Thank You Plaque—Detroit Friends of the Afro-Asian Institute; Israel Histadrut Campaign

"For outstanding achievement in the legal profession, dedication to the cause of civil and human rights, and his persistent struggle for equal justice for all."

- November 13, 1990

1991

Endowment Achievement Award—Council of Jewish Federations

"In recognition of creative and outstanding leadership to the endowment program."

- 1991

1992

Thank You Plaque—National Association for the Advancement of Colored People

"In recognition of your devotion to the preservation of our community's history."

- June, 1992

Thank You Plaque—Mark E. Schlussel, Former President of the Jewish Federation

"In grateful appreciation for your generous contribution."

- 1992

1993

Appreciation Certificate—The Jewish Community Archives

"In recognition of your devotion to the preservation of our community's history."

- June, 1992

Faculty Member: Federal Judicial Intellectual Property Law Seminar—Intellectual Property Law Institute

Appreciation of your participation.

- November 18-20, 1993

1995

Golden Torah Award—Yeshiva Beth Yehudah
"A great friend, humanitarian, statesman and leader . . . In recognition of his outstanding dedication to Torah and his legendary support of Jewish Education."

- October 22, 1995

Distinguished Brief Judge Plaque—Thomas M. Cooley Law Review
Distinguished Brief Judge

- 1995

1996

Distinguished Brief Judge Plaque—Thomas M. Cooley Law Review
Distinguished Brief Judge

- 1996

1998

Honorary Doctor of Laws—Detroit College of Law at Michigan State University
"Through his lifelong commitment to the spirit of justice and the power of education, through his on-going quest for civil rights for all citizens and through his scholarship regarding the law and its application, has brought great honor to this profession, the state, and this nation."

- January 25, 1998

The State of Israel's 50th Anniversary Award—State of Israel Bonds
"With deep appreciation for your devotion to the State of Israel and commitment to the Israel Bonds Program as we commemorate fifty years of Israel's independence."

- November 3, 1998

Member Certificate—American Judicature Society
Member of the Board of Directors

- 1992-1998

Appreciation Clock—State Bar of Michigan
In appreciation

- 1998

1999

Thank You Plaque—Detroit Metropolitan Bar Association & Wolverine Bar Association
"For outstanding leadership, tireless dedication, and personal sacrifice as a Judge of the U.S. District Court, E.D. Mich."

- December 10, 1999

Fifty Year Certificate—State Bar of Michigan
"Upon recommendation of its Board of Commissioners, the State Bar of Michigan hereby accords recognition to Hon. Avern Cohn in honor of having completed 50 years of continuous services as an attorney and counsellor at law."

- 1999

Distinguished Brief Judge Plaque—Thomas M. Cooley Law Review
Distinguished Brief Judge

- 1999

2000

The IAJLJ Pursuit of Justice Award—The American Section of the International Association of Jewish Lawyers and Jurists
"For proven commitment to Tsedek Tsedek Teerdof and the rule of law."

- 2000

2001

Thank You Plaque—Beaumont Tower Society
"In grateful appreciation for your financial support to Michigan State University."

- 2001

2003

Commemorative Plaque—Yeshiva Beth Yehudah
"On the Bar Mitzvah of his General Chairpersonship."

- November 16, 2003

Distinguished Leadership Award—American-Arab Anti-Discrimination Committee
"For his distinguished services, leadership, and commitment to justice in America."

- December 1, 2003

2004

Newspaper Article—The Sunday Oakland Press
"On the Bench is where Judge wants to Remain."

- February 15, 2004

Article Dedication—Law and Contemporary Problems, Fall 2004 Edition
"Cunningham would also like to dedicate this article to the Honorable Avern Cohn in honor of his 25 years of service as a United States District Judge for the Eastern District of Michigan, which have demonstrated that: "One of the basic principles, one of the glories, of the American system of justice is that the courthouse door is open to everyone—the humblest citizen, the indigent, the convicted felon, the illegal alien." (quoting Mahaday v. Cason)"

- 2004

Thank You Plaque—Jewish Apartments and Services: Strong Seniors Stay Young
In Gratitude

- 2004

2005

Distinguished Alumni Service Award—The University of Michigan
"For services performed on behalf of the University of Michigan or in connection with its organized alumni activities."

- October 6, 2005

2008

Equal Justice in Housing Award—Wayne State University Law School Fair Housing Education Program & the Fair Housing Center of Metropolitan Detroit
"In appreciation of your commitment to fair and equal application of Fair Housing Laws, your creative use of the court to enforce these laws, and the positive example you have provided to members of the legal profession."

- April 3, 2008

Congressional Tribute—110th Congress, Second Session
Congressional Tribute

- October 2, 2008

2009

Outstanding Achievement Award—State Bar of Michigan
"The Negligence Law Section of the State Bar of Michigan proudly confers this Outstanding Achievement Award upon Judge Avern L. Cohn for his outspoken and courageous support of the civil justice system, the right to trial by jury and for his long and distinguished service on the United States District Court, for the Eastern District of Michigan"

- September 18, 2009

Newspaper Article—Detroit Legal News
"Federal Judge to Mark Milestone on the Bench."

- October 9, 2009

Founders Award—Michigan State Bar Foundation
"For exemplifying the highest traditions of the legal profession and devoted service to the community."

- 2009

2011

Doctor of Laws, Honoris Causa—Wayne State University
"Upon the recommendation of the faculty of Wayne State University . . . In recognition of the achievements specified for the Degree."

- May 16, 2011

2012

Fair Housing Attorney Appreciation Award—Fair Housing Center of Metropolitan Detroit

- April 17, 2012

2013

Champion of Justice Award—The Michigan Association for Justice
"In appreciation of his commitment to the civil justice system and to preserving the rights of citizens."

- May 11, 2013

2014

Certificate of Appreciation—Historical Society of Michigan
"Recognizing his exceptional achievements in advocating and preserving Michigan history."

- July 23, 2014

Keepsake—Frankel Jewish Academy
"Generation to Generation."

- October 7, 2014

Hon. Sarah T. Hughes Civil Rights Award—National Federal Bar Association
Named after the renowned federal district judge from Dallas, Texas, the Sarah T. Hughes Civil Rights Award was created to honor that man or woman who promotes the advancement of civil and human rights amongst us, and who exemplifies Judge Hughes' spirit and legacy of devoted service and leadership in

the cause of equality. Judge Hughes was a pioneer in the fight for civil rights, due process, equal protection, and the rights of women. The Award will be presented each year to an attorney or judge whose career achievements have made a difference in advancing the causes that were important to Judge Hughes. Such work may include either ground-breaking achievement or a body of sustained and dedicated work in the area of civil rights, due process, and equal protection.

- 2014

2017

Newspaper Article—Detroit Legal News
"Breaking the Banks: Federal Judge Explores Detroit Banking Crises that Unfolded in 1933."

- February 24, 2017

Thank You Plaque—Neighborhood Legal Services Michigan
"For outstanding judicial leadership, dedication and contributions."

- November 11, 2017

Thank You Letter—Former President Jimmy Carter
"I just want to thank you for your fine service to our courting and to wish you an enjoyable holiday."

- December 20, 2017

2019

Happy Birthday Wishes—Former President Jimmy Carter
"We are proud of the 40 years you have dedicated to your remarkable career on the federal bench. You have served your country well in many capacities. I am honored to have this opportunity to share in the celebration of your life."

- July 23, 2019

2020

The Wade H. McCree, Jr. Award for the Advancement of Social Justice—E.D. Michigan Chapter of the Federal Bar Association

The McCree Award honors individuals or organizations who have made significant contributions to the advancement of social justice. These contributions may include advancing social justice in areas involving poverty, promoting economic or educational opportunity, or fighting discrimination involving race, gender, ethnicity, national origin, religion, or economic status. The recipient may be selected from any field of endeavor including law, social service, community organization, volunteer activities, journalism, academics or the like.

- 2020

The Dorothy Comstock Riley and Wallace C. Riley Award for Legal History—Michigan Supreme Court Historical Society

"Without you, all of us and our posterity would be immeasurably poorer in our knowledge of our state and its legal history."

- July 24, 2020

Detroit Bar Association—Sixteenth Annual Dennis W. Archer Public Service Award

- Nov. 19, 2020

2021

First Avern L. Cohn Distinguished Michigan Civic Historian Award—Michigan History Foundation

"Judge Cohn has never been afraid to take risks and change history … our jurisprudence and many individuals are better for Judge Cohn's judicial service."

- Michigan Chief Justice Bridget McCormack, March 26, 2021

Lifetime Achievement Award, Jewish Bar Association

- May 25, 2021

Not Dated

Thank You Plaque—Baruch U'Marpeh of Israel
"Please accept this modest gift as a token of appreciation for your life-saving generosity."

Thank You Plaque—Baruch U'Marpeh of Israel
"To our devoted patron . . . May you be blessed with good health, wealth, and nachas in merit of your generosity."

Thank You Plaque—Detroit College of Law at Michigan State University Benefactors Club
"In recognition of your significant contribution to the College."

Commemorative Plaque—Federal Bar Association
"Sustaining Member."

Thank You Coaster—United Community Services of Metropolitan Detroit
"In appreciation of your leadership."

Thank You Clock—Association of Certified Fraud Examiners
"Association of Certified Fraud Examiners Guest Speaker."

President's Award—Detroit Metropolitan Bar Association & Wolverine Bar Association
50-Year Member

Appreciation Certificate—Harry B. Hutchins Society, The University of Michigan
In Appreciation

Afterword

Editing this book has been truly a labor of love, and we have many people to thank for helping us. We benefited enormously from both the editing and legal help provided by retired federal Magistrate Judge Mona K. Majzoub, who selflessly read all of the case studies and helped make sure we had all the correct legal citations.

We knew her reputation and expected she would—but what was an unexpected bonus was that she also turned out to be an extremely fine editor, and caught many small errors and made countless suggestions that improved the writing. Judge Majzoub, who now runs her own firm, Mona K. Majzoub Dispute Resolutions PLLC, is a treasure.

Tara Villereal, Avern Cohn's judicial secretary, was also of immense assistance, and was never too busy to find a photo, case file or document we needed.

Magistrate Judge Kimberly G. Altman, who in her prior career was Judge Cohn's law clerk for twenty years, made time in her busy schedule to share memories and help lay hands on information that sometimes wasn't easy to find, even as she was changing careers and grappling with the challenges of the worst pandemic in more than a century.

David Ashenfelter, a Pulitzer-prize winning reporter who is now public information officer for the U.S. District Court for the Eastern District of Michigan, was also more than willing to help with this project.

Sheldon Cohn, the judge's eldest son, provided perspective and was helpful as well, as did talented filmmaker David Mayer, founder of Videoburst, whose film with the judge, *Avern Cohn, Memories and Mementos*, is an excellent compliment to this book.

This book would not be what it is without the firm guiding hand of Bill Haney, an author himself, a former publisher who has had his hand in more than 400 books, including two others which Jack has written; he improves everything he touches. Anne Zimanski, a professional illustrator and designer in Traverse City, gave this book its classy look.

Most of all, however, we need and want to thank this book's moving force: U.S. District Judge Avern Cohn, who has been more of an inspiration and has had more of a positive impact on lives, both in the courtroom and without (ours included) than this book comes close to capturing. We won't say the judge is *always* easy to work with … but we will say that working with him has been a pleasure and an honor not subject to appeal.

- Jack Lessenberry and Elizabeth Zerwekh
September 2021

About the Editors

Jack Lessenberry has been a writer and editor and political analyst for numerous publications, has hosted radio and television shows and taught journalism for many years at Wayne State University and the University of Michigan. He is the author of *The People's Lawyer: The Life and Times of Frank J. Kelley, the Nation's Longest-Serving Attorney General* (Wayne State University Press, 2015) and *Reason vs. Racism: A Newspaper Family, Race, and Justice* (BCI Press, 2020).

Elizabeth Zerwekh is a professional librarian and archivist, specializing in rare books and private collections. She has worked with Judge Cohn for years, and in addition to this book, played a major role in researching *Reason vs. Racism*.

They live in Huntington Woods and Charlevoix with their dogs Ashley and Chet, in homes overflowing with books.

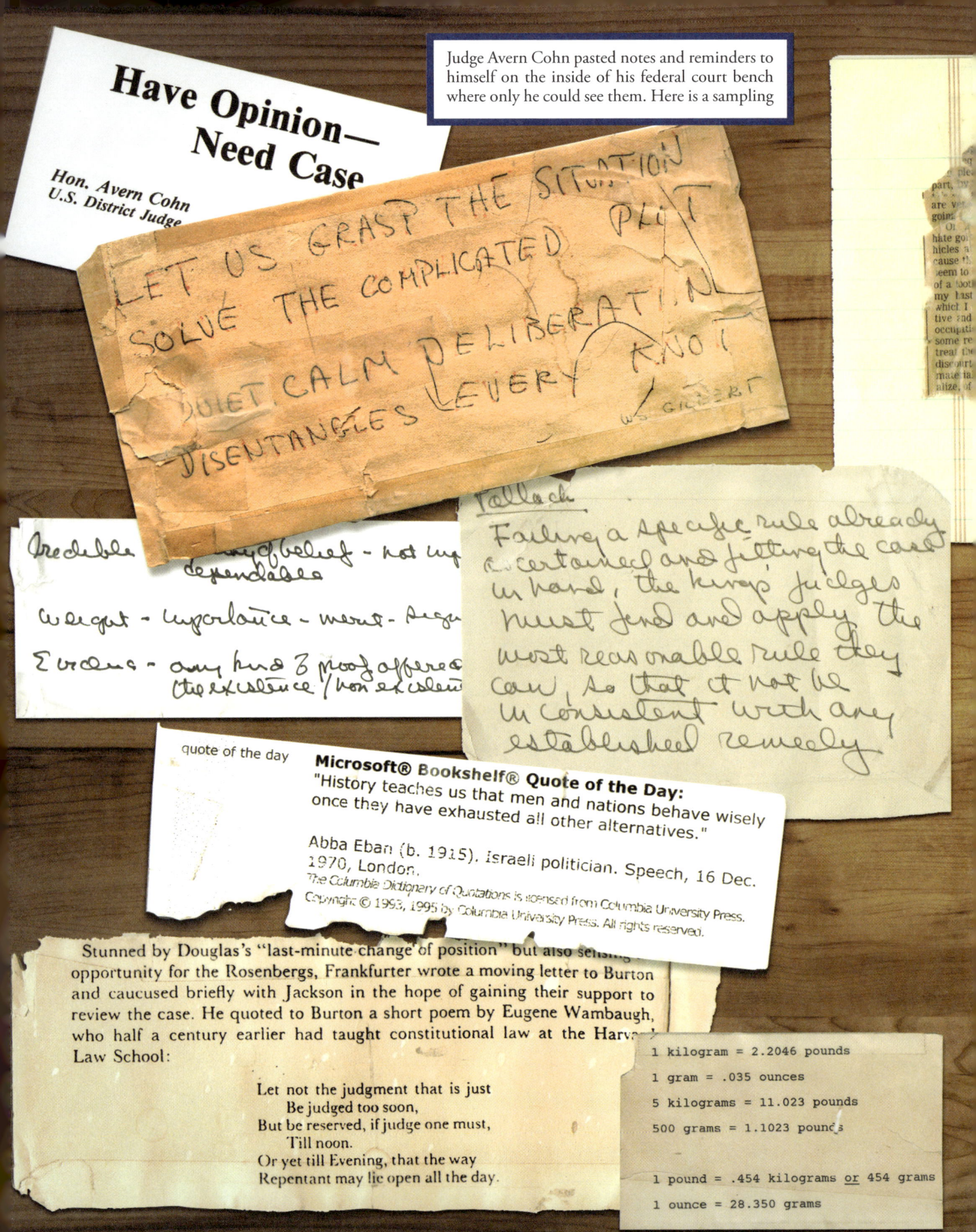

Judge Avern Cohn pasted notes and reminders to himself on the inside of his federal court bench where only he could see them. Here is a sampling

Have Opinion— Need Case

Hon. Avern Cohn
U.S. District Judge

LET US GRASP THE SITUATION
SOLVE THE COMPLICATED PLOT
QUIET CALM DELIBERATION
DISENTANGLES EVERY KNOT
— W.S. GILBERT

Credible — worthy of belief — not imp... dependable

Weight — importance — merit — sign...

Evidence — any kind of proof offered... (the existence / non existen...

Tallack

Failing a specific rule already ascertained and fitting the case in hand, the king's judges must find and apply the most reasonable rule they can, so that it not be inconsistent with any established remedy

quote of the day

Microsoft® Bookshelf® Quote of the Day:
"History teaches us that men and nations behave wisely once they have exhausted all other alternatives."

Abba Eban (b. 1915), Israeli politician. Speech, 16 Dec. 1970, London.

The Columbia Dictionary of Quotations is licensed from Columbia University Press. Copyright © 1993, 1995 by Columbia University Press. All rights reserved.

Stunned by Douglas's "last-minute change of position" but also sensing... opportunity for the Rosenbergs, Frankfurter wrote a moving letter to Burton and caucused briefly with Jackson in the hope of gaining their support to review the case. He quoted to Burton a short poem by Eugene Wambaugh, who half a century earlier had taught constitutional law at the Harva... Law School:

> Let not the judgment that is just
>   Be judged too soon,
> But be reserved, if judge one must,
>   Till noon.
> Or yet till Evening, that the way
> Repentant may lie open all the day.

1 kilogram = 2.2046 pounds

1 gram = .035 ounces

5 kilograms = 11.023 pounds

500 grams = 1.1023 pounds

1 pound = .454 kilograms <u>or</u> 454 grams

1 ounce = 28.350 grams